THE *TITANIC* AND THE *CALIFORNIAN*

THE *TITANIC* AND THE *CALIFORNIAN*

PETER PADFIELD

THISTLE
PUBLISHING

FOREWORD

In 1912, two official inquiries decided that, if my father had only taken proper action at the time, his ship, the *Californian,* could have saved many, if not all, of the 1,500 lives lost in the *Titanic* disaster. This book is the first ever to be written showing how impossible it is to come to such a conclusion if the available evidence is properly examined.

A monstrous accusation like this could easily have ruined my father, but curiously it had very little effect either on his subsequent sea career or his private life. But he was deeply and lastingly wounded by what he knew was a wholly undeserved slur on his professional reputation, which was always held in the highest regard by his employers and those who really knew him, both before and after this tragic event.

The official findings made him out to be an incompetent navigator and an inefficient shipmaster, but he was neither. He held the highest possible qualifications, and had been appointed to his first command, a passenger cargo liner, at the exceptionally early age of 29. The whole of his sea career proved that he was an outstandingly competent and successful officer and captain, and he was very proud of his record.

Although he was forced to resign from the Leyland Line, to which the *Californian* belonged, the Liverpool management (as distinct from the board of directors in London) had complete faith in him. Indeed, it was as a result of their reference that in 1913 he obtained another appointment as master with Lawther, Latta's, a London firm whose ships traded primarily to South America. Here he was almost immediately accepted as the company's most capable and trusted commander, being given their largest and newest ship, and he often used to say that the happiest years of his sea career were spent with this company.

I believe that there is a widespread misconception that my father did little or nothing in 1912 to try to clear his name. This is quite untrue, for he did everything possible to get the British inquiry reopened, and wrote to everyone who might have been able to help. He even wrote to Lord Pirrie, chairman of the company who built the *Titanic*, but the reply he received (that "it would be out of place" for Lord Pirrie to take the matter up) was typical of the attitude of many who might otherwise have been able to help him.

Articles in my father's defence were published in *The Reporter*, the journal of the Mercantile Marine Service Association, of which he was a member, and in the *Nautical Magazine*, while in the *Review of Reviews*, whose editor, Mr William T. Stead, had actually been lost in the *Titanic* disaster, Mr Filson Young drew attention to some of the major discrepancies between the evidence and the findings.

I feel quite sure that if it had not been for the First-World-War my father would have continued his efforts to clear his name, and that eventually he might have succeeded. But the war years proved that, now he was re-established in an excellent company, his professional interests had not suffered, nor did he ever meet anyone who referred critically in any way to the *Californian* and the official criticism of her alleged inaction during the *Titanic* disaster. All who really knew my father and who appreciated his personal integrity and ability as a shipmaster knew that he was innocent, and it was this knowledge that enabled him to bear the unfair burden of the charge.

When he left the sea, the events of 1912 cast no shadow over his long retirement and he led the normal life of any retired shipmaster, being completely contented and happy with the affection and companionship of his family. The *Titanic* was never referred to—it was of the past and, as far as he was concerned, the incident was closed.

But if his sea career and personal life had been relatively unaffected by the incident, his reputation as a shipmaster was still under a cloud so long as the official findings remained on record. Although he normally concealed his feelings about the matter it is obvious that it must have affected him deeply, and so it is easy to understand how distressed he was suddenly to discover in 1958, when he was 81, that not only was the

Californian's "guilt" now very widely believed, but that many authors and journalists were also concocting stories about the incident in which he was described in a completely different light from the true one.

Although I knew that he was upset by this discovery, I was still very surprised one day to learn that he had been over to Liverpool to inquire whether the Mercantile Marine Service Association still had the original file on the case, as he had decided to re-open it. This decision must have been a very difficult one to take, for now he was in failing health, and his desire to protect his reputation clashed with his anxiety to ensure that his private life was not upset. Nevertheless, he faced up to and accepted this risk, and it was consequently most fortunate for him that the M.M.S.A. was able to assume responsibility for the conduct of the case, thus sparing him much effort and worry. Indeed, it could be that, despite his initial apprehensions about the possible repercussions on his private life, my father actually found a new interest in what were to be the closing months of his life. Certainly he developed a supreme confidence that the action which had been initiated at his request would ultimately be successful.

The first major step in the campaign was the preparation of an article which it was intended should be released on the eve of the fiftieth anniversary of the *Titanic* disaster, in the hope of ensuring that any published references which might be made to the *Californian* would at least be accurate. Unfortunately, although my father was able to see the article in its final draft form, he died shortly before it was published.

Since then, the truth about the *Californian,* and my father's innocence of the charges levelled against him, have become more and more widely known. I hope that the publication of this book marks the opening of the final stages of this unhappy case, and I consider that its appearance fully justifies the confidence and faith held by my father that one day his reputation as a shipmaster would be officially restored.

STANLEY TUTTON LORD

INTRODUCTION TO THE 2015 EDITION

This book, written in 1965, was the first to seek to redress the injustice done Captain Stanley Lord of the *Californian* at the British Court of Inquiry into the loss of the *Titanic* in 1912. The book was written in anger – as I explained in the original Introduction which follows - anger directed at Lord Mersey, who presided over the Inquiry, and the senior law officers of the Crown and assessors who assisted him in making a scapegoat of Captain Lord to assuage public shock and anger and mask the government department and others chiefly responsible for the loss of life when *Titanic* sank – as this book makes clear.

Fifty years on this Introduction to the new edition is written in something like despair. Proliferating websites devoted to *Titanic* and *Californian*, including Wikipedia, reveal a marked and often malicious bias against Captain Lord, while Mersey and his preposterous distortions of the evidence at the Inquiry go unremarked. It is as if the work of Leslie Harrison, who presented the first formal petition to clear Lord's name, and so many others who have fought for justice for Lord over the years have been obliterated by the armchair jurists duped by Merseys' inventions, their own nautical and analytical incompetence or pure malevolence.

Since this book was written there has been an important addition to the navigational evidence. In 1985 Dr. Robert Ballard of Woods Hole Oceanographic Institute, Massachusetts, located the wreck of the *Titanic* on the ocean floor. The boilers, which must have plunged straight to the bottom when she went down, lay at 41° 43'N 49° 57'W; so, for the first time there was incontrovertible evidence of exactly where the liner sank

- not for where she struck the iceberg, for in the two hours thirty five minutes between striking the berg (23.45/14 April) and sinking (2.20/15 April) she drifted in the current.

During this time the *Californian* lay stopped considerably to the north of her at 42° 05'N 50° 07'W by Captain Lord's estimate. The latitude component was certain: Lord's chief officer, G.F.Stewart, an experienced navigator with an Extra-Master's Certificate, the highest qualification for merchant service officers, had taken a Pole Star sight at 19.30 on the evening of the 14th, and had confirmed his finding - 42° 05'N – with another Pole Star sight at 22.30 shortly after ice was sighted and the *Californian* stopped to await daylight. This is significant for the altitude of the Pole Star is virtually equal to the latitude at the point of observation. I inadvertently omitted Stewart's second Pole Star sight from this book, but his evidence at the British Inquiry (Question 8706) leaves no doubt on this important point.

The following morning Lord learned of the wireless distress messages sent by the *Titanic* during the night. He set off cautiously through the ice field, then took the *Californian* at full speed southwards towards the position given by the *Titanic*. It was too late. All survivors in boats had been rescued by the *Carpathia*. But she and floating debris from the liner were far to the east and south of the position given in the *Titanic*'s distress calls. Lord searched fruitlessly among the flotsam for some hours before resuming his course westward for Boston at 11.20. At noon all *Californian*'s officers were on the bridge taking sights; working back 40 minutes from the position established, Lord estimated the *Titanic*'s floating wreckage as lying in 41° 33'N 50° 01W.

So, we have one certain position – where the *Titanic* sank – and two positions with all the accuracy possible in that age of navigation by sextant and chronometer - which was considerable: these were *Californian*'s position - with the latitude certain - at 22.30 on the 14th, one hour and 15 minutes before the *Titanic* struck, and the position of the liner's floating wreckage at 11.20 next morning, the 15th, nine hours after she went down. This wreckage lay ten miles South (196°) of where she sank. Assuming this was the main floating wreckage field, the current must have been setting 196° at 1.1 knots – considerably faster than might have been expected; nevertheless, applying this current to both *Titanic* and *Californian* (after the 10.30 Pole Star sight on the 14th) the following chart can be constructed.

This places the *Californian* 19.5 miles from the *Titanic* when the liner struck the berg, well outside the distance either ship could see the other – over twice the separation Lord Mersey had judged; and since the South-setting current must have affected both ships equally from that time, they must have remained in the same relative positions and the same distance apart until the *Titanic* sank.

This is as near a definitive conclusion on the positions of both ships that night as will ever be achieved, and is consistent with the most reasonable conclusion reached in '*RMS "Titanic": Reappraisal of Evidence Relating to SS "Californian"* published in 1992 by the Marine Accident Investigation Branch (MAIB) of the Department of Transport, which had taken over responsibility for shipping from the Board of Trade. The 'Reappraisal' was commissioned as a result of Dr Ballard's discovery of the wreck of the liner, followed by much lobbying from Leslie Harrison and others. Fortunately the Deputy Chief Inspector of Marine Accidents at this time, Captain J.C.L.de Coverly, was intelligent, fair-minded and conscientious, qualities not well represented in the official correspondence on the *Californian* incident hitherto; consequently an Inspector was appointed to re-examine the evidence relating to the positions of the two ships and to consider whether the *Titanic's* distress signals were seen from the *Californian*.

The Inspector duly reported. He placed the *Californian* in 'about 41° 50'N 50° 07'W', some 8-10 miles from the *Titanic* when she struck the berg - although in his personal opinion the two ships were only 5-7 miles apart. He based his calculation on the presumption that a southerly current had affected the *Californian* since noon on the 14th and set her far to the south of her position as estimated when she stopped that night. No reason is given for his arbitrary dismissal of the Chief Officer's Pole Star sights which placed the ship on latitude 42° 05' N – 15 miles North of his estimate - when she stopped.

Not unnaturally Captain de Coverly disagreed with the Inspector's reckoning. In his opinion the full strength of the Southerly current was not felt by the *Californian* until she came close to the ice which caused her to stop engines for the night. He assumed she then drifted southwards for some five miles after the 19.30 Pole Star sight and before the *Titanic* struck the iceberg, and placed her at 42° 00'N 50° 09'W - between 17-20 miles from the liner when she struck. This, however, ignores the Chief Officer's 22.30 Pole Star sight. De Coverly probably missed this piece of evidence indicating that there had been no southerly drift up to that time. Nonetheless, he was clear that the *Titanic* when she struck could not have been seen from the *Californian* – unless by abnormal refraction - equally clear on the evidence from the *Titanic* that no one aboard the liner saw the *Californian* or any other ship until much later.

How the Inspector thought the *Titanic* was seen from the *Californian* when no one on the *Titanic*, neither lookouts nor officers, saw any other ship until about an hour later is a mystery that needs explanation. None was given in the 'Reappraisal' when published. Nor is any explanation given for the Inspector's rejection of the *Californian's* Pole Star sights.

The MAIB 'Reappraisal', when published, carried both the Inspector's and Captain de Coverly's very different conclusions, hence my comment above that my chart is consistent with 'the most reasonable conclusion' drawn in the report. Captain de Coverly did agree with the Inspector that *Titanic*'s distress rockets were seen from the *Californian*, but he did not believe this had penetrated Captain Lord's consciousness as he slept: 'I think the message from the Bridge simply did not get through.' He thus transferred the blame from Lord to the Second Officer on the Bridge who had failed to wake the captain from deep sleep.

The inclusion of both Captain de Coverly's and the Inspector's findings in the 'Reappraisal' on what seemed an almost equal footing left all questions in the air. The Press was baffled; no commentator picked out the essence of Captain Lord's exoneration. Above all, there was not and now could not be an official closure to the '*Californian*' incident' and the censure of her captain.

Despite this, I remain in no doubt that the British *Titanic* Inquiry was rigged by Lord Mersey, ably assisted by the Law officers appearing for the Board of Trade and abetted by the panel of assessors . Lord gave evidence as a witness only; there were no questions regarding his conduct before the Court; he was not a Party to the proceedings and was not legally represented. The question regarding his conduct was added after he went home. And after he was censured for not steaming to the rescue - an indictable misdemeanour - he was not prosecuted. It was a shaming day for British justice.

* * *

Since first publication of this book, and particularly since the coming of the internet, debate has raged between supporters of the late Captain Lord and others who damn him; but many dispassionate articles have also been published shedding scholarly light on aspects of the *Titanic* disaster. Here are a few from *The Titanic Commutator*, the journal of the *Titanic* Historical Society: Samuel Halpern's 'Light on the Horizon' analyses the ships' lights seen from both the *Titanic* and the *Californian* (vol. 32 No.181); Bill Wormstedt and others analyse the timing of *Titanic*'s first distress rockets (vol.33 No.188); Patrick Stenson in '*Titanic* meets Iceberg: The Evidence Revisited' and 'The Evidence Revisited Again' argues that the iceberg may have been as close as 170 yards to the *Titanic* before it was sighted (vol. 37 No. 198; vol.38 No.201); and there are countless others.

As for the doughty fighters for Lord's good name, the late Leslie Harrison was the first; he was utterly professional and, though vilified by the ignorant, extraordinarily tenacious; the late Rob Kamps, who edited Thomas Williams' *Titanic and the Californian* (2007), was equally committed and persistent until his untimely death; Senan Malony, author of *A Ship Accused* (2002) and other works on the topic, continues the struggle. Anyone who follows the immensely detailed evidence in *A Ship Accused* and continues to believe Lord blameworthy deserves compassion. My apologies to the many others valiant for truth I have not named.

Peter Padfield, Woodbridge 2015

INTRODUCTION TO THE 1966 EDITION

More myths have grown up around the *Titanic* disaster than possibly any other tragedy of the sea. The fate of the *Mary Celeste* is her nearest rival, but speculation about her is confined to only one set of mysterious circumstances, and the serious possibilities which arise out of them are limited. Not so with the *Titanic*. Despite two extensive inquiries held immediately after her loss there are many aspects of her one remarkable and truly titanic, uncompleted voyage which can only be guessed at.

For one thing only four men survived with useful information about her navigation and the ice warnings. These were the Second Officer, Lightoller, who had been in charge of the deck during the watch prior to the fatal one, the Fourth Officer, Boxhall, who was a junior officer on watch at the time of the accident, although inside the chartroom when it happened, the junior wireless operator, Bride, who had received some of the ice messages, and the chairman of the Line, J. Bruce Ismay, who had been kept informed by the Captain of the progress of the voyage and of one, at least, of the ice warnings.

But the Captain, all the senior officers with the single exception of the Second Officer, *all* the engineers and the managing director of her builders went down with the ship. These were really the key-men who might have been able to counteract the flood of conjecture and accusation which flourished after her loss like the seaweed in her plush-plastered staterooms below the Atlantic. In the months which followed the stories multiplied and fiction became indistinguishable from fact. The barnacles grew scabrous on the beautiful hull. The myths which had started as newspaper reports or survivors' tales and later as Court judgements became accepted, and have been repeated authoritatively but often inaccurately in a host of books down to the present day.

This book is an attempt to explore just one myth out of the many—the most pernicious of them all—a legal slander which affected a man's reputation for the rest of his life and which could have finished his professional career. The man was Captain Stanley Lord, master of the Leyland liner, *Californian*; the myth has come down the years from the original Court hearings in 1912 as "the *Californian* incident".

This is how it goes: on the night and at the time the *Titanic* went down the officer of the watch on the *Californian's* bridge saw rockets or flares apparently coming from a ship to the southward. He called the master—once, twice, three times—but Lord took no notice and slept on in his bunk while his ship lay stopped in plain sight of the sinking liner, and ignored all her calls for help.

It was a strange story—on the face of it a mad story, and scarcely believable about a British liner captain. But it *was* believed because people wanted to believe; it provided one man upon whom they could focus all their horror and despair at the outrage. And primarily it was believed because it was given authority by a British law lord—Mersey of Toxteth—sitting as president of the Court of Inquiry into the loss.

And it is here, in the courtroom of the British Inquiry that the sinister aspect of this story really begins. For it is impossible to read through the transcript of the evidence and the final judgement without realising that Mersey and his Court were not dealing with facts or law or justice when they heard Captain Lord so much as faithfully reflecting the temper of the outside world—a world staggering on its beam-ends with the magnitude of the drama, and howling for blood.

"Someone ought to hang over this *Titanic* business. Sixteen hundred men and women have been murdered on the high seas."[1]

In this atmosphere the story about Captain Lord was a very convenient story. . . .

Probably the first person to talk about him was a donkeyman from the *Californian*, Ernest Gill, a Yorkshireman who had briefly seen the lights of a near-by ship while walking on deck to call his mate just before twelve midnight on April 14th, and who had later, while off watch, seen

1 Horatio Bottomley in *John Bull*.

two rockets fired from about the same direction. He sold his story to a Boston newspaper. Other papers caught on. At the same time some of the officers and many of the crew and passengers who had survived the *Titanic* described seeing the lights of a "mystery ship" approaching and then turning away as the *Titanic* foundered and while continuous distress rockets were being fired. The story, hotter than wildfire, crossed the Atlantic; a few weeks later sections of the British Press, prejudging the case after seeing the *Californian* witnesses in the stand at the British Inquiry, leaped upon Lord and attacked him for inhumanity.

"No doubt it was a cold night, and it was not pleasant to turn out of a warm bed, to go on the bridge, and drive through the ice. But surely you might have taken the trouble to instruct somebody to call up the Marconi operator, and get him to try and find out what was the matter. Yet on your own evidence you slept on, and largely through your inaction 1,500 fellow creatures have perished. . . ."[22]

The story achieved its first substantiation in the Report of a special Senate committee which had been set up in Washington to inquire into the disaster. This committee began its sittings within a day of the arrival in New York of the pitifully few survivors, and rambled on for more than a month under the enthusiastic but dim chairmanship of a Senator William Alden Smith from the inland state of Michigan. It was not a technical investigation. Its brief covered all aspects of the disaster and to this the senators faithfully responded, conducting the questioning more on the lines of a conversazione than a responsible maritime Inquiry, an expensive and horrifying one which explored the highways and by-ways of human reactions to the disaster and threw odd lights on unexpected facets of emergency behaviour, but never really came to grips with the technicalities. They soon lost the confidence of the crew witnesses by their inability to understand the sailor's language. They were sniped at from all directions in their own country, especially by the Seamen's Unions, while informed opinion in England was equally sceptical of their competence to deal with anything but the broad human aspects of the tragedy.

But besides the crew and passengers from the *Titanic*, many of whom had seen the "mystery lights", three men from the *Californian* were called

2 *John Bull.*

to give evidence: these were the donkeyman who had started the story off, Captain Lord himself, and his wireless operator. Lord left after giving his evidence, unaware that the donkeyman's story was to be taken seriously. He had given his own version of the night's events quite simply, and his own log-book position which put his ship some 20 miles away from the signalled distress position of the *Titanic*. He had been treated gently, even courteously by the senators. He had not been asked any embarrassing questions, and had consequently no chance to reply to any suspicions which may have been lurking—which it turned out *had* been lurking—in the minds of the committee. He had no reason to suppose that he would hear anything more from them about his part in the tragedy.

And yet this is what was said: "The Committee is forced to the conclusion that the *Californian* . . . was nearer to the *Titanic* than the nineteen miles reported by her captain, and that the officers and crew saw the distress signals of the *Titanic* and failed to respond to them in accordance with the dictates of humanity, international usage and the requirements of law. . . . In our opinion such conduct, whether arising from indifference or gross carelessness is most reprehensible, and places upon the commander of the *Californian* a grave responsibility. . . . Had assistance been promptly proffered, or had the wireless operator of the *Californian* remained a few minutes longer at his post on Sunday evening, that ship must have had the proud distinction of rescuing the lives of the passengers and crew of the *Titanic*."

Although the committee was regarded by seamen and many landsmen as a farce, and although its findings were accompanied by what the *Daily Express* referred to as "the most amazing speech ever heard in any parliament in the world", and although the *Daily Mail* opined of Smith, "Where he descends to technical questions his now notorious want of knowledge of the sea renders his opinions absolutely worthless", his remarks about the *Californian* were nevertheless reported in great detail in most papers, and in many cases, notably the *Daily Mirror*, the significant points were underlined in bold type for greater effect. *The Times* reported the findings straight at some length without a word of doubt.

Meanwhile the British Inquiry, conducted by Mersey, assisted by five top nautical assessors had already been sitting for some weeks and had heard evidence from Lord and four of his officers. This evidence had been somewhat technical and infinitely confusing about bearings, distances, colour of lights and nature of vessels seen, and the press had consequently simplified it all and reported the few basic facts which they and their readers would understand. These were that rockets had been seen, that Lord had been called several times, and that he had done nothing. Anyone reading this without delving into where, how or exactly when these rockets had been seen, would naturally have drawn the obvious conclusions—as they did. Who, anyway, had the opportunity to delve?

But besides the apparently damning evidence from the *Californian* witnesses and especially, it seemed, from Lord himself, the president of the Court, Lord Mersey, declared his conviction of Lord's guilt at a very early stage when he remarked that it was in his mind that the ship seen from the *Californian had* been the *Titanic,* and the mysterious lights seen from the *Titanic had* been the *Californian.* This, too, was reported in bold type.

So it was no surprise to anyone when the Mersey Report confirmed what they already knew. "The night was clear and the sea was smooth. When she first saw the rockets the *Californian* could have pushed through the ice to the open water without any serious risk and so have come to the assistance of the *Titanic. Had she done so she might have saved many, if not all of the lives that were lost."*

Mersey had spoken; his sailor assessors had agreed unanimously. With a few sheets of immaculate prose the burden of guilt for the unnecessary loss of over fifteen hundred lives had been placed squarely on the back of Captain Stanley Lord, who remained thereafter until his dying day, "Lord of the *Californian*".

* * *

Not the least of the remarkable things about the story of the *Titanic* is that these two immensely lengthy and dramatic Inquiries which she occasioned have never been made the subject of a book. This omission forms a most incomprehensible gap in nautical literature. While the story of the tragedy itself has been repeated endlessly and with varying degrees of accuracy, the only publication about the British Inquiry has been *The*

Journal of Commerce edited transcript of the evidence (together with explanatory notes by Professor W. S. Abel) which appeared very shortly after the judgement. Since then nothing. Latterday authors have accepted Mersey's remarks as if they constituted an infallible pronouncement. This is made more surprising by the fact that there have been unbelievers ever since the Report appeared; one of the first was the said Professor Abel of Liverpool University who wrote what at the time must have been a courageously sceptical résumé of the evidence about the *Californian* incident in his introduction to the edited edition of the Inquiry.

"It also appears from the evidence," he concluded, "that the *Californian* observed the signals of distress which were sent up by the *Titanic*, but whether this was the actual vessel whose lights were seen from the sinking ship is a matter *the evidence does not show.*"

And quite independently, another man, a solicitor from Carbis Bay named A. M. Foweraker who had, unknown to Captain Lord, been taking a keen interest in what he considered were wrong deductions and legal anomalies in the case against Lord wrote detailed analyses of his conclusions in *The Nautical Magazine* and in the journal of the Mercantile Marine Service Association entitled "Pushed under the Wheels of the Juggernaut", and "A Miscarriage of Justice".

Lord himself was actively, but entirely unsuccessfully engaged in clearing his own name until the outbreak of the First World War, after the end of which, finding that public interest had died down and that his life was no longer seriously affected, he let the matter drop.

It probably wouldn't have been raised again during his lifetime had it not been for the publication of *A Night to Remember* in 1957. This book which was subsequently made into a film, told the story of the "cream of New York and Boston Society"—and their dogs—on board the doomed liner. It described the *Californian* incident as if from the lips of Mersey himself, and for good measure added a picture of Captain Stanley Lord holding a telescope, with a derisive caption below to the effect that he didn't make much use of it on the night the *Titanic* went down.

This was too much for Lord. He went immediately to his old Association, the Mercantile Marine Service Association, and put his case before the general secretary, Leslie Harrison. Mr Harrison investigated the transcript of the evidence and discovered, as had a very few before him, the astonishing fallacies on which the Court based its judgement. And from that time onwards, despite Lord's death in 1962, he had made strenuous efforts to clear Lord's name by means of publicity in the national press, articles in marine journals and advertisements for new evidence; as this book goes to press a formal petition is about to be presented to the Minister of Transport calling for a reopening of that part of the 1912 Inquiry relating to the *Californian*.

The *Titanic* story still exerts a powerful fascination and compels fierce rivalries: only recently a former Cunard commodore resigned from the Council of the Mercantile Marine Service Association rather than become involved in any attempt to clear Lord's name. And there are many other-Western Ocean men, in all other respects stout-hearted and true, who are so imbued with the *Californian* myth that they look upon it as an article of faith and refuse to examine the evidence on which it is based.

But just as dangerous perhaps are those who have buried the whole affair as past history, and who consider it a waste of time to resurrect the old agonies and arguments.

They are wrong. The conduct of tribunals and inquiries[3] has a burning relevance today. Firstly it is a continuing weakness of our legal system that there is, in most cases, no appeal from any public censure or incidental dirt which may attach itself to *witnesses* before Tribunals. Secondly, Press and Parliament alike are unable to investigate their findings if held *in camera*. Thirdly it is not unknown for Inquiries to be used simply as tools for dampening public unrest and substituting complacent assurances. Therefore while these issues are relevant in the light of the *Titanic* and contemporary Inquiries and while suspicion of an injustice as gross as the slander on Captain Lord remains, an examination of the conduct of this particular Inquiry cannot be either dated or unnecessary.

But the British *Titanic* Inquiry is important from another angle, for, while it exemplifies what can happen at any time when politics and the law get mixed up in a scandal, it also indicates that the image of the Press as a watchdog couchant, ready to spring to the defence of liberty in danger, or individuals suffering injustice—an image which it naturally likes

---

3 This is meant in a wider context than only *maritime* Inquiries.

to foster—may be seriously misleading where the popular appeal of the resulting story is in doubt. The fact is that the national Press, for one reason or another, swallowed the Mersey Report on the *Californian* incident whole. If they did this through nautical ignorance and not through apathy or design it still remains a criticism of their self-styled role as a curb on the worst excesses of the "establishment".

In this case the "establishment" was the Board of Trade, an invincibly conservative body which had allowed its regulations with regard to life-saving appliances to become dangerously out-dated, and which was already under raking fire over the loss of life after the liner *Oceana* had been sunk in collision the previous month.

The great vortex of shock created when the *Titanic* plunged to the bottom and left over 1,500 people to die by cold and drowning without hope of lifeboat accommodation—shock which to be adequately imagined has to be set against the apparent stability of those high old days of Empire before the First World War—quickly filled with anger. Much of the anger, probably the major share of informed anger, was directed at the Board of Trade whose administration had allowed this gigantic liner and her sister, *Olympic,* and others not so large to go to sea with such derisory lifeboat accommodation. It was not as if no one had told them. A question had been asked in the House two years before directing attention to the inadequate lifeboat accommodation on the *Olympic.* The official slightly supercilious reply had been, "The vessel has not only the statutory accommodation, but even more." Although the *Titanic* and the *Olympic* went to sea with boats sufficient for approximately one-third of their total complement they carried *more* boats than the statutory requirement!

The secretary of the Imperial Merchant Service Guild was able to comment on this lamentable fact, "The *Titanic* disaster is a complete substantiation of the agitation that our Guild has carried on for nearly thirty years against the system that precludes practical seamen being consulted with regard to boat capacity and life-saving appliances. . . . The *Titanic* disaster is an example on a colossal scale of the pernicious and supine system of the officials as represented by the Board of Trade."

When the British Inquiry was set up it was the Board of Trade which should have been standing trial alongside the White Star Line and its officers. And it is ironical that while they should have been answering the main charge of criminal negligence, it was the Board who, by virtue of their powers under the Merchant Shipping Act, were asking the questions, briefing the law officers of the Crown, and holding the reins of the Inquiry throughout.

As the Board of Trade was a government department, and as the government, by its *laisser-faire* attitude towards the Board and the big transatlantic liner companies, was implicated in the affair, the disaster was also a political question. But it was not an issue which could be turned to party gain, for the Tories, now in opposition, had done nothing to change the system during their own years in power. That the final reckoning had come during a period of Liberal rule was immaterial.

In these circumstances the Court was convened. All the pressures for an Inquiry designed to quieten public indignation and preserve the reputation of Britain's great transatlantic liner companies were on the surface, clear for anyone to see. The precedents for such an Inquiry had already been established. Mersey himself was tainted in some eyes with having been a member of the "whitewashing" Jamieson Raid Committee. And it is worth noting that the following year saw the extreme nadir of the Inquiry system when the Attorney-General, Sir Rufus Isaacs, who appears in this book leading for the Board of Trade, was under examination for his part in the share dealings known as "the Marconi Scandal".

***

A few words now about how this book came to be written: I came to the official transcript of the British Inquiry unaware of the background against which it has to be set, although not unaware, it must be admitted, of the campaign which Leslie Harrison was conducting on behalf of the late Captain Stanley Lord. Regarding the campaign with interest, I yet wasn't convinced one way or the other for I knew little of the circumstances and Harrison himself had warned against the dangers of studying some of the documents he had published without reference to the actual evidence given in Court.

So I came to the transcript with an open mind and my purpose was merely to collect material for one, or at the most two chapters of a book about collisions at sea. This idea was soon shelved. The *Titanic* became all-engrossing. Besides the remarkable drama of that unfinished maiden voyage—drama which comes more clearly through the old pages of the transcript than through most of the subsequent books about her—besides this there were the question marks, the unprobed basic facts, the crazy deductions, the distortions, the prejudice, the occasional bone-headed obstinacy of both witnesses and the Court refusing to accept facts which are so obvious outside and fifty years away from the Court room. The gaps in the evidence were tantalising; I began to suspect that however much historical detection work anyone put in, the whole truth of the *Titanic's* one voyage would never be known.

But more than this, my astonishment that Captain Lord was censured on the half-cock evidence I was reading grew with each day—and with it anger, not manufactured, literary anger, but the real blood-bubbling bile. This book was begun in anger.

It seemed to me then, without having studied any of the contemporary passions or prejudice, that the unbelievable conflicts of evidence which the Board of Trade and the Court glossed over, and the unbelievable mistakes of simplification, distortion, cannibalisation of various testimony, and even invention to which Mersey descended in his Report could only point to a "rigged" Inquiry.

This still seems to me a valid theory. For if it is rejected—and most Englishmen must surely reject it—it becomes extremely difficult to explain the Mersey Report on the *Californian,* or the speeches in Court by the law officers of the Crown acting for the Board of Trade, or their extraordinary failure to examine all the lookouts from the *Titanic* about the 'mystery' lights, or their failure to probe the exact position or the approximate heading of the *Titanic* when she foundered, or the time she was keeping, or, even more sinister, the failure of the Crown to prosecute Captain Lord afterwards for the serious misdemeanour Mersey had censured him for. If it is rejected it is difficult to explain how Mersey suddenly forgot his life's training at the Bar and censured a man, Captain Lord, who had not been made a party to the proceedings, who had not been served with notice of investigation, who had given evidence as a witness only, who had no legal representation apart from counsel holding a watching brief for the Leyland Line, and who had gone home long before the Board of Trade added the question which affected his conduct to the list before the Court. Any criticism of Lord was contrary to the whole spirit of British justice which demands that a man must be charged before being found guilty, and must be given every chance to defend himself. Lord was given no chance, for he wasn't told that his conduct was in question. And nor was it when he gave evidence. Mersey knew all this; he reflected on it aloud in questions to the Attorney-General, and yet he finally rejected it as *less important than finding Lord guilty*—finding him guilty moreover upon such insubstantial and conflicting evidence that it is difficult to understand how any intelligent man can reconcile it at all. And Mersey, unlike Senator Smith, was a highly intelligent man.

So, was the Inquiry rigged, and was Lord "framed"? Were the parties to what is almost certainly a flagrant miscarriage of justice also parties to conspiracy? Did Lord Mersey, Sir Rufus Isaacs, the Attorney-General, his colleague, Sir John Simon the Solicitor-General, and the Board of Trade together make it their business to see that the public had *someone* on whom to vent their anger?

It is an interesting speculation. And while it is extremely difficult to imagine an explicit agreement between Mersey and the government, represented by the law officers, it must be remembered that it was a system which was on trial as well as men. It was a system which was a direct result of the attitude of both the Board of Trade and the government itself—a system of running passenger liners fast through known ice regions (and through fog), and, perhaps more serious, a system which encouraged mammoth liners to go to sea with lifeboat accommodation for only a small fraction of the permitted souls on board.

So any theory of conspiracy is by no means as far-fetched as it may sound. Indeed the only stumbling block to any such theory (in my opinion) is the silence of the assessors, the majority of whom were practical sailors. It is well known that sailors as assessors are often harsher than they need be towards their own kind in misfortune before them, but the point here is not one of harshness—the point is conspiracy to indict one man for the loss of fifteen hundred lives. It seems impossible that the assessors would explicitly agree to this. What had they to gain by so doing, or to lose by keeping silent? And yet they must have seen the great gaps and flaws in the evidence—they more than the landsmen. The fact that they added their unanimous approval to the Mersey Report is so inexplicable that it must surely imply some national paralysis of reason brought about by the enormity of the disaster. This at any rate is the kindest theory for all concerned.

Since the publication of this book in England and the simultaneous presentation of the Mercantile Marine Service Association's Petition to the Board of Trade (see page 14) to try to obtain a re-hearing of that part of the British Inquiry concerned with the *Californian* and her Captain, the Board have issued a statement that they are "satisfied that there was no miscarriage of justice" towards Captain Lord. They have given no legal or technical reasons for thus summarily rejecting the Petition.

They cannot give any such reasons, because there are none.

The evidence at the British Inquiry provides two entirely separate proofs—besides many other evidential probabilities—that the *Californian* was *not* where Lord Mersey said she was. The first proof, which the Petition brought out clearly, is that none of the *Titanic's* lookouts saw the lights of any other ship either before they struck the berg or for some time afterwards, while the *Californian* had had the ship which Lord Mersey said was the *Titanic* in sight for over half an hour before that ship struck; further, that the coincidence upon which Lord Mersey rested so much of his case—that both the *Titanic* and the ship near the *Californian* stopped at the same time, 11:40—was only a coincidence because the British Court failed to probe the times which the two ships were keeping. When the times are examined it is seen that they did not stop simultaneously—according to the evidence heard before Lord Mersey's Inquiry.

The second proof is that the *Titanic's* fourth officer, Boxhall, whose testimony was never questioned and upon whose veracity much of the case against Captain Lord must have rested, stated that when firing rockets he was trying to communicate by signal light with the "mystery ship." As did the quartermaster, Rowe, who was with him at the time. The 2nd Officer of the *Californian* and his apprentice were also trying to communicate with a ship lying near *them*. Yet all four, Boxhall, Rowe and the two *Californian* men, stated that they elicited no response from the other ship. How, then, could it have been between the *Titanic* and the *Californian* that these men were trying to communicate?

With the navigational evidence of details *before* the disaster, these two points make it certain that the *Titanic* and the *Californian* were never in sight of one another on that night.

Fifty years and more after the tragedy, then, the *Titanic* has given rise to yet another mystery: how is it that the present Board of Trade are "satisfied" that there was no miscarriage of justice?

It must be remembered in this respect that it was the Board of Trade who conducted the original Inquiry, and the Board of Trade Counsel who pointed the finger at Captain Stanley Lord to divert attention from the Board's own shortcomings in the matter of Safety Regulations. It was the Board of Trade who, immediately after the Mersey Report, failed to study the case argued for Captain Lord by the Mercantile Marine Service Association, and dismissed it with a few official notes because "the solicitor was on holiday."

The author has drawn these contradictions to the attention of the present Board of Trade; they have replied that, while it is recognized that there was conflict on certain points, they are satisfied that there was evidence to justify the Court coming to the conclusions that it reached. The Board have not specified this evidence, nor have they answered any of the specific points submitted. The author suggests that there was no *evidence,* simply speculation and coincidence worked from erroneous times and unprobed positions.

Perhaps in the years to come the *Titanic* will be remembered as much for the stain on the fair name of British justice, which has so recently been perpetuated, as for the tragic circumstances of her loss.

CONTENTS

ILLUSTRATIONS

Following page 83

The *Titanic**
The *Californian*†
The *Titanic* sinking‡
Captain Smith*
Collapsible lifeboat with survivors*
Captain Stanley Lord
The Courtroom§
Lord Mersey*
Sir Rufus Isaacs (Lord Reading)*

Key to Acknowledgements

* The Radio Times Hulton Picture Library
† National Maritime Museum
‡ *The Illustrated London News*
§ *The Sphere*

CHARTS AND DIAGRAMS

ACKNOWLEDGEMENTS

My deepest thanks are due to Leslie Harrison, general secretary of the Mercantile Marine Service Association for all the help he has given unsparingly throughout my work on this book. Without his selfless enthusiasm, bright ideas, and encyclopaedic knowledge of many of the events of that tragic night in 1912, this book would have been a poor shadow of what it has become. Despite this I am sure he would not wish to be associated with *all* the views expressed!

I should also like to thank Wilton J. Oldham, author of that splendid book, *The Ismay Line,* for his help and encouragement, for his permission to use extracts from the book, and incidentally for his belief, as a man who knew Captain Lord, that Lord would have been incapable of the actions ascribed to him by two Courts of Inquiry. And I am grateful to Captain W. H. Coombs, C.B.E., for his detailed criticism of the typescript, and for his many constructive suggestions. As also to J. R. Ellis for his suggestions from the legal angle.

My thanks are due to Alan Villiers for permission to quote from his book, *Of Ships and Men,* to Lawrence Beesley for permission to quote extensively from his, *The Loss of the Titanic,* to Commodore Sir James Bisset, K.B., C.B.E., R.D., R.N.R., Ll.D., for permission to use some recollections from his book *Tramps and Ladies,* and to Frances Donaldson, who wrote *The Marconi Scandal,* for her help.

Memories are not infallible after more than fifty years and I have not sought out survivors for their recollections, but I am grateful to one survivor, Mr Dent Ray, for his long letter in response to the only such inquiry I made. And I should like to thank Mrs Russell Cooke, Captain Smith's daughter, for her comments on the typescript, and similarly thank Mrs

Lightoller, widow of the *Titanic's* Second Officer for her frank comments on the typescript and her recollections of her late husband, who incidentally, despite the gruelling experiences described in Part 1 of this book, commanded destroyers during the First World War, and was still actively afloat ferrying small craft for the Admiralty in the Second—a great record.

I should like to thank the proprietors of *The Daily Telegraph* for permission to use the chart of the ice floes drawn up by the officers of the *Birma,* extracts from the accompanying letter and extracts from their editorial on the Inquiry findings; and also Odhams Press for permission to quote the open letter to Captain Lord which appeared in *John Bull;* also to Nicholson and Watson for permission to quote from *Titanic and other Ships,* by Charles Lightoller. Thanks also to Arco Publishing Co., New York, and George Newnes Ltd. for permission to quote from Alan Villiers' *Of Ships and Men;* also to A. D. Peters & Co. and Cassell and Company for permission to quote from *Home from the Sea* by Sir Arthur Rostron; and also to William Heinemann Ltd. and Houghton Mifflin Company for their permission to quote from Lawrence Beesley's *The Loss of the Titanic;* also to The Journal of Commerce for permission to quote from *The Ismay Line* by Wilton J. Oldham. I would also like to thank the *Daily Express* for allowing me to quote extracts from their newspaper.

My thanks are due to Mr Skellon of the Ministry of Transport, and the staff of the Ministry of Transport Library who smoothed my path with the official transcript of the British Inquiry. Finally I thank the higher policy-makers at the Ministry of Transport for their refusal to grant me access to the *Titanic* files, thus tending to deepen suspicion that there is something in the conduct of the case which still needs to be hidden—thus strengthening the thesis of my book.[1]

---

1 Since the typescript went to print some of these files have come off the secret list. A brief description will be found in Appendix J.

PART 1

THE VOYAGE OF THE *TITANIC*

EXPLANATION

Part 1 is the story of the loss of the *Titanic* told in a time continuum embracing the day and night of the disaster and also the Inquiry which was held in London during the months following. The two series of events run side by side. Questions and answers from the Inquiry are printed in italics to illuminate the action in the words of the actors themselves. Where no name is given before the words they can be taken as being from the character appearing in the narrative immediately before.

Probably the only nautical jargon which it is necessary to know in order to understand Part 1 is that concerned with wheel orders: in the days before 1931, when the officer of the watch said "Starboard!" the Quartermaster at the wheel turned the spokes to *port,* and the ship's head swung to *port.* This was a pernicious system, stemming from the old tiller orders, and as not all ships were party to it (especially those ships of the lesser maritime nations) it led to many misunderstandings and not a few collisions. Rule Britannia!

CHAPTER ONE

APTAIN TITANIC—WESTBOUND STEAMERS REPORT BERGS GROWLERS AND FIELD ICE IN 42 N FROM 49 TO 51 W 12TH APRIL—COMPLIMENTS BARR.

Captain Smith received this message from R.M.S. *Caronia* soon after breakfast on the morning of Sunday, April 14th, the fourth day out from Queenstown for New York. His splendid new command which was justifying all the high hopes placed in her was then in approximately 43° 35'N, 43° 50'W, South of the Flemish Cap in the North-Western Atlantic Basin, 500 odd miles ESE of Cape Race, Newfoundland, and nearing the cod fishing banks—the Grand Banks. She was steering a course of S 62°W true, along the correct Southern outward track to "the comer", 42°N, 47°W, where she was due to alter course up to S 85°W true. Just to the North of this track and still some 250 miles away lay the bergs, growlers and field ice of the *Caronia*'s message.

The engine revolution repeater on the bridge showed 75 revolutions per minute; the "Cherub" patent log which was streamed from the port side of the docking bridge right aft was registering 45 nautical miles steamed every two hours—corrected for permanent error, this gave her a speed of just under 22 knots.

Twenty-two knots—the world's largest liner—46,328 tons gross, 852 feet 6 inches long by 92 feet 6 inches beam, and displacing 52,310 tons—an astronomical momentum. Trials on her sister *Olympic* later that year showed that it would take 3 minutes 15 seconds to take all way off from 74 revolutions full ahead to full astern, during which time she would travel over 3,000 feet, or about half a nautical mile.

Under Captain Smith were seven deck, or navigating, officers, all mature seamen holding Master's Certificates. The Captain himself, the Second and Fourth Officers all held Extra Master's Certificates. The watches were arranged so that there was one senior officer—either the Chief, First or Second—in charge of the deck, and two junior officers with him, besides the quartermaster who took the wheel and the lookouts. The senior officers stood four hours on and eight off, the times of their change-over displaced two hours from the change-over times of the junior officers who did "four on, four off", and stood the "dogs" in the evening so that their watches altered each day. This was the practice on the crack White Star liners.

WATCH LISTS

		TITANIC			CALIFORNIAN	
		Captain SMITH			Captain LORD	
		Senior officer of watch	Junior officers of watch	Lookouts	Officer of watch	
2 p.m.			3rd officer PITMAN			2 p.m.
A P R I L	4	CHIEF OFFICER WILDE	5th officer LOWE			4
			4th officer BOXHALL 1st D O G			
			6th officer MOODY		CHIEF OFFICER STEWART	6
6 14th	6		2nd			
		2ND OFFICER LIGHTOLLER	3rd officer PITMAN 5th officer LOWE D O G	HOGG EVANS		8
	8		4th officer BOXHALL	JEWEL SYMONS	3rd OFFICER GROVES	10
	10	1ST OFFICER MURDOCH	6th officer MOODY	LEE FLEET		12 midnight
midnight 12				HOGG EVANS		
A P R I L	2 a.m.				2ND OFFICER STONE	2 a.m.
	4					4
15th	6				CHIEF OFFICER STEWART	6
	8					8

On Sunday, April 14th the senior officers' watches were: Murdoch (First), 10 a.m. to 2 p.m., Wilde (Chief) 2 p.m. to 6 p.m., Lightoller (Second) 6 p.m. to 10 p.m., then Murdoch again from ten o'clock. The Juniors were: Pitman (Third) and Lowe (Fifth) from 12 midday until 4 p.m., Boxall (Fourth) and Moody (Sixth) from 4 p.m. to 6 p.m. (the first "dog"), Pitman and Lowe from 6 to 8 (the second "dog") and then Boxhall and Moody from 8 until midnight. It is not necessary to go further.

At 12.30 midday, Lightoller relieved Murdoch for lunch after noon sights had been taken. About a quarter of an hour afterwards he saw the stocky, full-bearded figure of the Captain approaching, holding a Marconigram, which he thrust towards him.

Lightoller looked at it and saw it was an ice warning. This was in fact the message from the Cunarder *Caronia*, which had reached them earlier that morning. He made a mental note of the meridians 49 to 51, and handed it back.

The Captain stared out ahead at the smooth sea which sparkled in the spring sunshine, and shortly afterwards went out through the chartroom, which was just abaft the wheelhouse, and down to his table for lunch.

When Murdoch returned at one o'clock Lightoller told him about the ice message, and had the impression, although it was nothing more concrete than that, that it was news to him. He handed over the course and speed, "Everything the same", and went below to have his own lunch.

CAPTAIN SMITH TITANIC—HAVE HAD MODERATE VARIABLE WINDS AND CLEAR FINE WEATHER SINCE LEAVING. GREEK STEAMER ATHENAI REPORTS PASSING ICEBERGS AND LARGE QUANTITIES OF FIELD ICE TODAY IN LAT 41 51 N LONG 49 52 W. LAST NIGHT WE SPOKE GERMAN OILT-ANK STEAMER DEUTSCHLAND STETTIN TO PHILADELPHIA NOT UNDER CONTROL SHORT OF COAL LAT 40 42 N LONG 55 II W. WISHES TO BE REPORTED NEW YORK AND OTHER STEAMERS. WISH YOU AND TITANIC ALL SUCCESS—COMMANDER.

This message from the *Baltic*, which until the advent of the *Olympic* and the *Titanic*, had been one of the "big four" White Star liners, was received and acknowledged by the *Titanic* about a quarter to two in the afternoon, when the ship herself was in about 42° 35'N, 45° 50'W. The ice was nearer now; less than 200 miles ahead of them. Captain Smith had the message in his hand while walking along the 1st Class promenade-deck after lunch. J. Bruce Ismay, the Chairman of the White Star, taking the maiden voyage of his latest and proudest answer to the Cunard (his answer indeed to all the other transatlantic passenger companies) just as he had taken the maiden voyage of the *Olympic* the previous year, was on the deck. The Captain handed the message to him without a word and went on his way. They knew each other well, these two men. Captain Smith had been in command of the *Olympic* until this voyage, which was to be his last as he had reached the retiring age;[1] he was a confident, outgoing man, confident in himself, and confident like his generation in the irresistible march forward of man's scientific and mechanical genius, and of Britain's supreme destiny. He was popular with the passengers and popular with the crew; as Lightoller was to write later, "a man any officer would give his ears to sail under".[2]

"Broad, bluff, hearty, you would think at first sight, 'Here's a typical Western Ocean Captain,' Lightoller went on, 'and I'll bet he's got a voice like a foghorn.' But he had a pleasant, quiet voice and an invariable smile— a voice he rarely raised above a conversational level, although when he barked an order it made a man come to himself with a bump. He was one of the ablest and most experienced of the Atlantic skippers." He was also the highest paid. At a time when top Cunard commanders were receiving about £600 p.a. and top P & O men about £900, Smith was getting £1,250.

Ismay was not surprised to have the message thrust at him. Captain Smith often gave him messages—some important, others of only incidental interest. He read it briefly. Then he stuffed it in his pocket, bringing it out only to show two women who were curious, and afterwards pushing it back again and forgetting about it.

At two o'clock Wilde relieved Murdoch on the bridge. At 4 p.m., Boxhall and Moody relieved Pitman and Lowe as juniors. Boxhall, going into the chartroom, saw the *Caronia*'s message on the board and marked it on the chart with a cross which came very slightly to the North of the course line after "the corner" had been turned. The Captain's night order book, open on the chart table, contained instructions for the course to be altered at 5.50 to S 86°W true. Boxhall pricking off the position with the dividers, thought that they should reach the corner at about five o'clock, and assumed that the additional southing and westing which would be made good by holding on until 5.50 was probably in order to go further South than the reported ice. In fact it only took the *Titanic* about 8 miles below the course line, and the additional one degree more Northerly

---

1 Ismay had specially asked Smith to command the *Titanic* on her maiden voyage although he had already retired.
2 *Titanic and Other Ships*, Charles Lightoller.

course, S 86°W instead of that laid down of S 85°W, would bring her very gradually up to the line again.

At ten minutes to six Boxhall reminded Wilde about the change and Wilde ordered the quartermaster to steer N 71°W. This was the compass heading necessary to make the true course ordered.

The quartermaster swung the wheel over to port, watched the compass card follow it more gradually, but steadily as the ship was steady, and then eased the spokes over in the opposite direction. Wilde watched her head swing over to starboard.

Lord Mersey: "Mr Attorney, am I right in supposing that she ran right into the locality where the ice was after the warning that the ice was there?"

Attorney-General: "Yes."

Lord Mersey: "According to the indication made for me by my colleagues upon this chart, if that is to say, the figures given to me by the Attorney- General are right, it looks as if she, having had warning, made for the ice. . . ."

There was a general change over on the bridge at six o'clock. The junior officers changed, Lightoller relieved Wilde, and the quartermaster was relieved by his mate, Robert Hitchins.

"Going N 71°W."

"Was she a good steering ship?"

Hitchins: *"Fairly well, yes."*

"Up to the time of the collision did she vary from her course at all?"

"Not that I am aware of. Not more than a degree on either side."

At about ten minutes past seven Captain Smith found Bruce Ismay sitting in the smoke room and asked him for the *Baltic's* message so that he could post it for the information of the officers. Ismay remembered it suddenly and dug in his pocket, and handed it to him.

Up on the bridge Murdoch, who was relieving Lightoller for his dinner, watched the stars appearing one by one, faint at first, growing stronger in the gathering dusk. By the time Lightoller took over again they were out in their hundreds without a cloud to shadow them, and a midnight blue had crept up from the Eastern horizon. Lightoller took his sextant and called out for Lowe to stand by the chronometers.

Some miles to the North and West the *Californian,* outward bound from London to Boston was also steering a Westerly course. At 6.30 that evening she had passed icebergs. At 7.30 she radioed this to the *Antillian.*

TO CAPTAIN ANTILLIAN—6.30 P.M. APPARENT SHIP'S TIME. LAT 42 3 N 49 9 W. THREE LARGE BERGS FIVE MILES TO SOUTHWARD OF US. REGARDS LORD.

The *Titanic* was less than 44 miles from the ice. Her time was running away.

It is not clear what was happening in the Marconi office on the *Titanic* when this message went out. The junior operator, Bride, had gone down to dinner at seven, relieved by his senior, Phillips. When he returned he chatted for a while. When the *Californian's* message was going out to the *Antillian,* when, in fact, he might have recently returned from his meal, he was, according to his evidence at the Inquiry, writing up his accounts. He heard the message but didn't take it down. When the *Californian* a little while later called him and said they had a service message about ice he wrote the latitude and longitude down and took the message to the bridge. According to the *Californian's* operator the *Titanic* man replied that he already had the message and the *Californian* did *not* repeat the position. Whether this message was ever brought to the notice of the watch-keeping officers is extremely doubtful.

Soon after seven the *Titanic's* lamp-trimmer, Samuel Hemmings reported to Murdoch on the bridge that all lights were placed, and Murdoch told him to go forward and close the fore scuttle hatch which was allowing a faint glow through from below. He wanted nothing to interfere with vision from the bridge or crow's-nest, and remarked to Hemmings that they were in the vicinity of ice. Hemmings went to carry out the order.

At eight o'clock Robert Hitchins was relieved at the wheel and Boxhall and Moody relieved the junior officers. Boxhall began working up the star sights which Lightoller had taken, three stars for the latitude, three for the longitude, while Lightoller himself kept his eyes on the horizon ahead. After a while he called to Moody and asked him to work out when they might expect to reach the ice region.

Moody disappeared and came out later to tell him they would be there by eleven o'clock. Lightoller, with the meridians 49 to 51 still firmly in his mind, had already worked out mentally that they would be approaching the position at 9.30, but he didn't say anything, and assumed that Moody had seen a different report. By this time the dusk had given way to complete darkness—no moon, a flat calm sea and the stars striking fiercely through the cold atmosphere and reflected in the water. The only wind was made by the ship's progress.

The temperature was dropping fast. At seven when Lightoller had gone down for his meal it had been 43°, at half-past seven 39°, and as nine o'clock approached, it reached 33°. He called to Hitchins, now stand-by man, and told him to go forward to the carpenter. "Give him my compliments and tell him the thermometer is very low. He should look after his water in case it freezes."

"You do not think that indicates anything?"

"Nothing whatever. You may have it any time in the year, summer or winter, going across the Atlantic. It is not quite so noticeable in winter because the air is generally colder."

Lord Mersey: "That may be, but is it not the fact that when you are approaching large bodies of ice the temperature falls?"

"Never in my experience, my Lord."

"It does not go up I suppose?"

"Well, though it may seem strange it is quite possible for it to go up if the ice happens to be floating in slightly warmer water, or if the wind were to come from the southward."

"A continuous drop of 10° F in two hours, does that not indicate anything at all as regards the probable presence of ice?"

"Absolutely no indication whatever."

Soon after he had sent Hitchins away he saw the Captain making his way towards him. "It's cold, mister."

Lightoller told him what the temperature was, and that he had sent word around to the carpenter and the engine-room.

"There's not much wind."

"It's a flat calm," Lightoller replied. "It's a pity the wind hasn't kept up while we're going through the ice region."

"In the event of meeting ice there are many things we look for. In the first place a slight breeze. Of course the stronger the breeze the more visible

will the ice be, or rather the breakers on the ice. Therefore at any time when there is a slight breeze you will always see at night time a phosphorescent line around a berg, growler or whatever it may be; the slight swell which we invariably look for in the North Atlantic causes the same effect, the break on the base of the berg, so showing a phosphorescent glow. All bergs, all ice more or less, have a crystallised side . . . it has been crystallised through exposure and that in all cases will reflect a certain amount of light, what is termed ice blink, and that ice blink from a fairly large berg you will frequently see before the berg comes above the horizon."

"It's quite clear, though." The Captain was getting his night eyes. He could see the stars rising and setting all around the horizon with absolute distinctness.

They discussed the ice reports for a while and Lightoller said, "In any case there'll be a certain amount of reflected light from the berg."

"Oh, yes." The Captain had no doubts about it. "Even if the blue side is towards us we'll see the white outline."

Lightoller had no doubts either. He had done this hundreds of times. True it was a dark night without a moon but visibility was sharp and he'd seldom seen clearer weather. It never occurred to him to discuss a reduction in speed.

The Captain stayed talking with him for some twenty minutes before he left. As he walked away he said, "If it becomes at all doubtful let me know."

Lord Mersey: "And then did you understand and do you represent that if the slightest degree of haze arose it would at once become dangerous?"

"Well, it would render it more difficult to see the ice, though not necessarily dangerous. If we were coming on a large berg there might be a haze, as there frequently is in that position where warm and cold streams are intermixing. You will very frequently get a little low-lying haze, smoke we call it, lying on the water perhaps a couple of feet."

Lightoller called to Moody and told him to phone up to the crow's nest and tell them to keep a sharp lookout for ice, particularly small ice and growlers.

Moody went to the receiver and twizzled the bell handle. "Keep a sharp lookout for ice," he said, when the lookout man replied, "particularly small ice." He hung up.

Lightoller was near him. "And growlers."

Moody picked the receiver up again and repeated the message correctly.

"*Cannot you tell us at all whether that message was in any way caused or suggested by the conversation you had with the Captain?*"

"*It was not. I see your point, that having been talking with the Commander I should naturally take this precaution, but I may say that it was in no way suggested by the conversation with the Commander.*"

FROM MESABA TO TITANIC—IN LAT 42 N TO 41 25 N LONG 49 W TO 50 30 W SAW MUCH HEAVY PACK ICE AND GREAT NUMBER LARGE ICEBERGS ALSO FIELD ICE. WEATHER GOOD CLEAR.

This was received and acknowledged by Phillips on the *Titanic* soon after 9.30. He was very busy with Cape Race at the time, sending and receiving passenger's messages, and directly he had sent the acknowledgement he continued transmitting to them.

The *Mesaba's* operator heard him sending. He timed the acknowledgement signal, dated it, wrote in the office sent to and initialled it, then noted in his log that he was standing by, waiting for the *Titanic's* answer. The answer never came.

This message, a vital and very startling one, far more positive in delineation of area, which extended well South of and right across the *Titanic's* course line, and far more dramatic than any of the previous ones, *never reached the bridge.* Had it done so it would have told the navigators that the *Titanic* was already in among the bergs.

Lightoller walked out near the end of the exposed wing of the bridge which was actually just the forward end of the boat-deck and settled himself against the rail where he had a clear view ahead outside the shrouds and backstays to the mast. He remained there with his binoculars by him for the rest of the watch.

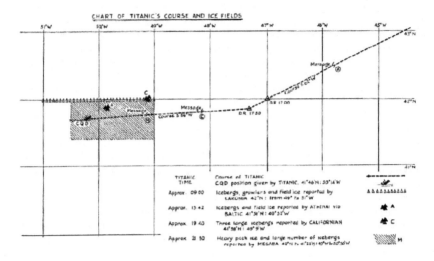

CHART OF TITANIC'S COURSE AND ICE FIELDS

TITANIC TIME	Course of TITANIC	
	CQD position given by TITANIC. 41°46'N : 50°14'W	•————•
Approx. 09 00	Icebergs, growlers and field ice reported by LAKONIA 42°N : from 49° to 51°W	🚢
Approx. 13 42	Icebergs and field ice reported by ATHINAI via BALTIC 41°51'N : 49°52'W	▲ A
Approx. 19 40	Three large icebergs reported by CALIFORNIAN 41°59'N : 49° 9'W	🚢 C
Approx. 21 30	Heavy pack ice and large number of icebergs reported by MESABA 42°N to 41°25'N : 49°W to 50°30'W	░░ M

"*In your experience when you have used glasses, have you in fact found ice with the help of glasses?*"

"*Never. I have never seen ice through glasses first. Never in my experience. Always, whenever I have seen a berg I have seen it first with my eyes and then examined it through glasses.*"

Murdoch came on deck at ten o'clock with a scarf and an overcoat on, working his arms across his body. "It's pretty cold."

"It is—it's freezing." By that time the thermometer had fallen a further degree to 32°. "We might be around the ice any time now." Lightoller handed over the course and then told the First Officer that the Commander had been on deck and had asked to be called if there was anything doubtful.

Then he went to make his rounds before turning in.

"*This is the first time in my experience of the Atlantic in twenty-four years, and I have been going across the Atlantic nearly all that time . . . of seeing an absolutely flat sea.*"

Lord Mersey: "*Do you mean that there was no swell at all?*"

"*I mean to say that the sea was so absolutely flat that when we lowered the boats down we had to actually overhaul the tackles to unhook them, because there was not the slightest lift to the boat to allow for slacking, unhooking.*"

"You have had great experience of the North Atlantic at all times of year. Just tell me, when a liner is known to be approaching ice, is it or is it not your experience usual to reduce speed?"

"I have never known speed to be reduced on any ship I have ever been in the North Atlantic in clear weather on account of ice."

These officers of the White Star were hard men. They were first and foremost sailors brought up in a still rough, tough school—the great majority from sailing ships. They were no strangers to sudden disaster. Lightoller himself had been wrecked on a desert island very early on in his career and had served in a variety of trades and ships before going for his interview for the White Star. He was to write later, "These ships are not only the cream of the service but the cream of the mercantile marine, and it is considered a feather in one's cap to be appointed to one. Therefore, despite the rigorous conditions and the powers of endurance one has to exhibit, there is never a word of complaint. Time and again I have seen the ship driven into a huge, green wall of water, crowned with that wicked, curling breaker, which it seemed utterly impossible for anything to withstand. An immediate dash is made for the nearest stanchion, and gripping this with might and main, one awaits the crash. Not infrequently the steel-fronted bridge, stanchions and rail are driven back and nearly flattened to the deck."[3]

Such were the hard-driving traditions of the company. The mails and the passengers came first.

Here are extracts from the Captain's report to the company from one of the first four White Star liners which inaugurated the transatlantic trade of the company, the first *Republic*, 3,707 tons:

At sea.
February 3rd, 1871.

Gentlemen,

Since leaving Liverpool we have had nothing but bad weather. In my letter from Queenstown I told you of detention from leakage in the upper between decks, forward of the saloon; I am sorry to say it still continues, and we have many

---

3 *Titanic and Other Ships*, Charles Lightoller.

other difficulties to contend with; the saloon and staterooms have been flooded through the new ventilation; the windows of the wheelhouse have been dashed in by a sea, and compass unshipped and broken, etc.; the stanchions of the bridge and bridge compass carried away, gangway abreast of saloon unshipped and carried aft, chocks of two boats washed away, and keel of number 4 boat started; wooden cover of forward ventilator washed overboard, a great deal of water washing down companion-way into women's quarters aft, said hatch companion is a nuisance. . . . The officers and men are getting worn out; Mr Steele and the boatswain are laid up. . . . We have had all hands on deck the best portion of the time since we left. Mr Williams hardly leaves the deck, and I was compelled to order him below this morning, fearing I should have him knocked up. . . . The turtle back was completely caved in; the beams from the hatch forward all gone, most of them in two or three places; the riveting has gone more or less . . . the new ventilators, as before mentioned, are a perfect failure, drowning the passengers out. . . .

February 7th. It is still blowing a heavy gale; but the ship having lightened, there is no longer any difficulty in driving her. . . .

February 8th. We encountered a terrific gale in about latitude 47 and longitude 42 W, our decks were swept, all boats but two entirely destroyed, one of the two left open right out, the engine room skylight smashed and driven right in on top of the cylinders: this skylight has never been properly bolted or secured. Mr Williams, the 2nd Officer, whose pluck and endurance have been beyond all praise, was securing a sail over a fidley (great quantities of water having gone down and put all the lee fires out) was caught by number 4 boat as it was dashed, a perfect wreck, inboard, one of the davits unshipping and coming with it, and crushed against the railing round the funnel; his left thigh broken a little above the knee; his left ankle was dislocated; we fear some of the ribs broke. We trust the accident may not prove fatal, but only time will tell us; he shows amazing pluck and is at present doing well; if he does not recover he will be a very great loss to the company for men like him are very few and far between. No canvas was set during the gale, it was ordered at one time but the utter worthlessness of the crew, skulking and stowing away, crying like children, made it difficult to do anything. . . .

A sea struck the mizzen boom and broke it clean in two; imagine where a sail would have been! We steamed against the gale about 20 revolutions, making from one and a half to two knots. I tried her slower but could not keep her to the sea . . . the rails of the promenade deck have been mostly swept away, telegraphs broken and thrown down, top of standard binnacle washed overboard, forward gangway ditto, large ventilator, three davits ditto, doors and windows, shutters and all, smashed in bodily. . . .

Our carpenters are precious little account in bad weather, and a very slow lot at any time; our crew often have a lot of curs; to have got a sail up, or cut away for use, I should have had to ask assistance from the passengers; to have got one up from below would have been impossible. . . .

The only boat we have saved was insecurely lashed, and that, strange to say, proved her salvation; there was something to give; we were unable to cook for two days, indeed not properly for two and a half. . . . Pray condemn bad weather ventilators; passengers will stand a little closeness, but not wet; and it has fairly ruined carpets, paint, cushions, etc., etc. . . . The crew (excepting only the seamen) officers, engineers and stewards, firemen and coal trimmers, have behaved splendidly. When the lee fires were put out, the watch below turned out without being ordered, kept below and worked like men. . . .

I had one seaman (so called) rope's ended for stowing away in the coal bunkers for the fourth time; it had become really a serious question; we could only get four men of the starboard watch the other night. I therefore consulted with the officers and the Chief Engineer, and we decided the safety of the ship requires decisive measures, and that after this we will strip and flog every man stowing away while on watch; the crew were mustered and notified, and an entry made to that effect in the official log. . . .

I remain, etc.,

Digby Murray.

I have omitted, I see, urging the necessity of a communication with the engine room perfectly independent of telegraph, there should be bells or gongs from forward wheelhouse; during a great portion of the gale we had no communication with the engine room . . . the only way we could communicate was by shouting down the fidley to the firemen. It made Mr Fair (the Chief Engineer) too very uneasy, as he could not tell what was happening on deck, or at what speed he was required to drive; indeed he expressed an unhappy uncertainty as to whether we might not all have been overboard. . . .[4]

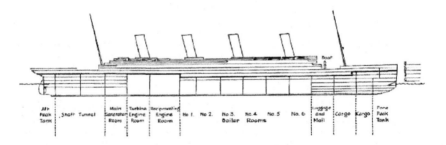

Such were the conditions in which the senior officers certainly and the junior officers probably had been trained.

Up in the crow's-nest on the foremast Archie Jewel and Symons had been relieved by Lee and Fleet. They passed on the message about keeping a sharp lookout for ice—and growlers in particular—and then climbed

---

4 *The Ismay Line*, W. J. Oldham

down. Lee took the starboard side and Fleet took the port side. The stars were very clear overhead. The white paint on the fo'c'sle bulwarks made a dim outline below them, the wash curved out on either side and caught suddenly here and there the light from a star, trembling and tumbling away, and astern the water was bathed in a pale glow from the passenger decks. But they couldn't see astern except around a canvas screen, and they dare not look or their eyes would be affected by the blaze of light.

Down in the bowels of the hull nearly 30 feet below the waterline an army of trimmers and firemen with thin singlets and trousers and grimy white caps or handkerchiefs knotted over their hair, shovelled coal from the side bunkers, and fed it into the furnaces, gaping fire from the lower part of each cylindrical boiler. The heat was intense. Air was forced in by twelve electric fans, but the men sweated still—the sweat ran in trickles over their bare, grey-white shoulders and down the tight muscles of their arms.

The most forward stokehold was in the fifth watertight compartment, 193 feet from the bow so that it started almost immediately below and some 90 feet down from the front of the bridge. This was number 6. Abaft it were five more boiler-rooms, numbered from 5 to 1. The forward five contained twenty-four boilers, each 15 feet 9 inches in diameter and 20 feet long with three furnaces at each end of each boiler. Rows and rows of rivets along the seams of the metal and great bolts in lines above the furnaces where the steam tubes passed—built steel cradles to hold the boilers in position above the "plates" and strong steel stays to prevent athwartship movement. The after compartment contained five more single-ended boilers of the same diameter, but only 11 feet 9 inches long and with three instead of six furnaces each. All were built for a working pressure of 215 lb. to the square inch. On this night the gauges flickered around 210. The shovels grated on the coal. In the preceding twenty-four hours nearly 700 tons had been consumed.

Aft of number 1 stokehold was the reciprocating machinery room with the great four-crank, triple-expansion engines, one to port and one to starboard of the central aisle. Steam from the boilers entered the high-pressure cylinders which had a bore of 54 inches and drove the pistons 6 feet 3 inches before passing into the intermediate cylinders—84-inch bore—and from there to the low two-pressure cylinders each side—97-inch bore—expanding all the time, and finally exhausting into the next watertight compartment aft where they drove the Parsons reaction turbine, which was directly coupled to the centre-line propeller shafting. The *Titanic* was a triple screw vessel, one shaft from each engine. She had been designed and laid down as a 21-knot ship with reciprocating engines only, but while on the stocks the success of the comparatively recent invention of marine steam turbines had been so conclusively proved on smaller ships that she was adapted for them. She was capable of speeds far in excess of 21 knots.

Abaft the turbine room, which also contained the main condensers and circulating pumps, was the generator room, and then the three shafts ran in their tunnels beneath two cargo holds and the after peak ballast water tank to emerge beneath the counter—the counter which swept up gracefully from the straight stem post and the shallow curve of the rudder, unchanged in outline from the days of the clipper ships.

These watertight compartments in the belly of the ship were about 60 feet long—with the exception of the shorter number 1 boiler-room—and were entered one from another through openings which had watertight doors suspended above them like ribbed and blunted guillotine blades. The doors were kept up by clutches held in position with powerful electro-magnets, and they could be lowered independently by levers beneath each, or dropped all together by operating a single switch from the bridge. In this case a warning bell sounded and the rate of drop was checked by cataracts so that the opening took some 30 seconds to close—time enough for a few men to dart through. If any men should be left behind there were escape ladders leading upwards.

Almost as many men were needed to keep the machinery running as to serve the needs of the passengers—325 against 494. Compare this with the fifty odd sailors on deck. Below the men on the stokehold "plates" was the cellular double bottom, 6 feet in depth and extending around the turn of the bilges 7 feet up the ship's side. Two bilge keels 300 feet long and 25 inches deep pointed out each side.

The *Titanic* was a pool of light gliding across the black mirror of the sea. The public rooms were ablaze; below them the windows and portholes showed up spasmodically in long lines. There were eight accommodation decks in all. Beneath the boat-deck was the main First Class deck—A deck—500 feet long with thirty-four staterooms forward and then the reading room, the entrance and staircase, the lounge, the smoking room, elaborately and intricately decorated and furnished, dark panelling and Victorian curlicues, carpets, deep club chairs and cigar smoke—in others the faint, lingering perfume of the ladies, fur stoles and the rustle of evening dresses, slap-slap of the cards crisp on the baize table before stiff, white shirts. There were millionaires and multi-millionaires aboard. Patricians above the turmoil, noise, sweat, grime, fiery heat, oaths, crudities, brief grins, coughs, rattle of the coal and dust and scrape-grate-scrape of the long-handled shovels in the din 80 feet below. All in the steel body of one immense liner.

The A deck public rooms extended at irregular widths from 72 to 24 feet across the deck, leaving wide sections of teak planking out to the side rails. A metal screen with great windows extended from the forward end of this deck almost 200 feet aft, and considerably further aft than the four boats on each side which were slung beneath davits immediately above. The two forward boats were the emergency boats, more manoeuvrable than the full-bellied lifeboats astern of them, and kept swung out in readiness all the time. There was open deck to the rails astern of these boats, and then four more lifeboats each side under davits at the after end of the deck.

The bridge was forward; abaft it was the wheelhouse, then the chartroom, and on the starboard side was the navigating room and the Captain's suite. The officers' quarters stretched in this deckhouse aft of the first funnel to the second funnel, and on the centre line abaft the forward funnel casing were the Marconi operators' quarters, the room containing their apparatus and the "silent room" where they sat their watches. Wires led from connections on the roof above to the main aerials. Also on this roof were two collapsible boats, one on each side. These were merely rafts in the shape of boats, virtually flat-bottomed and enclosing air inside with canvas screens which could be erected to form the sides. These sides were laced down when stowed. There were two more collapsible boats just inboard from the emergency boats, one on each side.

All told the *Titanic* carried fourteen 65-man lifeboats, two 40-man cutters or emergency boats, and four Englehardt collapsibles for about forty-seven persons each—a total capacity for 1,178 people. The ship herself had accommodation for 2,435 passengers (although she was carrying only 1,318) and about 885 crew—3,320 persons when full.

Attorney-General: "*The table referred to in the foregoing (Board of Trade) Rules shows the minimum number of boats to be placed under davits and their minimum cubic contents. When the gross tonnage is 10,000 and upwards the minimum number of boats to be used under davits, 16.*"

Lord Mersey: "*What was the tonnage of the Titanic?*"

"*She had a gross tonnage of 46,328.*"

"*It does not matter what size over 10,000 tons a vessel may happen to be, 16 boats is the minimum number?*"

"*Yes, my Lord, that is how it stands.*"

The first scale of lifesaving appliances in 1854 had been based upon gross tonnage. This had continued ever since and had been perpetuated by the Rules of June, 1899.

Lord Mersey: "*The serious point to my mind here and the one which I want to have cleared up is this: why did the Board of Trade leave this table which finished at 10,000 and upwards in existence for 18 years without any revision—that is the point?*"

Sir Walter J. Howell for the Board of Trade: "*It was to encourage shipowners to have more watertight bulkheads—what was said in effect is that if you put in so many bulkheads we will not require you to carry so many lifeboats. . . .*"

"*When the Committee came to examine the lifesaving appliance rules they were instructed by the Board of Trade to divide the ships up into classes, and that was a clear indication that they were to take size as the basis of their consideration. If it had been intended that they were to take the number of persons on board as their basis they would not have been told to divide the ships up into classes. There would have been no necessity to do anything of the sort.*"

"*What classes?*"

"*That was precisely the question they had to settle.*"

"*Either you do not understand my question or I am not sufficiently intelligent to understand your answers; I do not know which it is. I want to know why, when they were applying themselves to the question of how to provide for the safety of a number of lives, they excluded the number of lives from consideration and took into consideration only the tonnage of the ship?*"

"*I should be sorry to say that was the only thing they took into consideration, but it was the main consideration. . . . The main basis they took was the tonnage of the ship, because that indicated her size. A consideration running through it all was the number of lives on board, so they took both. . . .*

"*One consideration was can we take the basis of persons on board, or is it better to take the basis of size as indicated by gross tonnage—and they came to the conclusion that it was better to take the basis of size as indicated by gross tonnage.*"

"*But why?*"

"*Because they thought so I suppose.*"

"*But why did they think so?*"

"*I cannot tell you.*" (Sir Walter was the secretary of the Committee.) "*I cannot tell you what other persons thought.*"

"*But cannot you give me any notion?*"

"*I was trying to do so just now.*"

"*Well, what is it?*"

"*The reason was that they were told to divide the ships into classes. If they were told to do that, why should they say the basis is lives, because that would not require the division of ships into classes. You would simply say ships of all classes are to carry boats sufficient to save all on board.*"

"*Suppose you had to divide your vessels into classes it would mean that you would have one class for emigrants carrying the largest number of passengers; another class would be passenger ships; another class would be cargo ships, and then I suppose you would also have the home trade passenger ships?*"

"*Yes, every sort of ship, every class of ship . . . you would say every ship going to sea . . . is to carry sufficient boats to save everyone on board.*"

It is a fact that a cargo ship has to carry enough boats for double her number—or enough on each side for her entire complement?"

"*Yes.*"

Lord Mersey: "Therefore, so far as lifeboats are concerned a man is safer upon a cargo ship than upon an emigrant ship?"

"*Yes.*"

Sir Alfred Chalmer's, holder of a Master's certificate, nautical adviser to the Board of Trade Marine Department, 1896 to 1911: "I considered the matter (of lifeboats) very closely from time to time. I first of all considered the record of the trade—that is to say the record of casualties—and to see what immunity from loss there was. I found it was the safest mode of travel in the world, and I thought it was neither right nor the duty of a State Department to impose regulations upon that mode of travel as long as the record was a clean one. . . ."

Sir Norman Hill, chairman of the Merchant Shipping Advisory Committee: "In the last twenty years there have been 32,000 voyages made across the Atlantic by passenger ships, that is 1,600 per year, casualties involving loss of life or loss of ship in 25 cases, and in those 68 passengers and 80 crew were lost—a total of 148 persons. In the same period there were 233 casualties to other ships, in which 17 passengers and 1,275 crew were lost—a total of 1,292 persons. . . . I do not know the total number of ships involved. . . ."

Sir Alfred Chalmers: ". . . Secondly I found that as ships grew bigger there were such improvements made in their construction that they were stronger and better ships, both from the point of view of watertight compartments and also absolute strength, and I considered that was the road along which the shipowners were going to travel, and that they should not be interfered with. I then went to the maximum, that is down the table—16 boats and upwards, together with the supplementary boats and I considered from experience that that was the maximum number that could be rapidly dealt with at sea (supposing only one side available) and that could be safely housed without encumbering the vessel's deck unduly. In the next place I considered that the traffic was very safe on account of the routes—the definite routes being agreed upon by the different companies which tended to lessen the risk of collision, and to avoid ice and fog. Then there was the question of wireless telegraphy which had already come into force on board of these passenger ships. . . . Then another point was the manning. It was quite evident to me that if you went on crowding the ship with boats you would require a crew which were not required otherwise for the safe navigation of the ship, or for the proper upkeep of the ship, but you are providing a crew which would be carried uselessly across the Ocean, that would never be required to man the boats. Then the last point, and not the least, was this that the voluntary action of the owners was carrying them beyond the requirements of our scale and when voluntary action on the part of shipowners is doing that, I think the State Department should hold its hand before it steps in to make a hard and fast scale for that particular type of shipping. I considered that that scale fitted all sizes of ships that were then afloat, and I did not consider it necessary to increase it, and that was my advice to Sir Walter Howell. . . . It would be putting an undue strain on the masters and officers by fitting more boats . . . they could not possibly get more people into the boats in case of a disaster. . . . It is better to leave it to the discretion of shipowners—they constantly exceeded the requirements. . . . Although the Rules were necessary in 1880 they are not in need of revising for vessels of the Titanic's size. . . . Shipowners carried unnecessary lifesaving gear on their ships to induce people to travel in their boats. . . . It is not desirable to encumber the deck of a ship with unnecessary things. . . ."

Alfred Young, holder of a Master's Certificate, succeeded Sir Alfred Chalmers as nautical adviser, B.O.T. He had been involved in the Committee which drew up a letter dated April 16th, 1912, containing the following sentence: "The Board are of the opinion that a very careful and thorough revision of the table (lifeboats) should now be made."

"Did you hear Sir Alfred Chalmer's evidence?"

"I did."

"Did you agree with it on this point?"

"Not absolutely, with regard to the degree of extension."

"You think there should be an extension?"

"I do."

The Rt. Hon. Alexander Montgomery Carlisle, former general manager, Harland and Wolff (the builders): "The designs of Olympic and the Titanic were entirely worked out by Lord Pirrie. The details, the decorations, the equipment and the general arrangements all came under me. . . . When working out the designs for the Olympic and Titanic I put my ideas before the davit constructors (Welin) and got them to design me davits which would allow me to place, if necessary, four lifeboats on each pair of davits, which would have meant a total of over forty boats." (Producing designs.) "That is the one for consideration which I put before Lord Pirrie and the directors of the White Star. Then when I pointed out that I expected the Board of Trade and the Government would require much larger boat accommodation on these large ships I was authorised to go ahead and get out full plans and designs so that if the Board of Trade did call upon us to fit anything more we would have no extra trouble or expense . . ." (Pointing.) "There they are as fitted in the Union Castle Line. That was done in 1909—that was on the Edinburgh Castle I think. . . . The davits on the Titanic were of this type (pointing) it represents 32 boats—16 double (of course only one boat was actually carried) . . . I estimate all 32 could be lowered in 30 minutes. . . ."

"Who decides the number of lifeboats that shall be carried?"

"The White Star and other friends give us a great deal of liberty, but at the same time we cannot build a ship any bigger than they order, or put anything in her more than they are prepared to pay for. We have a very free hand and always have had—but I do not think that we could possibly have supplied any more boats to the ship without getting the sanction and approval of the White Star."

Harold Sanderson—director White Star Line: "In fact the Titanic carried more than necessary under Board of Trade requirements. . . ."

Before the Titanic sailed, Axel Welin had read a paper on boat davits to the Institute of Naval Architects, in which he described the latest davit introduced by his company and now fitted to the White Star liners Olympic and Titanic. This davit enabled an upper and a lower boat to be handled on the same falls; the usual difficulty of recovering the falls after the launch of the first boat had been overcome by fitting a non-toppling block. The davits had been ordered and used by the White Star as an insurance against possible changes in the regulations which would require the carrying of additional boats.

CHAPTER TWO

Still to the North and West of the *Titanic*, the *Californian* steamed westwards at something under 12 knots. Captain Stanley Lord had been about the decks all day and actually on the bridge since soon after eight o'clock when his Third Officer had relieved the Chief Officer. He was a much younger man than Captain Smith, but, like him, had learnt about the sea in sailing ships, and like him held an Extra Master's Certificate, which he had obtained at the early age of twenty-three.

At about 10.15, peering forward over the bridge wing, he thought he saw a brightening along the western horizon extending across on both sides of the bow. Unlike Captain Smith, this was his first time in ice. He watched it for a while, screwing up his eyes and then training his glasses in an arc, trying to detect something positive from it. He could see the silhouetted head and shoulders of the lookout up on the stem head; there was another man in the crow's-nest. Out on the other wing, his Third Officer looked out over the canvas dodger.

At 10.21 he strode towards the wheel and pulled the handle of the telegraph over to "Stop", then "Full Astern".

"Hard a-port!"

As the bow began to swing off to starboard the lookouts sang out, "Ice ahead!" The bow started to grate against small pieces of loose floe ice, and when they looked down over the side they could see they were surrounded with it. Captain Lord went across to the port wing and saw the edge of the field ice between a quarter to half a mile away, lying directly across their old course.

Eventually the ship came round on a heading of ENE and as the turbulence from the reversing propellers reached forward to the bridge Lord went to the telegraph again and rang "Stop."

At about 10.30 he left the bridge to the Third Officer and went below to the main deck, where he stayed for a while, throwing cobs of coal on to the surrounding ice in an attempt to assess its thickness. He sent for the Chief Engineer and told him that he intended to remain stopped until daylight.

"Keep main steam handy, though, in case we start bumping the ice."

At about this time on the *Titanic*, Bruce Ismay, who had dined with his friend, the ship's Doctor, earlier that evening, switched off his light and lay down in bed. There was a gentle throbbing from the main engines way down below—muffled through the furnishings—only a background vibration.

She was a thoroughbred, like her sister.

"Everything on board the ship worked most satisfactorily," he had written after the maiden voyage of the *Olympic*, "and the passengers were loud in their praises of the accommodation and table. . . .

"The only trouble of any consequence on board the ship arose from the springs of the beds being too 'springy'. This, in conjunction with the spring mattresses, accentuated the pulsation in the ship to such an extent as to seriously interfere with passenger sleeping, and we cabled asking you to communicate with Pirrie that, if he sees no objection, we would like to have lath bottoms fitted before the next voyage, and hope this can be arranged.

"The trouble with the beds was entirely due to their being too comfortable. . . ."[1]

The two great ships which were to be followed by a third, *Britannic,* had been conceived in 1907 when the Cunarder, *Lusitania,* was showing her paces and the *Mauritania* was still building. Bruce Ismay and Lord Pirrie, the head of Harland and Wolff, had dined quietly with their wives at the Pirries' house in Belgrave Square, and after the meal the two men had drawn up rough plans of the three "big" ships. At that stage they had three funnels only, and three or four masts. Details were altered afterwards, but the overriding considerations never changed—these ships were to be the epitome of comfort and elegance—fast, but not unduly so; not so fast that they would be uneconomical to run or uncomfortable for their passengers. The White Star had built up its outstanding position on the North Atlantic by regard for its passengers. The "big" ships were to be the last word.

The following year, to help finance the building, the company issued £1,500,000 worth of shares, which was the eventual price of just *one* of the sisters—an immense sum in those days. Harland and Wolff converted an area in which there had formerly been three slipways into two huge ones, and then later in the same year the *Olympic*'s keel was laid down, and afterwards the *Titanic*'s beside her. The two sisters grew together. On May 31st, 1911, the *Olympic* was handed over to her owners, and on the same day the *Titanic* was launched. To appreciate what this meant—how these graceful giants must have looked to contemporary eyes it is necessary to realise that each was half as big [1] again as the world's largest liners, the *Mauretania* and the *Lusitania* and the Press spared no praise in their lavish eulogies.

Harland's, whose genius had made them possible, had enjoyed a special relationship with the White Star from the very beginning of the Line's association with the North Atlantic. In 1867 T. H. Ismay, Bruce's father, had bought the firm of Wilson and Chambers after it had gone into liquidation. This firm had built, under the heavy mortgage which eventually crippled it, a fleet of some of the finest and fastest clipper ships which ever spread their 'royals' on the Australian run—ships as famous in their day and in their trade as their successors on the Atlantic were soon to become—and from their house flag—a five-pointed white star on a red burgee—the name of the Line was derived.

Some two years after the acquisition Ismay, with encouragement and financial backing from an uncle of Wolff's, formed the Oceanic Steam Navigation Company with the express purpose of entering the North Atlantic trade, and immediately commissioned four ships to Harland's design from the recently formed partnership of Harland and Wolff, iron shipbuilders, in Belfast. The first of these was the *Oceanic* of 3,707 tons. She had her main First Class saloon amidships, a considerable novelty, and the deck over it extended out to the extreme beam for the first time

---

1 *The Ismay Line,* by John Oldham.

on any ship, and had the lifeboats housed on it. She had a short raked funnel and four raked masts, the forward three carrying square sails, and the after one carrying just a spanker. From the main mast flew the red burgee with the great white star extending out almost to the edges. Her cabins were light and airy with larger portholes than had been customary; her low lines and narrow beam gave her more of the appearance of a yacht than a steamer, and from the day in 1871 when she inaugurated the firm's Liverpool-New York service she and her sisters, *Atlantic, Baltic* and *Republic,* captured the cream of the passenger trade, out-dated all existing ships on the run, and hotted up the already fierce competition across the Western Ocean.

The ships had been built on a cost plus basis. All the subsequent ships built by Harland and Wolff for the White Star were ordered on the same basis; the builders were given *carte blanche* to produce the finest ships, and after they had produced them they added a percentage to the cost which was their profit. No other builder ever received an order from the White Star. No line in direct competition with them ever had any ships built by Harland and Wolff; this was the agreement between the heads of the two firms.

As their ships increased in size and magnificence the guiding principle of the White Star remained, as it had started, the safety and the comfort of the passengers. This had been expressed as early in 1871, before the inaugural voyage of the first *Oceanic,* in the company's letter to the Commander, Captain, later Sir, Digby Murray.

February, 1871.

Dear Sir,

When placing the steamer *Oceanic* under your charge, we endeavoured to impress upon you verbally, and in the most forcible manner we were capable of, the paramount and vital importance above all other things of caution in the navigation of your vessel, and we now confirm this in writing, begging you to remember that the safety of your passengers and crew weigh with us above and before all other considerations. We invite you to bear in mind that while using due diligence in making a favourable passage to dismiss from your mind all idea of competitive passages with other vessels, concentrating your whole attention upon a *cautious, prudent,* and ever watchful system of navigation, which shall lose time, or suffer any other temporary inconvenience, rather than run the slightest risk which can be avoided. We are aware that, in the American trade, where quick passages are so much spoken of you will naturally feel a desire that your ship shall compare favourably with others in this respect, and this being so we deem it our duty to say to you most emphatically that, under no circumstances can we sanction a system of navigation which involves the least risk or danger. . . .

This principle, so forcibly stated here, was later embodied in the *Regulations for the safe and efficient navigation of the company's steamships:*

Responsibility of Commanders. The commanders must distinctly understand that the issue of the following instructions does not in any way relieve them from entire responsibility for the safe and efficient navigation of their respective vessels; and they are also enjoined to remember that, whilst they are expected to use every diligence to secure a speedy voyage, they must run no risk which might by any possibility result in accident to their ships. It is to be hoped that they will ever bear in mind that the safety of lives and property entrusted to their care is the ruling principle that should govern them in the navigation of their ships and no supposed gain in expedition, or saving of time on the voyage, is to be purchased at the risk of accident. The Company desires to establish and maintain for its vessels a reputation for safety, and only looks for such speed on various voyages as is consistent with safety and prudent navigation.

Poor Ismay! As he went to sleep that night there was less than an hour to run before the most shattering tragedy that ever struck his, or any other, steamship company.

* * *

Sometime about eleven o'clock or very soon after Captain Lord of the *Californian* and his Third Officer both saw a ship approaching from a distance—it might have been a star at first, the night was so brilliant—but soon there was no doubt that it was a ship under way. Captain Lord went along towards the wireless operator's room to ask the Marconi man, Cyril Evans, what ships he had. He met him coming out on deck and pointed the steamer out to him as he asked the question.

Evans looked at the lights for a moment, trying to adjust his eyes to the night. "Only the *Titanic*."

"That isn't the *Titanic*," Lord replied. Afterwards he said, "Better tell the *Titanic* we are stopped surrounded by ice." He had already worked out a dead reckoning position 42° 5'N, 50° 7'W, by running the course and speed up from the noon sights, which had been subsequently checked by a pole star latitude, and this he gave to Evans.

Phillips, in the big ship, was hard at work still with the passenger's messages through Cape Race. He heard the *Californian*, which in comparison with that station was almost on top of him, come in with a bang, drowning out the fainter signals from Newfoundland.

KEEP OUT, he signalled, and Evans, appreciating the position, closed his station down for the second time that night and went to bed shortly afterwards. He had been up and on long periods of duty since seven o'clock that morning; he was the only operator on board.

"What did you understand by this signal?"

"It meant he did not want any interference . . . this is a normal thing . . . one does not take it as an insult or anything."

In the *Titanic's* crow's-nest Reginald Robinson Lee, taking the starboard side, thought he detected a slight haze around the horizon ahead, which had not been there when they had come on duty. He also thought that his mate, Frederick Fleet, said, "Blimey, if we can see through this we'll be lucky."

Frederick Fleet: "There was a slight haze extending from ahead to about two points on the bow."

"You have heard what Lee said you remarked at the time. Did you say that?"

"I did not."

Whatever degree of haze it was that the lookouts thought they saw it was not seen from the bridge. It may have been an indistinctness along the horizon, for other men that night were finding difficulty in seeing just where the sea ended and the sky began; there did not seem to be any dividing line. The stars rose straight up out of the darkness. Had Murdoch, on the bridge, thought that there was any substantial degree of haze he would undoubtedly have called the Captain and suggested a reduction in speed.

"There never was a better officer," Captain Edwin Jones told Alan Villiers[2] later. He had shared the bridge of another White Star liner with Murdoch, and had first-hand experience of his remarkable presence of mind. "Cool, capable, on his toes always—and smart toes they were. I remember one night—we had just come up on the bridge to take over the watch when the lookout struck the bell for a light on the port bow. It was that awkward moment before you have your night vision, for we had just come up to take over from the First Officer and his junior. Murdoch went at once to the wing of the bridge. I didn't see anything for a while, I don't think I ever did see that light until it was almost on top of us.

"But Murdoch did! And realised on the instant what it was and precisely what sort of ship was showing it and what she was doing. I never forgot what he did. Before I knew what was happening he rushed to the wheel, pushed the quartermaster aside and hung on to the spokes. The First Officer was still on the bridge.

"'Hard-a-port!' the First shouted, suddenly seeing the light again *very* close.

"Murdoch kept the ship on her course.

"'Hard a-a-a! My God, we'll be into her!' shouted the First Officer, and then 'Midships the helm! Steady! Steady as she goes!'. . .

"But Murdoch had not shifted the helm. That was why he had jumped there, fearing a confusion of orders leading inevitably to a collision. As he stood there, coolly keeping the ship on what we all then realised was the only possible collision-free course, a great four- masted barque, wind

---

2 *Of Ships and Men,* by Alan Villiers.

howling in her giant press of sails, came clawing down our weather side. We watched horrified. Would she hit us? But she went free. Just—but she went free! It was a matter of yards.

"If Murdoch—or the quartermaster at the wheel who, of course, was there to obey orders and not to question them—had put that wheel over we'd have been into that sailing ship. We couldn't have helped it. If he had altered to port we'd have hit her with our bow: if to starboard, with our stern. Our only chance was to keep our course and speed—to go straight. She was one of the great modern steel windjammers, 3,000 tons of her. She could have cut us down.

"We were only two days out of New York at the time. None of us had seen a sailing ship there before. Remember, even the biggest sailing ships carried only dim sidelights—oil lamps generally stuck in towers. They were hard to see. We were looking down—she had a good breeze and was making twelve knots. Under all sail the swelling arch of her foresail would have hidden the sidelight from us. But Murdoch saw—just one glimpse. It was enough for him. In a split second he knew what to do. We others would have been too late. Upon the instant he had her figured out! Good thing he did too.

"That man let nobody down on the *Titanic*, I'm sure of it."

Murdoch stared out ahead. The *Titanic* drove on at 22 knots.

Sir Ernest Shackleton—polar explorer: "The range of visibility entirely depends upon the height of the iceberg. Take an iceberg of about 80 feet high and the ordinary type of iceberg that has not turned over, you could see that in clear weather about 10 to 12 miles."

"At night?"

"Not at night, no. I would say, providing it was an ordinary iceberg, about five miles on a clear night."

"You said provided it was an ordinary iceberg?"

"Yes . . . there are many bergs I have seen that appear to be black, due to the construction of the berg itself, and also due to the earthy matter and rock that are in all bergs. In fact in the South many of these so called islands must have been big bergs with earthy matter on them. Again after a berg capsized if it is not of close construction it is more porous and taking up the water does not reflect the light in any way."

"Have you seen ice of this particular dark character to which you refer in the North Atlantic?"

"Yes, twice . . . once on the outward route, once on the homeward . . . about April I think, 1897, and again in May, 1903, and again in June, 1910, but that was further North."

"How far would you see one of these dark bergs on a clear night, assuming it to be 60 to 80 feet high?"

"It might be only three miles, depending on the night and depending almost entirely on the condition of the sea at the time. With a dead calm sea there is no sign at all to give you any indication that there is anything there. If you first see the breaking sea at all, then you look for the rest and you generally see it. That is on the water line. I do not say very high because from a height it is not so easily seen; it blends with the ocean if you are looking down at an angle . . . if you are on sea level it might loom up. . . ."

Murdoch stood against the forward rail 60 feet above the sea, and some 20 feet above him Lee was having difficulty in *piercing through* the haze. Fleet could see perfectly well and was not worried.

Sir Ernest Shackleton: *"When we navigated in thick or hazy weather there was always one man on lookout and one man as near the deck as possible."*

"That is thick or hazy weather?". . .

"Yes . . . or even clear weather, just the same."

"Do you think it is an advantage in clear weather to have a man stationed right ahead at the stem as well as in the crow's next?"

"Undoubtedly if you are in the danger zone—in the ice zone."

"And supposing you were going at 21¾ to 22 knots?"

"You have no right to go at that speed in an ice zone."

Sometime after 11.30 the watchers on the *Californian* saw the ship, which they had been observing, stop. The Captain told the Third Officer to try and morse her.

Frederick Fleet saw a dark shadow on the water immediately ahead of the *Titanic's* bow. He grabbed the bell rope to his right and struck the hammer three times (object dead ahead), then moved across Lee to pick the receiver of the bridge telephone off its hook.

Moody answered. "Bridge here."

"Iceberg right ahead."

"Thank you." Moody hung up quickly and turned towards Murdoch, who was peering ahead from the wing trying to make up his mind which way to turn. "Iceberg right ahead!"

Murdoch leapt for the telegraphs and rung them over to "Stop", shouting, "Hard a-starboard!" Then he rang "Full astern!", almost in the same movement.

Robert Hitchins at the wheel glanced up at the wheelhouse clock on the forward bulkhead as he put all his weight on the spokes. It was twenty minutes to twelve. Moody was beside him, seeing the order carried out.

In the crow's-nest Lee had seen it as Fleet spoke into the telephone.

"It was a dark mass that came through that haze and there was no white appearing until it was just close alongside the ship, and that was just a fringe at the top . . . that was the only white about it. . . ."

It was about quarter of a mile ahead when the bows, still travelling through the water at 22 knots began to swing slowly to port. To the watchers on the ship the berg slid inexorably towards them, moving gradually, gradually over to starboard as the hem began to have effect; it towered up 40 or 50 feet from the flat sea.

Boxhall was coming out of the chartroom when he heard the telegraphs ringing, and he stood in the wheelhouse temporarily blinded by the dazzle he had just left. Hitchins was still heaving the spokes round with every ounce of his energy. He felt it jam as it came hard over. He pressed down to make sure, but it wouldn't move.

"Wheel hard over!" he called.

"Hard a-port!" Murdoch said.

Everyone on the bridge felt a slight shock as she struck right up under the bows below the waterline 10 feet above the keel to starboard. The ship drove on, the head still swinging slowly. The ice tore a gash in the forepeak, number 1 hold, number 2 hold, the baggage and mail hold, number 6 boiler-room, number 5 boiler-room—a jagged intermittent wound stretching 300 feet in less than ten seconds before she disengaged.

CHAPTER THREE

Lee, in the crow's-nest, thought they might just clear the dark mass as the bow veered, but it came right on and the visible portion above water struck before the foremast and little chips flaked off and scattered over the rail and in the scuppers on the well-deck. It had just been a shape ahead, but as it shot past astern it was picked out stark white in the glare from the passenger decks.

Down below in the stokeholds the shock was like thunder—the roar and ripple of thunder, louder the further forward the men were. When the impact came they were shutting down the dampers on the orders to "Stop engines" from the bridge.

In number 6 boiler-room Frederick Barret heard the crash very close and when he looked up water was bursting in from the ship's side about 2 feet above the plates. He heard the watertight door alarm bells ringing and then he and his mate were scrambling through into number 5, as the door dropped behind. In number 5 the water was entering through the bunkers at the ship's side.

To William Lucas, asleep in his cabin forward, the collision was like a ship running up on gravel—a crushing noise. Joseph Scarrot, standby A.B. on the 8 to 12, was also forward and felt a sudden vibration as if the engines had been racing full astern from ahead. When he darted out on deck he saw the sparkle of ice in the scuppers and way astern and to starboard the dark shape of the berg like a lion couchant with its head towards the ship. He thought the stern was circling away from it as if the helm was hard a-port.

George Rowe, quartermaster, and an ex-Royal Naval Petty Officer, was right aft and just felt a slight shock, a deflection almost, before the berg swept by very very close to starboard. He ran up the ladder to the docking bridge and took the patent log reading—260 miles.

Boxhall, up on the bridge, blinking still to get his night eyes, hadn't seen anything positive of the ice. He saw Murdoch pull the lever to close the watertight doors and when he looked round Captain Smith was beside him, coming forward from his quarters.

"What've we struck?"

"An iceberg, sir," Murdoch replied. "I hard-a-starboarded and reversed the engines—I was going to hard a-port round it but she was too close——"

"Have you closed the watertight doors?"

"Yes."

"Rung the alarm bells?"

"Yes, sir."

The Captain strode through to the starboard wing and Murdoch followed.

After a short interval the Captain returned and put the telegraphs to "Half Ahead", and the stand-by quartermaster, Olliver, was sent below to call the carpenter. Boxhall too hurried down into the Third Class passenger accommodation forward on F deck, which was just one deck above the waterline, to see if he could gauge the extent of the damage. He passed sailors and firemen wandering sleepily out of their quarters, wondering what had happened, but there was no alarm that he could see and no signs of damage. He made a quick inspection, but he didn't go low enough. When he started back he came up on the well-deck and seeing a few men gathered there with ice in their hands, he took a piece from one of them and examined it briefly, then threw it over the side. There were other chunks and slivers by the rail but nothing bigger than an ordinary cooking basin, nothing very alarming He returned to the bridge and reported what he had seen.

By this time Olliver had returned too and had been sent down with a message on a folded slip of paper to the Chief Engineer, who was in the engine-room. When he arrived the engines had been stopped. He gave the message to the Chief and stood waiting, expecting an answer while the man read it and gave some orders to the men near by. The Chief noticed him standing there, and asked him what he was waiting for.

"A return message."

"Tell the Captain I'll get it done as soon as possible."

With that Olliver left and went back to the bridge. The Chief Officer, Wilde, was up by then, and told him to go forward and tell the Bosun to rouse the crew out and get all the boats uncovered. He left and delivered the message. When he returned the Sixth Officer, Moody, wanted the boat muster list so that he could assemble the men at their proper boats. He went forward again.

In the meantime Lightoller, who had not been quite asleep when the jar came, had heard the grinding noise which followed and immediately realised that they had struck something. There had been no violence though, and as he lay and thought about it he wondered if perhaps the propeller blades had struck. Maybe they had stripped the blades, because as he listened in the darkness he felt that the engines had stopped. He rose from his bunk, thrust a coat around his shoulders and went out on the port side of the boat-deck. When he looked forward he could see Murdoch standing quite still, silhouetted against the night in his normal lookout position on watch. He walked to the side rail between the boats and saw that the ship had slowed right down. She was only making about 6 knots—the water was just drifting past the hull, not frothing and creaming as it usually did. He turned and went back to his quarters and through to the starboard side, where, looking forward, he saw Captain Smith outlined in about the same position as Murdoch had been to port, very still, just looking out ahead.

The Third Officer, also in pajamas with his greatcoat wrapped around his shoulders, came out from behind him, rubbing the sleep from his eyes, and asking whether they had hit something.

"Yes, evidently," Lightoller replied. He glanced forward again at Captain Smith's reassuring bulk, and shivering from the intense cold on deck, hurried back to his cabin.

"Judging the conditions normal, I turned in."

Lord Mersey: "What on earth were you doing? Were you lying down on your bunk listening to the noises outside?"

"There were no noises. I turned in my bunk, covered myself up and waited for somebody to come along and tell me if they wanted me."

The Third Officer, too, returned to his bunk and lay down, and near at hand the Fifth, who had not been awakened, slept peacefully.

So vast was the *Titanic* that those officers off watch on the boat-deck, and indeed the passengers still awake in the lounges and smoke rooms had no conception that anything serious had happened. The ice had caressed her and the wound had been inflicted by stealth 20 feet and more below the waterline, tearing the fresh paint and the metal as it careered past, sliding to the next compartment and puncturing it and the next and the next.

As she drew to a stop half a mile or more from the berg she was a doomed ship. She had about two and a half hours to live, and there was nothing anyone could do to prolong that time. She was sinking then, and though the engineers, to their undying glory, gave their lives to a man to save her, she was past saving.

The engineers, indeed owing to their position down in the guts of her, were the first to be aware of danger. While the passengers returned to their cards or their drinks, and Lightoller returned to the warmth of his bunk, the juniors had been despatched to arouse all those off watch, and those already down below were preparing to raise all steam on the pumps. The men had been ordered back to their "stations". Frederick Barret, who had escaped into number 5 as the water rushed into his own stokehold, climbed the escape ladder above the watertight bulkheads and went to the next escape forward down into number 6 again, which was his "station". He heard the water swirling below him and a tremendous roar of steam from the red hot coals as it reached the furnaces. He couldn't see very much through it, but he caught glimpses in the dim lighting as he probed cautiously lower and lower—glimpses of the water, dark and full, reaching half-way up the sides of his boilers. He turned and ran up the ladders again and then down into number 5.

Here they had seen the wound in the ship's side in the nearly empty starboard bunker, had seen the sea entering steadily, spurting in a great arc from the pressure as if from a firehose, and they had closed and clamped the bunker door on it.

The engineers were opening the after watertight doors with the independent gears beneath each so that they could communicate through the undamaged compartments, and the men were throwing water over the forward boiler furnaces to draw them. The steam hissed as it had in number 6 and made it difficult to see what was going on further than a few feet away. Barret was ordered to lift a manhole door which gave access to some pumpline valves. He and his mate Harvey did so and were waiting for further orders when Shepherd, one of the engineers, came tearing through that dim, hazy aisle between the boilers and fell down the manhole and broke his leg. Barret and Harvey heaved him up and carried him, wincing with pain, through the steam to the pump room, where they laid him on a bench and stayed with him.

It was about this time that Barret first noticed a slight dip in the plates beneath his feet, an almost imperceptible feeling of 'wrongness' as if his balance was slightly affected, and he thought it felt as if she was going down very slightly by the head.

"Had you ever remarked on it to Mr Shepherd or any of them?"

"No we never passed any remarks; the engineers never had time to pass remarks; they were working all the time."

Captain Smith knew it was serious then; he had been in touch with the Chief Engineer, and afterwards despatched Boxhall forward again to tell the carpenter to sound around. Boxhall met the carpenter halfway. He had his sounding line and lead in a coil over his arm, and an anxious expression.

"We're making water fast," he said. "Where's the Captain?"

"He's up on the bridge."

The carpenter hurried by without a word. Boxhall carried on forward, down another set of steps and saw the mail clerk, Smith, hurrying towards him.

"Where's the Captain?" the man asked. "The mail hold's filling."

Boxhall told him and pressed on, quickening his steps, down to G deck. When he got to the hold the hatchboards were off and two mail bags were on the deck where they had been pulled out, dark with water, and heavy. He saw the water was 2 feet from the deckhead below, and he could hear it coming in, rushing like a stream. There were mail bags floating in it. He flashed his torch around.

Samuel Hemmings, the lamp-trimmer, had been aroused in his cabin forward by the shock of the collision, and had become aware of a strange hissing noise almost immediately. He had left his bunk and gone right up to the storeroom forward of the chain locker (for the anchor cables) but had found no evidence of damage—only this hissing still. So he had climbed the ladder to the space under the foc's'le head where the filling pipes and air pipes for the forward tanks were located. Here the noise was louder and he soon discovered that it was air being forced out from the air vent from the 4-foot tank in the forepeak below. Air being forced out could only mean that water was being forced in.

The Captain received the reports one after the other—and worse each time.

"Now my Lord, my submission upon this part of the case," continued the Attorney-General, "upon which I have concluded what I desire to say now, is this, that in view of all those facts and circumstances to which I have called your attention that preceded the sighting of the berg, a reasonably prudent navigator ought to have reduced his speed; and I say further that he ought to have doubled his lookout, and that reasonable precautions to have taken would have been both . . ."

Joseph Barlow Ranson, Commander, S/S Baltic: "We go full speed whether there is ice reported or not . . . this is the practice of all liners on this course. . . ."

John Pritchard, Commander Cunard, 18 years between Liverpool and New York: "As long as the weather is clear I always go full speed. . . . My ship is the Mauretania. *. . . During the night time when I expect to meet ice I would not double the lookout if it was clear weather."*

Hugh Young, Extra Master, 37 years in command, Anchor Line between Glasgow and New York: "Assuming the conditions on this night I would not have reduced speed. . . . My fastest vessel was the City of Rome—17 knots. . . ."*

William Stewart, 35 years in command, Beaver Line, later taken over by Canadian Pacific: "My last vessel was the Empress of Britain—speed 18 knots. *. . . I would not have reduced speed so long as it was clear. . . . In clear weather we have the ordinary lookouts. . . ."*

John Alexander Fairfull, 21 years in command, Allan Line across the North Atlantic: "My practice is in accordance with theirs—all except that when we have got to the ice track in an Allan steamer, besides having a lookout in the crow's-nest, we put a man on the stem head at night. . . ."

Andrew Braes, Extra Master, 17 years in command Allan Line across the North Atlantic: "My practice is similar to theirs—just the same. I never slowed down so long as the weather was clear. . . . I never knew any other practice. . . ."

Arthur Henry Rostron, later Sir Arthur, Commander Cunard Carpathia: "If it is a perfectly clear night and I was sure of my position and everything else, unless I knew there was a lot of ice about, I should feel perfectly justified in going full speed . . . I would take special precautions by putting men in the eyes of the vessel. . . ."

Did Murdoch, that capable and clear-thinking officer, have any doubts as he listened on the bridge to the swelling evidence that the ship under his charge had inflicted a death blow upon herself—did he examine himself in the awful moments before the need for action became crystal clear, and drove thoughts away?

Charles Lightoller: "Of course we know now the extraordinary combination of circumstances that existed at that time, which you would not meet again once in a hundred years; that they should all have existed just on one particular night shows of course that everything was against us. . . .

"In the first place there was no moon . . . then there was no wind, not the slightest breath of air. And most particular in my estimation is the fact, a most extraordinary circumstance, that there was not any swell. Had there been the slightest degree of swell I have no doubt that berg would have been seen in plenty of time to clear it. . . .

"The berg into which we ran must have been in my estimation a berg which very shortly before capsized and that would leave most of it above water practically black ice. . . .

"When I went on deck after the collision the night was clear, there was no haze. . . ."

Lightoller heard a quick knock on his door, and then Boxhall was inside and had switched the light on. He said very quietly, "You know, we have struck an iceberg." Lightoller saw him standing just inside the curtain, wrapped bulkily in his dark overcoat. "The water is up to F deck in the mail room."

Lord Mersey: "Well, that was rather alarming was it not?"

"He had no need to say anything further then, sir."

Down by the mail room First Class Stewardess Mrs Annie Robinson, who had previously been in the *Lake Champlain* when that vessel had struck a berg, was looking down the companionway from E deck which led in the direction of the squash racquets court. She could see two mail bags, and the water climbing almost visibly from step to step. The mail man had just hurried off, leaving her and a few stewards and the carpenter with his lead line watching, hypnotised.

"The man looked absolutely bewildered—distracted—he did not speak."

"He looked alarmed?"

"He certainly was."

After a while the mail man returned with the Captain and another man and Mr Andrews. Mr Andrews was the builder's representative on board. He had taken over from the Rt. Hon. Alexander Carlisle as managing director of Harland and Wolff before the *Titanic's* completion, and was making the voyage with a gang of fitters and shipwrights from Harland's to make the final adjustments and to watch performance. By his bed in his cabin were rolled-up plans of the ship, his table was littered with papers he had been working on since leaving—often late into the night. He knew the ship intimately and structurally.

Andrews and the Captain had come by way of the engine-room and a glimpse into number 5 boiler-room before ascending again to F deck. By the time they saw the water advancing up the stairs to meet them from the mail and baggage holds they knew that at least three compartments had been broached and the ship could not live. She had been designed to float with any two flooded—no more.

Andrews knew and the Captain knew and the carpenter probably guessed, but the passengers and some of the crew still had a long time to go before the full extent of the disaster became apparent to them, and when it did, for most it was too late.

Andrews saw Mrs Robinson, and told her to put her life-jacket on.

She looked startled.

"Put it on and walk around and let the passengers see you."

"It looks rather mean."

"No—put it on."

His voice was firm and carried authority, but still she hesitated.

He lowered his tone so that the few people around would not hear. "Well—if you value your life put it on."

As soon as the facts had been established, no time was wasted. The Bosun himself had been through the sailors' quarters like the sound of a gale, rousing them out of their bunks and exhorting them to look alive and get up to the boat-deck. Murdoch, on the bridge, had set the alarm bells ringing through the crew accommodation. The head stewards in the various classes were told to arrange for the passengers to be roused and told to dress in warm clothes and put life-jackets on, and they in turn told off the bedroom stewards to look after the passengers in their own sections. Thomas Andrews at a very early stage took it upon himself to give instructions to the Third Class stewards that all steerage passengers were to be shepherded on deck.

But the *Titanic* was unsinkable. Everyone knew this. And no one told them she was going to go down. Many of them would not have believed it if they had been told. And there was little indication to the First and Second Class passengers and those steerage who were further aft than the water that anything really serious was amiss. The stewards had been told not to alarm anyone—true the passengers had been ordered to wrap up warmly and told to bring their life-jackets, but no doubt this was a sensible precautionary measure. The *Titanic* was unsinkable. She was honeycombed with watertight compartments. She had hit a berg and the crew were taking precautions. She wasn't sinking—there was no reason to suppose anything of the sort. The decks were solid underfoot—steady as a rock—and there was Mr Andrews over there by the main staircase talking reassuringly to a group of questioning ladies——

The Attorney-General: "Had the passengers been told there was grave danger when this was known to the Captain, Mr Andrews and the Chief Engineer, instead of orderly manoeuvring by the stewards leading the women and children there might well have been a rush for the boats, a panic which would have more disastrous consequences. I believe no passenger, however ignorant of the perils of the sea, who knows his vessel has been in contact with an iceberg, and that an order is given for the lifeboats to be uncovered and lowered, and women and children are to get in first, would have failed to realise that there was, at least, a grave state of things on board that vessel."

F. Dent Ray, a First Class Saloon Steward, had turned in early that night after a particularly tiring day on his feet. He had woken briefly as they struck, the thought had crossed his mind that maybe they had dropped a blade from the propeller, but anyway it was nothing to do with him, and he huddled up under his blankets and the new overcoat he had put over them to keep out the cold, and tried to get to sleep again. He was rudely brought to life by a fellow steward telling him to get up.

Ray thought it was a poor time for jokes. All he wanted to do was get back to sleep.

"We've hit a berg," the other man said—"Here," he thrust a chunk of ice on Ray's bunk. "Come on!"

The Second Steward, Dodd, was framed in the doorway.

"Everyone on deck! Look alive now!"

Ray moved. When he arrived at the boat-deck the noise was intense as the engineers blew off steam from the boilers. It was a continuous, deafening roar that struck him with almost physical violence as he emerged from the stewards' stairway by the third funnel. He stood there, numbed with the sound and the cold that pierced through his clothes and his flesh. There were odd groups of people standing with scarves and thick overcoats and fur stoles and life-jackets, looking bewildered. There were others moving at the boats, shadows in the dim lighting up there. But it was too cold to stay a moment longer. He turned and hurried back down the stairs to find some more clothes.

The Fifth Officer, Lowe, was awakened by the sound of voices in the alleyway outside his cabin. He thrust something over his pajamas and looked out and saw a small knot of women with life-jackets sheltering from the cold on deck. He darted back inside and began to pull his clothes on.

At twelve o'clock the watch changed in the crow's-nest. It is a significant pointer to the attitude of the crew at this stage that both the lookout and the wheel (later) were relieved in the normal way. The ship was sinking beneath them—but imperceptibly—and Hogg and Evans climbed to the crow's-nest up the ladder inside the mast and relieved Lee and Fleet, who afterwards made their way down, and along C deck to their quarters, and then up to the boat-deck. Also at twelve, Bride, the junior wireless operator, relieved Phillips who told him he thought they had hit something. Bride was not due on until 2 a.m., but Phillips had had a rough night previously with messages to and from the passengers, and it had been agreed that Bride would take over early. In the event, with the obvious activity elsewhere, they both remained on duty.

Out on deck, under the funnels which were roaring steam like a hundred locomotives, Lightoller, Murdoch and the Chief Officer, Wilde, were shepherding the crew to the boats around the deck by mime, and by mime again making clear that the covers were to be unlaced and the gripes chopped free. It was impossible to make themselves heard above the uproar. The crew were straggling up in twos and threes, without any real sense of urgency to begin with, and few of them knew which boat to go to as there had been no real boat drill before leaving, and all were, obviously, new to the ship.

The junior officers were on deck helping too. Pitman, the Third, met Moody, who had been on watch when they struck, and asked him what they had hit. "A berg—but I didn't see it."

Pitman went forward down to the well-deck to have a look at the ice, which he had been told about, and there met firemen coming up from below saying their quarters were flooded. He returned to the boat deck on the starboard side and helped to clear away number 5 boat. Besides the crew at this boat was one passenger in a very excited state who was doing his best with the lashings and urging everyone to greater efforts.

"There's no time to lose!"

Pitman did not recognise him then, but this was Bruce Ismay. He was one of the few who knew. He had gone to the bridge soon after feeling the shock of collision and had learnt from Captain Smith that the damage was serious. On going below afterwards he had met the Chief Engineer who had told him that she was making water fast, "—but the pumps should control it." He had returned to his cabin and then, finding inaction in such a situation impossible, had made another sortie to the bridge where he found the Captain and Thomas Andrews after their tour of inspection. By this time they must have known the full extent of the disaster. They must have known that six watertight compartments were flooding and that over one-third of the ship from the bow aft would soon be full. They could not know how soon this was going to happen, but from the speed with which the water had risen in probably the most seriously damaged forward cargo holds, it is unlikely that they expected to see daylight on board the *Titanic*. They had told Ismay. Now he was doing his best to save some of the lives for whom he must have felt, at least in part, responsible.

On the bridge someone had spotted a light. The lookouts had not reported it, and it is difficult to know who it was that saw it first or what time it was seen, but it was some time after twelve. Boxhall was helping with the boats when it was reported to him and he went forward to the bridge and joined a group of people there who were pointing it out. Boxhall himself first saw it half a point to port. Then he was sent into the chartroom to work out a position to send out with the distress message.

The 7.30 star fix, he knew—now 7.30 to 11.46 at 22 knots along S 86°W true. He took up a pencil.

CHAPTER FOUR

CQD CQD CQD.

Cape Race heard the distress call, as did the *Frankfurt,* Nordeutscher Lloyd, who was the first to answer soon after 12.15.

OK STAND BY.

CQD LAT 41 46 N LONG 50 24 W.

Out on the boat-deck the men, still surprisingly sparse among the comparatively few boats, had cleared the covers and lashings away and were ready to swing them out if need be. They wondered whether it would be necessary.

Lightoller sought out the Chief Officer, and found him coming across the deck between the funnels. "Shall we turn the boats out?" He had to cup his hands into the man's ear to make himself understood.

"Wait."

Lightoller went back to the port side where his men were standing by, moving all the time to keep themselves warm. There were a few passengers about them, but most had decided it was warmer inside and many had returned below. He saw the Captain walking along the deck from the wireless operators' room and, approaching him, asked again whether they should turn the boats out.

"Yes, swing them out."

While he was working to get this done at the forward group of boats on the port side, which by tacit agreement with the other senior officers, he had taken charge of, he became aware of the group on the bridge, and looking out past the emergency boat, he saw the light which they were studying. It was about two points on the bow then, he thought—a clear white light, or possibly group of white lights at a distance; he couldn't stop to examine it.

"Easily now—easily—" he shouted, trying to attract the attention of the man at the after davit. There weren't too many seamen here.

CQD SOS TITANIC. COME AT ONCE. WE HAVE STRUCK A BERG. ITS A CQD OM1 POSITION 41 46 N 50 14 W.

This was the corrected position as worked out by Boxhall. The *Frankfurt* had already answered; now two British ships came in, and much closer. The Canadian Pacific *Mount Temple,* bound West and on a course slightly to the southward of her normal track to avoid the ice, acknowledged the signal and sent her own position 41° 25'N, 51° 14'W, and the Cunard *Carpathia,* whose operator, the only one on board, had been due off watch at twelve o'clock, and was at that moment stooping to undo his shoelaces preparatory to turning in- but with his headphones still over his ears such was his enthusiasm in those early days of wireless—also acknowledged.

Captain Arthur Rostron of the *Carpathia* was in bed.

"And the First Marconi operator came up to my cabin and came right up to me and woke me—well I was not asleep as a matter of fact—and told me he had just received an urgent distress call from the Titanic—*that she required immediate assistance—that she had struck ice——"*

"Are you sure it is the *Titanic* that requires immediate assistance?" he asked.

"Yes, sir.

The Captain levered himself up and stared at the man. Wireless was still in its infancy then. The normal range of the *Carpathia's* set was a mere 130 miles although they could do better in good conditions, and the concept was still strange, and the reliability questionable—at least to those not schooled in its mysteries.

"You are absolutely certain?"

"Quite certain."

After that he wasted no time. "All right. Tell him we're coming along as fast as we can."

---

1 "It's a distress call, old man."

The wireless operator dashed back to his set and the Captain went forward to the chartroom, laid off his distance from the evening's star fix, drew the course from there to the *Titanic,* and gave orders for the ship to be turned on to a north-westerly course. While he was doing it the wireless man came up again after checking the position from the *Titanic* "—41° 46'N, 50° 14'W."

The Captain ordered a course of N 52°W, and sent for the Chief Engineer. Fifty-eight miles to go—normal speed 14 knots—just over four hours. The Chief would be able to push her along a bit though.

***

CQD MGY (TITANIC) SINKING. CANNOT HEAR FOR NOISE OF STEAM.

CQD MGY I REQUIRE ASSISTANCE IMMEDIATELY. STRUCK BY ICEBERG IN POSITION 41 46 N 50 14 W.

MGY TO DFT (FRANKFURT) MY POSITION 41 46 N 50 14 W. TELL YOUR CAPTAIN TO COME TO OUR HELP. WE ARE ON THE ICE.

CARONIA TO BALTIC. MGY STRUCK ICEBERG REQUIRES IMMEDIATE ASSISTANCE.

FRANKFURT TO MGY. WHAT IS THE MATTER WITH U.

MGY TO FRANKFURT. WE HAVE COLLISION WITH ICEBERG. PLEASE TELL CAPTAIN TO COME.

FRANKFURT TO MGY. OK WILL TELL. MY POSITION 39 47 N 52 10 W.

MGY CQD CQD . . .

Captain Smith had asked Phillips and Bride to be quick with the CQD when he had come in first; they had caught the urgency of the situation.

Outside on deck Lightoller was asking the Chief Officer whether he should put the women and children in the boats. He had his first one, number 6, swung out and lowered to the boat-deck rail.

"No!"

On the other side of the deck in the same position number 5 had been swung outboard and lowered to the side rails, and Ismay hovered by it, beside himself with anxiety for the passengers, and bewildered at the lack of urgency displayed by the officers. What he didn't realise was that only a few of the senior men and Thomas Andrews and himself knew the full extent of the damage. The engineers knew of course, but they were way down below, keeping up steam for the pumps and generators.

"Come on—let's get the women and children in—fill her up—fill her up——"

Pitman wondered who this excitable fellow was. "We'll wait for the Commander's orders," he said, and went forward to the bridge to ask Captain Smith himself.

The Captain was on the port side among a group of men who included Boxhall, the quartermaster of the watch, some stewards, all gazing out at the distant light. He turned briefly at the question.

Yes, carry on.

Boxhall said, "Is it really serious, sir?"

"Mr Andrews tells me he gives her from an hour to an hour and a half."

Pitman went back to the boat.

"Come along ladies——"

They were reluctant to go—those who still braved the night outside— and had to be coaxed and encouraged by him and Ismay and the Fifth Officer, Lowe, before they would leave the safety of the *Titanic*'s deck for this small craft which hung by ropes above a 60-foot drop to the sea. These women were mostly from the First Class cabins. Many hung back and refused to leave their husbands—others wondered if it was all really necessary.

The *Titanic*'s clocks were to have been put back 47 minutes that night, which time was to be split between the "8 to 12", and the "12 to 4" watches in the proportions 23 minutes and 24 minutes. At 12.23, therefore, Hitchins at the wheel had been relieved by Quartermaster Perkiss. No one had relieved Rowe down aft though, and at 12.25 he saw his excuse to ask what was happening—there was a lifeboat out on the starboard side. He rang through to the bridge and said, "Do you know there is a boat being lowered?"

Boxhall answered. "Is that the Third Officer?"

"No. I am the Quartermaster."

"Come up to the bridge then—and bring the detonators with you."

Rowe found the box of detonators and carried them forward.

The *Mount Temple* was still steaming westwards, and John Durrant, the Marconi operator was back at his earphones after delivering his message to the Captain. He could hear the *Titanic* still sending out the CQD and other ships answering, and the *Carpathia* breaking in, COMING TO YOUR ASSISTANCE. Shortly afterwards he received word from the bridge and noted in his log, "12.26 (maybe 12.40 *Titanic* time) Ship's course turned, going to their assistance." Captain Henry Moore had ordered a course of N 65°E true and doubled the watches in the engine-room.

Murdoch and Wild were dividing their attention between the forward and the after sections of boats on the starboard side. Archie Jewel, one of the "8 to 10" lookouts, had helped to turn out numbers 5 and 7, and he now stood by while Murdoch tried to find more women to go in them.

Archie Jewel: "Well, we put all the women in that was there, and children. Up to that time there was not many people; we could not get them up—they were rather afraid to go into the boat, they did not think anything wrong. . . ."

"Were there men passengers there too?"

"Yes, we had some men passengers . . . some of them got into the boat—I do not know how many. There were three or four Frenchmen there—I do not know whether they got into the boat. . . ."

"Was there any excitement?"

"No, sir. None at all. Very quiet."

The Captain came around from the port side of the deck, where he had ordered Lightoller to put the women and children in the boats and lower away, and himself tried to coax away the women's fears, helping them into number 7, and calling out for more to be sent from the other decks. By the time he left to return to the bridge number 7 was becoming full. The bulky life-jackets worn by the women made it appear fuller than it was. Murdoch detailed Archie Jewel and three other sailors to go down with the boat and when they were settled at each end, gave the order to lower away.

The evacuation was beginning. For those about to be spared it was half-hearted and fraught with doubt.

To the south-east and west-south-west, almost equidistant from the *Titanic,* two first-class passenger liners were racing towards her with doubled watches in the stokeholds, working up some two or three knots more than their normal maximum speed, their wireless operators tuned in and anxious for any signal that would tell them of her situation. Neither probably realised how desperate it was. And somewhere to the North, less than half their distance away, the *Californian*'s Second Officer watched the strange ship which Captain Lord had pointed out to him when he came on watch. He could see her red sidelight and one masthead light. He estimated her to be about 5 miles off.

* * *

When Boxhall had come from the wireless office after taking the corrected position to the operators he had gone straight to the port wing of the bridge to see what had happened to the light which everyone had been watching. He had found it unchanged—if anything a trifle clearer and possibly further over to port. To the naked eye it was just a white light. Examining it through the glasses he had made out the two white masthead lights of a steamer angled towards him as if she would be showing her port side light had it been near enough to see. He had despatched one of the near-by seamen for distress rockets, and told the Captain. The Captain had replied, "Yes—carry on."

Now, shortly after Archie Jewel and his boat-load of women had been lowered in spasms past the blazing saloons on the starboard side of the ship, he jerked the lanyard to fire the first rocket.

Flash! Cannon-sound of the explosion—searing upwards the luminous trail arcing up—up way over the foremast and exploding into dozens of bright white stars, spreading and dropping slowly, slowly fading, drifting—leaving the image of the flash briefly on the retina.

An excited burst of voices from the decks and more people were crowding forward to get a closer view.

Lowe at the starboard boats, saw Ismay, beside him, and the whole deck lit up brightly for a moment. He didn't know who Ismay was then— he was just a passenger lending a hand, and giving a lot of orders; he didn't like passengers giving orders.

Lightoller, loading up number 6 boat on the other side with reluctant women, pointed out the white light over towards the horizon to reassure them.

"D'you see her—that ship over there. Probably she's a sailing-ship. The breeze should spring up at daybreak and she'll be able to come and pick us up from the boats——"

He himself judged the vessel, whatever it was, to be within 5 miles of them, and some two points on the port bow. During the intervals he was watching she didn't appear to move—neither coming towards them nor turning away.

Robert Hitchins, the quartermaster who had been relieved at the wheel, had the light pointed out to him by Lightoller as they helped the women forward over the rail, he inside the boat and Lightoller on deck. He also judged it to be some 5 miles off and two points to port. Lightoller kept on calling out for more for the boats, but although there appeared to be knots of people in the dim lighting by the deck-house they hung back, and Hitchins heard them talking among themselves, saying they would rather stay aboard the ship than trust themselves to a small boat; he could see women among them.

The Second had already ordered a man and a boy into the boat in place of seamen, who were scarce on that part of the deck and all needed to lower the boats, and at length he gave the order to drop her right down to the sea. Hitchins felt the boat giving beneath him, first one end, then the other, then both together in a series of jerks as the falls ran round the sheaves. When they reached the water it was flat as a pond. He released the hooks with the quick release gear and as he looked up afterwards Lightoller was pointing away and shouting down orders. He thought he was telling him to row for the light, which when he turned, was still in the same position, burning through the clear atmosphere, low on the horizon now they had reached water-level.

He pushed off and tried to organise some rowers from among the women, clumsy in life-jackets, who sat anywhere among the benches and oars and lashed rowlocks and the mast and sails which lay centrally across the thwarts. There were only about forty in a boat certified for sixty-five, but it looked crowded enough to him. There was one other sailor, and with him and the man and the boy and a few of the women on the oars he steered a course away from the ship towards the light. When he looked back the *Titanic* was great, wall-sided, solid with rows and rows of lights—her straight stem and curving stem and the four reaching funnels dark against the myriad bright stars behind. She was solid and comforting in that wide expanse of loneliness and ice-dark water. The flares which exploded at intervals above her raked masts were as meaningless and ephemeral as fireworks.

On the boat-deck Lightoller transferred his attention to the next boat astern, number 8. He could feel a slight tilt in the deck now—the beginnings of a port list. Wilde, too, had noticed it and was ordering the passengers to the starboard side to try and get the weight across.

Lightoller could hear the strains of ragtime music from behind him as he worked. The band, who had been playing in the lounge below, had assembled on the boat-deck by the entrance to the main stairway down to the First Class accommodation—eight of them in motley clothing. Lightoller didn't like jazz as a rule but he was glad of it on this night, and it seemed to help everyone. It lent an air of normality to the unbelievable things that were happening.

On the other side of the deck Ismay had watched number 7 boat reach the water with Archie Jewel in charge, and was now urging on the officers to greater efforts with number 5, the next boat ahead.

"Lower away—lower away——"

Lowe was exasperated. "If you'll get the hell out of the way we can get on with the job!"

The Chairman of the Line turned away silently.

***

Down in number 5 boiler-room the water was building up its pressure inside the bunker which sealed the gash in the ship's side from the stokehold. The bunker door was the weak point. Frederick Barret was still down there with the engineer, Shepherd, when it burst and the sea came tumbling down the aisle between the boilers like a river in flood, carrying lumps of coal and debris before it.

"Do you know yourself where it was the water came from?"

"I did not stop to look."

The watertight doors to the boiler-rooms further aft were closed, however, and the flood was contained after the first triumphant burst-through, although the sea still forced its entrance through the narrow gash in the bunker.

Further aft all hands were keeping up the pressure on the boilers so that the pumps could work full out, and so that the lighting would not fail and cause panic among the passengers. Many of the men not on watch at the time of the accident had been on deck before being ordered below and had seen the preparations for getting the boats away—some knew that women and children were being disembarked, and if some know anything in any ship all know. In number 4 boiler-room water was gradually rising up and visible through the manholes for the valve connections—and then it rose over the 'plates'. Whether this was damage to the hull or water from above the watertight decks is not known.

"My Lord, one cannot peruse the evidence in this case without, I think being very much struck by the discipline of the crew taken as a whole. . . . To take one instance and I think a very, very striking one . . . of Dillon and Cavell, trimmer and fireman, who were in number 4 boiler-room; they had been on deck, and there were others, who had been ordered below in a vessel which they knew was in great jeopardy, and who heard the order had been given from the bridge to uncover the boats and to man them and to fill them with women and children. All these men on board knew they were in grave peril and yet it is one striking fact that they did go down, apparently without any question, without a murmur, they go down below to work on board that vessel and down below in the hold when the water was coming in as we know, in number 4 boiler-room, till the water was up to their knees, when they were ordered to come up on deck through the escape . . . they were not even seamen, and on the whole I do not think one is saying too much when we say that the behaviour of those men was heroic . . . .

"One is also struck in reference to the evidence about the engineers. Not a single engineer was saved. . . . There they are right down in the vessel, and during a time of peril they did not come up in this case until, if at all, all hope of safety had disappeared. . . ."

The water was gaining fast.

Pitman had been ordered away in number 5 boat by Murdoch and told to look after the starboard side boats generally as they came down and then make for the gangway when hailed. As his boat and number 7 pulled away and stood off some 20 yards, and while number 6 from the port side pulled in an opposite direction towards the distant vessel's light, the occupants of all these boats began to notice the rows of cabin lights—incredibly they were no longer parallel with the water—they were sloping down towards the bows. At first the starboard boats remained close to the bulk of her and watched as number 3 came slipping down the side, a small, pale shape with the deck lights picking out anonymous heads and the sailors higher up than the rest at the bow and stem, ready to slip her when she reached the water—slap! She was free and they were struggling to raise some oars and push away from the side. Soon afterwards all the starboard boats began to pull further away from the side, and they went on pulling until they were some 200 yards from her, and drawing the later boats after them as they came away from the falls.

Down in one of the alleyways on F deck the Assistant Second Steward, Joseph Wheat, was talking with a group of Turkish Bath attendants when they noticed a trickle of water approaching from forward. Wheat had already seen to the closing of the watertight doors on the deck they were on so he knew it must have come from the deck above, and as, some while previously, he had seen the water rising up the stairs from the squash racquets court right forward to F deck, he guessed that it must have risen up the next flight to E, and then aft. It was more than a trickle now, but not so much as a stream.

Dent Ray had seen this earlier when he had returned on deck by way of the main First Class stairway after wrapping up more warmly. He had a good idea of the gravity of the situation because he had seen the Pursers taking the valuables from the safes.

The Third Class passengers were moving aft now, those who had been quartered forward, moving deep down in the tunnels of the ship like ants dragging their baggage with them, not comprehending any immediate peril and anxious only to escape from the water which was flooding their cabins and their few worldly possessions. The cry had already gone round for all women to be passed up to the boat-deck and some were being gathered by the stewards of their sections, but others, the married ones, as with the First and Second Classes, were anxious to remain with their families. No one had told them the ship was going to go down.

"My Lord, the striking figures, and figures which will no doubt engage the Court's attention during this Inquiry, are that 63% of the First Class were saved, 42% of the Second Class, and only 25% of the Third Class. . . ."

W. D. Harbinson—Counsel for the Third Class passengers: "I wish to say distinctly that no evidence has been given in the course of this case that would substantiate a charge that any attempt was made to keep back the Third Class passengers. There is not one atom or tittle of evidence upon which any such allegation could be based, and I do not for one moment say that the Third- Class passengers were deliberately kept back or were kept back at all in the sense that any effort was made to prevent them reaching the boat-deck . . . I desire further, my Lord, to say that there is no evidence that when they did reach the boat-deck there was any discrimination practised either by the officers or the sailors in putting them into the boats. . . ."

Attorney-General: "One reason that occurs to me, and that I suggest is worthy of consideration, is that these Third Class passengers were emigrants. . . and they would certainly be carrying all they possessed with them. To leave their cabin or to leave the vessel with all their little property on board and to go into a boat would be a thing that they would naturally be loth to do, more loth probably than a person whose property was not all in the vessel. . . . When you bear in mind here that you have emigrants, and that they were asked to leave and to get into boats at a distance no doubt of some 65 feet, and to be lowered in these boats into the water, probably many of them not having been on a vessel before, and certainly not a vessel of this character, I think one can readily understand why it is that the Third Class passengers refused to leave the ship, and remained on the ship in a larger number proportionately than the First or Second Class passengers. There is one other reason, not an important one, which is of course that their quarters, according to the construction of the ship, were in a less favourable position undoubtedly for reaching the boats than either the First or Second Class passengers."

John Edward Hart, Third Class steward, had been instructed by Mr Kieran, the Third Class Chief Steward, to rouse all his people and see that they had life-jackets on—whereupon Mr Kieran had gone aft superintending the other sections. Having gathered all those in his section of cabins, mostly unmarried women and married couples—for the steerage was strictly segregated in these ships—Hart waited with them in the alleyway. Most had warm clothes and life-jackets on but some refused the life-jackets. After a while Mr Kieran had returned. Later still, at maybe 12.30, the instructions had been given, "Pass your women and children up to the boat-deck." Not all had wanted to go. The family groups particularly, with their cases and bags had been most reluctant to part company, and eventually he had left with a group of thirty or so who were willing to make the journey. He had led them aft along the alleyways to the after well-deck, then into the Second Class accommodation by the library, to the stairs of the barber's shop, and so to the First Class stairs up to the boat-deck where he had emerged between the funnels. The journey, although circuitous, had been made comparatively fast for all the normal barriers which he came to between the Third and Second and Second and First Class sections of deck had been unlocked.

Lightoller was loading up the after boat, number 8, of his four when they arrived almost opposite to it. Hart therefore left his charges there and made his way down to the Third Class again, meeting groups of stewards with their batches of womenfolk behind them, meeting too Third Class men who were trying to reach the boat-deck but were prevented by other stewards from doing so. He was delayed by them.

At one of these strategic entrances between the Third and Second Class accommodation, Paul Maugé, secretary to the Chef of the Restaurant *à la carte,* was struggling with some stewards who would not let him through. He had been awakened soon after the collision by the alarm bells ringing and had promptly risen and gone up on deck, passing Captain Smith by the engine-room entrance. The Third Class alleyways had been buzzing with rumour and speculation then, and amove with families clutching their children and their baggage, and others with pieces of ice in their hands who had come down from the well-deck forward. He had made his way up to the boat-deck and seen the sailors preparing the lifeboats, seen

Captain Smith again up there, encouraging the women into the starboard boats as they hung back, and had then returned below to find his chief.

The Chef was still in his cabin with several other cooks.

"There is some danger—we must get up."

The Chef lost his temper.

"You mean he was agitated at what you told him?"

"Yes . . . he lost himself . . ."

He and the Chef then made their way out in the same direction as Hart had, to the Third Class decks at the stern, telling the other cooks to wait until they returned, and from there had tried to reach the Second Class accommodation forward of them.

"Two or three stewards were there, and would not let us go. I was dressed and the Chef was too. He was not in his working dress, he was just like me. I asked the stewards to pass. I said I was the secretary to the Chef and the stewards said, 'Pass along—get away.' So the other cooks were obliged to stay on the deck there—they could not go up. That is where they die

"They let me pass, me and the Chef, because I was dressed like a passenger. I think that was why they let me pass. . . ."

Maugé and the Chef went on towards the boat-deck; Hart returned to gather some more women. Both had been obstructed—both had seen the stewards doing their duty at the meeting of the two classes where there would normally have been barriers or locked doors, and both had carried away different impressions of what those stewards were trying to do—which is not really surprising, for by then there was more awareness of danger, certainly in those lower corridors where the water was gaining access and driving everyone aft.

Without stewards like Hart the Third Class passengers who had been restricted to their low decks throughout the voyage could not—except by long processes of trial and error—have found their way along the labyrinthine alleyways and up the "snakes and ladders" after stairways with their baggage to the upper decks. Many of them still carried their baggage despite admonitions against it.

"Come along, girls—come along—hurry along please!"

There were more boats in the water now, the starboard numbers 7, 5 and 3—the latter sent away under the charge of the Third Officer—pulling out to starboard, their occupants watching the lines of portholes dipping into the water forward, the stem raising slightly—imperceptibly upwards, so slowly that it was impossible to see it rising, but like the hour hand of a clock, always in a different position after an interval. On the port side number 6 boat with Hitchins in charge was still making for the light on the horizon and close behind was number 8 with Hart's steerage women, and a First Class bedroom steward, Alfred Crawford, who had been told by the Captain before he left the ship to row for the light, the light which, when pointed out, he had recognised as the two masthead lights of a steamer. The lovely Countess of Rothes was at the tiller, encouraging the rowers and giving them a running commentary on the light ahead. Crawford could see the *Titanic* as he rowed—she was abnormally low in the water—sending off rockets every four or five minutes, explosions of white stars way up past her bows, high in the air. He turned round every now and then to glimpse the ship they were pulling for, but it wasn't getting any nearer.

Boxhall was watching her too from the bridge. In the intervals between firing the rockets he trained his glasses on her and began to make out her sidelights—both the green and the red. She was coming for them, end on to them, approaching slowly, but surely approaching because when he had studied her first he had only seen the mast lights. George Rowe, the quartermaster who was helping him with the rockets only saw one white light; the Captain was up beside him sometimes, asking what the ship was doing. When she had approached to what he judged to be some 5 or 6 miles he started morsing. He went on morsing in between firing rockets for a long time and someone said she was answering. He tried to see through the glasses, but guessed it was only the lights flickering—nevertheless he asked Rowe to keep on calling her up while he had her under observation through his glasses. There was no reply.

The Second Officer of the *Californian* was again watching the ship to the South of him through his glasses. At 12.45—or maybe about 12.55 *Titanic* time—he had seen a flash in the sky somewhere over her which he had thought at first might have been a shooting star; they had been common that night. So he watched her, and very soon he saw three more flashes at short intervals over her, and then, in company with the apprentice who returned from preparing a new log line, another one, all of them over her and about half the height of her mast lights. He knew they were rockets or signals of some sort, but was puzzled by their low altitude and by the fact that there were no flashes or explosions of any sort visible or audible from the deck of the vessel. He kept her under observation and then at about 1.10 blew down the speaking tube to call Captain Lord who was asleep in full dress on the chartroom settee below, and told him what he had seen.

At this point it is necessary to give a brief description of this section of the *Californian*'s accommodation. The chartroom was to starboard and immediately behind the lower enclosed wheelhouse which ran along the forward end of the main accommodation deck. Above was the open bridge on which the officers stood their watches, with wings extending out to the ship's side. The voice pipe from this upper bridge went down to the Captain's bunk which was against the port bulkhead of his cabin, which was to port and abreast of the chartroom. It was an extraordinarily clumsy arrangement altogether because the Captain's cabin had *no windows;* there was a door which led into the chartroom, and from the chartroom one door led into the lower wheelhouse and another opened aft into a cross alleyway which led to the deck. Thus, when Lord was awakened by the whistle from the voice pipe, he had to get up from the chartroom settee, go into his cabin and take the cap off the voice pipe by his bunk on the port side. And while there he could not see anything. When he heard from the Second Officer about the rockets he had asked him whether they were company's signals. The second replied that he didn't know—there had been no colours in them.

"Call her up then and find out what ship she is. When you know send the apprentice down." Lord replaced the cap over the pipe and returned to the chartroom and lay down again.

As he went to sleep he heard them ticking away above him on the key for the morse lamp, which, like all ships of the day, including the *Titanic,* was an all-round white light raised above the bridge.

The Second Officer and the apprentice flashed the other ship repeatedly but received no reply. Both of them saw that she was altering her bearing from SSE through South, while the *Californian* herself was swinging from an easterly direction towards the South—stationary still.

Several ships besides the *Carpathia* and *Mount Temple* were still listening-in on the drama. The Cunard *Caronia,* the Allan Line *Virginian,* the White Star *Baltic,* the *Frankfurt* still sending messages, and a day's steaming distant, too far to be of any assistance, her own sister, *Olympic* was altering round and sending extra men down below to the stokeholds.

TITANIC TO OLYMPIC. CAPTAIN SAYS GET YOUR BOATS READY. GOING DOWN FAST BY THE HEAD.

BALTIC TO CARONIA. PLEASE TELL TITANIC WE ARE MAKING TOWARDS HER.

Lightoller had ordered the passengers by him on the port side to go below to A deck and embark from there, where it would be easier to keep the boats triced in to the rail, but after receiving a report that the metal windows were still in position, had countermanded the order and tried to get the passengers up again. He also ordered the Bosun's Mate and several sailors to go below and open the forward gangway doors in the ship's side so that more passengers could be put in the boats nearer the water. Wilde had done the same for the after gangway doors. Many of the boats were by no means full when they were lowered from the boat-deck, and the Commander was circling the rails with a megaphone shouting to them to come round to the doors to take on more people.

Lord Mersey: "It appears to me that you would be very unlikely to order the forward gangway doors to be opened. You might get the ship's head so deep in the water that she might ship water through that gangway door?"

Lightoller: "Of course, my Lord, I did not take that into consideration at the time; there was not time to take all these particulars into mind. In the first place at this time I did not think the ship was going down."

"Were there still women on the boat-deck?"

"Yes."

"Was the discipline good?"

"Excellent."

"The men passengers behaving themselves well?"

"Splendidly."

George Symons, an A.B., was working on the davits on the other side of the deck under Murdoch and the Bosun. Lowe was there and Ismay, and between them all they had swung the boats out and lowered them without fuss and with routine precision, only being delayed by the shortage of people to put in them. The davits had worked better than Symons ever remembered—of course they were new. They had lowered numbers 7, 5 and 3—exhausting the supply of women and children each time and then putting men in; now they were working on the emergency boat, number 1. Murdoch told Symons to hop in and get the plug fixed and was just about to lower it with only five trimmers from the stokehold, one other sea-man and himself aboard when two women came running towards them; one was Lady Duff Gordon and the other her secretary, Miss Francatelli. Behind them came Sir Cosmo Duff Gordon, who approached Murdoch and asked if he might go too. The deck was completely clear of passengers by this time and Murdoch hurried him towards it, "I wish you would."

Sir Cosmo climbed in, and after him two Americans who had appeared. Murdoch called out to Symons, "Take charge of this boat. Make all those under you obey you," and then to the A.B.'s on the falls, "Lower away!"

It was while lowering this boat that Lowe first became aware of the ship's lights on the port bow. Someone pointed it out to him, and when he looked he saw her two masthead lights and her red sidelight. Boxhall was still firing off rockets at intervals and someone was flashing the morse lamp at her.

Symons had seen the light before being lowered and thought it was probably a cod-fisherman. When his boat reached the water he and the other sailor slipped the hooks and then organised the trimmers with oars, Symons himself taking the tiller.

"After I left the ship I gave the order to pull away. We were pulling very hard—we were pulling very steady—a moderate pull. After I gave that order we pulled away I should say about 200 yards, and I told them to lay on their oars. . . ."

Some of the men left on deck as number 1 pulled away started heav-ing the collapsible boat outboard to the emergency boat's davits, and erecting the canvas sides. Among them was Ismay, still working enthu-siastically. Others, including Lowe, made their way up the gentle slope of the deck towards the after boats, none of which had as yet gone down. Lowe himself crossed over to the port side as he went and helped Moody, the Sixth Officer, filling up numbers 12, 14 and 16. Wilde was in charge of the deck at this time, which was now filling up with more passengers than there had been forward, and there was less difficulty in finding women to embark. The stewards and others were holding a line against any men who might want to get in the boats, and passing the women along. At one stage a crowd of men, some of whom did not understand English, rushed number 14 past the stewards and were only held back by Joseph Scarrot, A.B., threatening them with the tiller. Soon afterwards number 10 went down, and then 12, 14 and 16 very quickly one after the other and some of them very full. Before they went Lowe stepped into number 14 and took charge.

"Did you go by anyone's orders?"

"I did not. I saw five boats go away without an officer and I told Mr Moody on my own that I had seen five boats go away and an officer ought to be in one of those boats. I asked him who it was to be—him or me—and he told me, 'You go—I will get in another boat.'"

Scarrot, A.B.: *"When Mr Lowe came and took charge he asked me how many were in the boat. I told him as far as I could count there were 54 women and 4 children, one of those children being a baby in arms. It was a very small baby which came under my notice more than anything because of the way the mother was looking after it, being a very small child.*

"I told Mr Lowe that I had had a bit of trouble through the rushing business, and he said 'All right'. He pulled out his revolver and he fired two shots between the ship and the boat's side, and issued a warning to the remainder of the men that were about there. He told them that if there was any more rushing he would use it. When he fired the two shots he fired them into the water."

Lowe: *"While I was on the boat-deck just as they had started to lower, two men jumped into my boat. I chased one of them out and to avoid another occurrence of that sort I fired my revolver as I was going down each deck, because the boat would not stand a sudden jerk. She was loaded already with about 64 people on board her, and she would not stand any more . . . I was taking a risk lowering her with that many . . . the risk of buckling in the middle. . . ."*

FRANKFURT TO TITANIC. OUR CAPTAIN WILL GO FOR YOU.

CARONIA TO TITANIC. BALTIC COMING TO YOUR ASSISTANCE.

OLYMPIC TO TITANIC. MY POSITION 4.25 GMT 40 52 N 61 18 W. ARE YOU STEERING SOUTHERLY TO MEET US.

TITANIC TO OLYMPIC. WE ARE PUTTING THE WOMEN OFF IN BOATS.

OLYMPIC TO TITANIC. WE ARE LIGHTING UP EVERY BOILER AND MAK-ING FOR YOU AS FAST AS WE CAN.

TITANIC TO OLYMPIC. WE ARE PUTTING PASSENGERS OFF IN SMALL BOATS.

On the bridge Boxhall stared hopelessly at the steamer ahead. It had seemed to be coming for them, but now the mast lights had widened their distance apart and instead of the red and green sidelights he could only see the red. She didn't seem to get any closer. He kept on sending up rockets but with less enthusiasm than before and he had stopped morsing.

"—she turned round—she was turning very, very slowly—until at last I only saw her stern light. . . ."

The after boats on the starboard side were going down one after the other with Moody and Murdoch or Wilde filling them, and Wilde making sorties below to gather more passengers at A deck where they were stopped in their descent. Paul Maugé and the Chef had been on the Second Class decks for a while after coming through the barrier of stewards, and seeing the first of these dropping past, hurried up to the boat-deck.

"We saw a boat going down . . . it was going to the water, but it was between two decks when I jumped . . . it was stopped between two decks . . . about ten feet . . . yes but before that I did ask the Chef to jump many times, but the Chef was too fat I must say—too big you know. He could not jump . . . and when I was in the lifeboat I shouted to him again in French 'Sautez!' . . . he said something, but I could not hear because at the same moment a man said to me 'Shut up!' . . ."

Maugé's troubles were not over, however, for as they passed an open deck, a man stretched out his arm and grabbed him and tried to pull him out of the boat. He resisted and soon they had dropped down out of reach.

Number 9 had reached the water, 11 was following it, and then number 13 with the lookout man, Lee, in charge stopped at A deck to fill up with more passengers. About this time Hart, the Third Class steward, arrived up on the boat-deck with his second batch of steerage women, some twenty or twenty-five of them, and looking around, could only see boat number 15 left, so he made for it. By the time he had seen his charges in, it was full—or it looked full to him. There were other women hanging back on the deck there, but they refused to go—refused time and again to repeated encouragement. There were four men in the boat besides about fourteen of the crew, and he asked Murdoch whether he should get in.

"Who are you?"

"Hart, sir. Steward—Third Class."

"Yes—hop in then."

Soon afterwards Murdoch gave the order to lower away to A deck, and while there they embarked five more women, three children and a man with a small baby in his arms. Then they were lowered to the water, arriving almost on top of number 13, which had to hurriedly push away and in doing so nearly became awash with a flow of water being pumped from the engine-room.

All the after boats were now down. On the port side forward Lightoller was scouring the decks for passengers for number 4, and Boxhall had been ordered down from the bridge by the Captain to take away the emergency boat, number 2. The Quartermaster, George Rowe, who had been helping him, had been ordered to the collapsible boat C on the starboard side, where sailors, stewards, the saloon barber, Wilde, Murdoch and Ismay, having erected the sides and hooked on the falls which had previously been used to lower the emergency boat, were filling it with passengers— all women. Besides the three boats thus being prepared there were only three more collapsibles left, two stowed and lashed down, one on each side of the top of the officers' deckhouse inboard of the working groups, and another just inboard of Boxhall's emergency cutter on the port side of the deck.

The boats in the sea were fanning out from the ship, the oars poking out from their sides crossed and disorganised and the passengers gazing back at the great bulk of the sinking liner, hypnotised by the sight of her. Lawrence Beesley, a passenger in boat number 13 tried to describe the scene afterwards and came to realise how totally inadequate language was to convey to some other person who was not there any real impression of what he saw.[2]

---

2 *The Loss of the Titanic,* by Lawrence Beesley.

"... the whole picture is so intensely dramatic that, while it is not possible to place on paper for eyes to see the actual likeness of the ship as she lay there, some sketch of the scene will be possible. First of all the climatic conditions were extraordinary. The night was one of the most beautiful I have ever seen: the sky without a single cloud to mar the perfect brilliance of the stars, clustered so thickly together that in places there seemed almost more dazzling points of light set in the black sky than background of sky itself; and each star seemed in the keen atmosphere, free from any haze, to have increased its brilliance tenfold and to twinkle and glitter with a staccato flash that made the sky seem nothing but a setting made for them in which to display their wonder. . . . The complete absence of haze produced a phenomenon I had never seen before: where the sky met the sea the line was as clear and definite as the edge of a knife, so that the water and the air never merged gradually into each other and blended to a softened, rounded horizon, but each element was so exclusively separate that where a star came low down in the sky near the clear-cut edge of the waterline, it still lost none of its brilliance. As the earth revolved and the water edge came up and covered partially the star as it were, it simply cut the star in two, the upper half continuing to sparkle as long as it was not entirely hidden, and throwing a long beam of light along the sea to us.

"And next the cold air! Here again was something quite new to us: there was not a breath of wind to blow keenly round us as we stood in the boat, and because of its continued persistence to make us feel cold; it was just a keen, bitter, icy, motionless cold that came from nowhere, and yet was there all the time; the stillness of it—if one can imagine 'cold' being motionless and still—was what seemed new and strange.

"And these—the sky and the air—were overhead; and below was the sea. Here again something uncommon: the surface was like a lake of oil. . . . The sea slipped away smoothly under the boat, and I think we never heard it lapping the sides, so oily in appearance was the water. So when one of the stokers said he had been at sea for twenty-six years and never yet seen such a calm night, we accepted it as true without comment. Just as expressive was the remark of another: 'It reminds me of a bloomin' picnic!' It was quite true; it did: a picnic on a lake, or a quiet inland river like the Cam, or a backwater on the Thames.

"And so in these conditions of sky and sea and air we gazed broadside on the *Titanic* from a short distance. She was absolutely still—indeed from the first it seemed as if the blow from the iceberg had taken all the courage out of her and she had just come quietly to rest and was settling down without an effort to save herself. . . . From the first, what must have impressed all as they watched was the sense of stillness about her and the slow, insensible way she sank lower and lower in the sea like a stricken animal.

"The mere bulk of the ship viewed from the sea below was an aweinspiring sight. Imagine a ship nearly a sixth of a mile long, with four enormous funnels above the decks, and masts again high above the funnels; with her hundreds of portholes, all her saloons and other rooms brilliant with light, and all round her, little boats filled with those who until a few hours before had trod her decks. . . .

"The thing that ripped away from us instantly, as we saw it, all sense of the beauty of the night, the beauty of the ship's lines, and the beauty of her lights—and all these taken in themselves were intensely beautiful—that thing was the awful angle made by the level of the sea with the rows of port-hole lights along her side in dotted lines, row above row. The sea-level and the rows of lights should have been parallel—should never have met—and now they met at an angle inside the black hull of the ship. . . ."

The boats crept gradually, erratically away. The *Titanic* inched her bows lower and lower, the waterline creeping towards the fo'c'sle head, the stern lifting, the port side dipping, the decks angling, the water inside her swelling aft as it was forced in through the torn plates deep down on the starboard side, the pressure mounting as she settled, the tremendous weight of the sea dragging at her—dragging her down.

OLYMPIC TO TITANIC. WHAT WEATHER HAVE YOU.

TITANIC TO OLYMPIC. CALM AND CLEAR.

FRANKFURT TO TITANIC. ARE THERE ANY BOATS AROUND YOU ALREADY.

BALTIC TO TITANIC. WE ARE RUSHING TO YOU.

CAPE RACE TO VIRGINIAN. PLEASE TELL YOUR CAPTAIN THIS. THE OLYMPIC IS MAKING ALL SPEED FOR THE TITANIC BUT HIS POSITION 40 32

N 61 18 W. YOU ARE MUCH NEARER TO TITANIC. THE TITANIC IS ALREADY PUTTING WOMEN OFF IN BOATS AND HE SAYS THE WEATHER IS CALM AND CLEAR. THE OLYMPIC IS THE ONLY SHIP WE HAVE HEARD SAY GOING TO THE ASSISTANCE OF THE TITANIC. THE OTHERS MUST BE A LONG WAY AWAY FROM THE TITANIC.

***

In the engine-room and stokeholds the engineers were fighting a one-sided and inevitably losing battle with the pumps. The generators were still turning and keeping her decks ablaze with light even though some of those lights forward were now under the water. The watertight bulkheads were still holding against the pressure; aft of number 5 boiler-room the water was rising only slowly over the floors.

Thomas Patrick Dillon, trimmer: "We got the order 'All hands on deck' . . . I went to the well-deck on the starboard side and heard them singing out, 'Any more women on board?' The last boat was just leaving the ship, and we chased two women up the ladder to the boat-deck.

"After that did you see any passengers standing about?"

"Yes, but no women."

"What did you do then?"

"I went on the poop."

" Who was there?"

"Some of the crew and passengers, but no women. I waited there till the ship sank."

"How long were you on the poop?"

"About fifty minutes."

"Was there any commotion?"

"No. No disorder whatever."

C collapsible on the starboard side was crowded with women, mostly Third Class passengers who had been driven up on deck. The water was approaching B deck below them, only some 20 feet now, where there had been a drop of 60. The forward well-deck was awash, and the after part of the foc's'le was an island beyond, deserted, with the mast rising dark against the night and the backstays leading down to the ocean. Wilde ordered the boat to be lowered, and then, seeing Ismay and another passenger called Carter, who had also been helping, he ordered them in, and then repeated the order to lower. There were only the men who had been helping with the boats left on the deck then, and those who were not lowering immediately turned their attention to the collapsible on the roof of the officers' deckhouse. Among them was the saloon barber, Mr A. H. Weikman.

"I helped to launch the boats and there seemed to be a shortage of women . . . I saw Mr Ismay helping to load the boats. . . . He got in along with Mr Carter, because there were no women in the vicinity of the boat. This boat was the last to leave, to the best of my knowledge. He was ordered into the boat by the officer in charge. I think that Mr Ismay was justified in leaving in that boat at that time."[3]

J. Bruce Ismay: "As the boat was going over the side, Mr Carter, a passenger, and myself got into it. At that time there was not a woman on the boat-deck nor any passengers of any class, so far as we could see or hear the boat had between 35 and 40 in it, I should think, most of them women. The rest were perhaps four or five men and it was discovered afterwards that there were four Chinamen concealed under the thwarts in the bottom of the boat. . . .[4]

Mr A. Clement Edwards, M.P.: "Now it has been given in evidence here that you took an actual part in giving directions for the women and children to be placed in the boats. Is that true?"

"I did, and I helped as far as I could."

"If you had taken this active part in the direction up to a certain point, why did you not continue and send to other decks to see if there were other passengers available for this last boat?"

"I was standing by the boat; I helped everybody into the boat that was there, and as the boat was being lowered I got in."

"That does not answer the question. You had been taking a responsible part, according to the evidence, and according to your own admission, in directing the filling of the boats?"

"No, I had not—I had been helping to put the women and children into the boats as they came forward."

3 Affidavit, April 24th, 1912, to American investigation.
4 Statement made by J. Bruce Ismay, April 21st, 1912.

"*What I am putting to you is this, that if you could take an active part at that stage, why did you not continue the active part and give instructions, or go yourself to the other decks or round the other side of the deck, to see if there were other people who might find a place in your boat?*"

"*I presumed there were people down below who were sending the people up.*"

"*But you knew there were hundreds who had not come up. That is your answer, that you presumed that there were people down below sending them up?*"

"*Yes.*"

"*And does it follow from that that you presumed that everybody was coming up who wanted to come up?*"

"*I knew that everybody could not be up.*"

"*Then I do not quite see the point of the answer.*"

"*Everybody that was on the deck got into that boat.*"

Lord Mersey: "*Your point, Mr Edwards, as I understand is this—that having regard to his position, it was his duty to remain upon that ship until she went to the bottom. That is your point?*"

"*Yes—and inasmuch——*"

"*That is your point?*"

"*Frankly that is so. I do not flinch from it a little bit.*"

C collapsible dropped slowly to the ocean lapping B deck and because of the list to port it scraped its inboard bilge keel all the way down the riveted side as it went. She was unhooked and the men put out the oars and slowly, with fumbling movements, rowed away towards the other boats on their side which had been lowered before and which were still pulling further from them. Ismay sat with his back to his ship, pushing an oar before him, unwilling to turn and face the death of his grand conception. Beneath his brusque exterior he was a shy and sensitive man. He rowed with his back to the *Titanic*—stricken—and drifting towards a terrible remorse that he had been spared.

Somewhere to the North Captain Lord of the *Californian* lay asleep on his chartroom settee. Ismay and Lord, but particularly Ismay, were soon to be hounded and pilloried and subjected to possibly the most violently scurrilous personal attacks ever mounted by a sensation- hungry Press against its chosen scapegoats.

Symons, in charge of starboard emergency boat number 1, containing Sir Cosmo, his ladies, and trimmers to a total of twelve persons, looked anxiously back at the angled ship.

"—and just a little while after that, after I saw that the ship was doomed, I gave the order to pull a little further and so escape the suction . . . because her foc's'le was well under water then . . . you could see her starboard side light which was still burning, was not so very far from the water, and her stern was well up in the air . . . just her foremost light had disappeared, and her starboard light left burning was the only light, barring the masthead light on that side of the bridge that I could see. . . .

"Being the master of the situation I used my own discretion. I said nothing to anybody about the ship being doomed, in my opinion. I pulled a little farther away to escape—if there was any suction. . . . The other boats were around us by that time, and some were pulling further away from us. . . ."

Suction! the fear that grew in the night. Leaving Southampton the *Titanic* in passing the *New York*, which was tied up alongside, had drawn her out from the quay towards her until only prompt action by tugs and Captain Smith had averted a collision. If she could suck in a great ocean-going passenger liner, what would be her effect on the lifeboats, minute against her as she sank. Imagination boggled at the tremendous vortex she would leave behind.

The seamen, stewards and engine-room ratings in the boats without officers could not be expected to know anything scientific about the effects of suction, and once whispered, the word must have had a terrifying effect. Even the officers couldn't know exactly what would happen. They, too, pulled away. On the starboard side Pitman ordered Archie Jewel's boat to be lashed to his, 200 yards or more from the sinking ship.

By this time on the port side, Boxhall, with his emergency boat, number 2 filled with some twenty odd women and one man, besides three of the crew and himself, was keeping his boat standing by some 100 feet from the side, watching number 4 still in the davits but only one deck above the sea, being loaded up. He heard Captain Smith shouting at him through a megaphone to come round in to the starboard side, and, himself pulling the starboard stroke oar and at the same time trying to show a girl at the tiller how to steer, and a foreigner at another oar how to row, they made a slow course around the high stem to the other side. The propellers were showing now. James Johnson, who had been night watchman on duty in the First Class accommodation that night when they struck watched the people clustering on the poop. There were hundreds there. There had been others, women among them, walking away from the boat he was in as it had been lowered—back along the boat-deck.

"Going back to their berths do you mean?"

"No, I do not think they were—they did not seem to realise that there was anything wrong. They were going down to the deck below."

The boat reached a position some 200 feet away from the ship's side just abaft the starboard beam. They could still see the people up on the lighted decks, and hear the band faintly. Boxhall rested on his oars and thought he detected suction—they seemed to be drifting in towards the *Titanic*'s counter. He ordered the men back to the oars—they turned and rowed off towards the north-east, and after a while Johnson thought he heard the ripple and suck of water along ice. They couldn't see anything.

"You mean you pulled away from the ship?"

Boxhall: *"Yes."*

TITANIC TO ALL SHIPS. ENGINE ROOM FULL UP TO BOILERS.

By this time the power for the transmitter was failing and it was the last that was heard of the *Titanic* by any other ships except the *Asian*—a faint SOS—and the *Virginian* which picked up a very faint CQD almost half an hour later. Both Bride and Phillips had been ordered by the Captain to clear out long ago. Both stayed at their posts.

Outside the deckhouse men were working at the collapsibles. On the starboard side they had the oars from the top of the house to the deck below, on which they were trying to slide the raft, and on the port side Lightoller and his men, who had just lowered number 4, were dragging the lower raft D, which had been stowed just inboard of the emergency boat, to a position underneath the davits.

"It takes a little time to swing your davits in and hook on . . . nothing very difficult. . . .

"We had very great difficulty in filling her with women. As far as I remember she was eventually filled, but we experienced considerable difficulty. Two or three times we had to wait and call for more women—in fact

on one, I think, perhaps two, occasions someone standing close to the boat said, 'Oh, there are no more women,' and with that several men commenced to climb in. Just then or a moment afterwards whilst they were still climbing in someone sang out on deck, 'Here are a couple more'. . . . If I am right I think this happened on two occasions. . . . The men gave up their places. . . .'

Eventually they had her filled, and with no men except two (described as Filipinos or Chinese!) who had stowed under the thwarts. Some of the crew stepped in, and Lightoller ordered most of them out to lower it. A deck was under water now, and the boat only dropped a few feet before those left in her slipped the hooks; some of the men jumped back in. Lightoller ordered the rest of them up to the roof of the officers' quarters to bring the last collapsible down, and almost immediately afterwards noticed the sea coming out on the boat-deck from the entrance to a crew ladder just forward of him. The deck was sloping well down to port and steeply forward now so that the men on the starboard side under Murdoch and the other deck officers were finding it impossible to drag the last collapsible, which they had dropped from the top of the deckhouse, up the slope to the davits. Instead they were overhauling the falls towards the boat.

Captain Smith still had his megaphone and was walking by the rails further aft trying above the sound of the band to attract the attention of the boats which were pulling away.

And the passengers still stood in quiet groups on the deck.

Lightoller: "The men passengers were preserving splendid order . . . I could not see any women left. . . ."

The Attorney-General: "My Lord, really speaking with the rarest exception in this case everybody on board seems to have behaved in this moment of gravest peril realising, as they must have done, that they were in imminent danger of losing their lives, with a calmness and a devotion to duty which I hope will always be remembered to the credit of those who sail on British vessels. My Lord, in the same connection, I think one ought also to remember the passengers—the accounts which have been given of the women who refused to leave their husbands—took their chance and must have known perfectly well what it meant. . . . It must also not be forgotten, my Lord, that the men, with the exception of, I think, only one instance in which evidence was given of a rush by the Second and Third Class passengers to one boat which was checked, as your Lordship will remember by Mr Lowe——

"Your Lordship will remember again one other significant fact, that although the stewards and crew were marshalled to keep the line and to prevent the male passengers from getting into the boats, and to take care that only women and children got into the boats, the evidence is that they had nothing to do—that the passengers stood there and made no attempt in any way to get into the boats. . . .

"My Lord, this becomes of greater significance when you present to yourself the picture in that vessel, of the ship sinking by the head, the water always getting further and further mastery over the ship, the boats going away one by one, and the realisation of those who remained on board that ship that there was no possibility of their leaving the vessel.

"There is some evidence that when the news came through as Bride received it that the Carpathia was coming to their assistance that the news was taken by him to some of those on board the vessel. It may be that this caused a good many to prefer to remain on board the vessel, but one does not know exactly how much was known of that. . . ."

None of the people in boat number 13 with Lawrence Beesley had heard about the *Carpathia*. But some of the stokers knew that the *Olympic* was steaming to their rescue—the *Olympic*, her sister—but the *Olympic* was further than any of them.

"The sea will be covered with ships tomorrow afternoon," said one of the stokers. "They will race up from all over the sea to find us."

CHAPTER FIVE

Captain Smith with his megaphone in his hand walked forward past the empty davits on the starboard side of the boat-deck, downhill towards the bridge. The water was only a few feet below. The band was loud behind. Just ahead of him he saw Murdoch directing a group of men who were working on the last collapsible on that side, watched by a few passengers behind.

He stopped briefly to encourage them. "Well boys, do your best for the women and children, and look out for yourselves," and continued on towards the bridge.

On the other side of the deck, Lightoller's crew, joined now by the two wireless operators, and assisted by the list of the ship, pulled and heaved and punched their collapsible down from the top of the deck-house. They were desperate men. There wasn't much time. As it landed just astern of the sea rising like a tide from the ladder ahead of them they fell on it and leaped for the lashings. If they could just get the sides up there would be no need to put it under the davits—the sea would float it off for them.

Lightoller himself left them to it and climbed up to the roof of the deckhouse to glimpse what was happening on the starboard side. He saw Murdoch and Moody there, working with the men, saw that someone had managed to hook on the after falls some way from the davits, saw Murdoch overhauling the for'd fall, saw the men beginning to pull up the canvas sides—saw the water rise suddenly around their legs and over— scrambling men——

Edward Brown on the after falls felt the water coming as she dipped her bridge under, and leaped inside the boat and hacked away at the falls with a knife, calling out to the man forward to do the same. He glimpsed the passengers, who had been watching them, struggling in the water and felt himself being washed out of the boat—he was under the surface, ice cold, others all around him—someone dragging at his clothes——

Weikman, the saloon barber, was in the water too and striking out desperately when a pile of rope fell on him. He struggled to free himself.

The port collapsible was swept off at the same time. Bride saw his senior, Phillips, standing on top of the deckhouse as he fumbled with the lashings—then he was lying on his back in the water under the capsized boat, fighting his way out.

Captain Smith went down on his bridge. Wilde, Murdoch and Moody of the deck officers perished, and many of the crew and passengers there—and moments later, as the flood swept aft, the musicians were stilled.

Lightoller, alone of the senior officers, survived.

"She seemed to take a bit of a dive, and I just walked into the water. . . . Well, I was swimming out towards the head of the ship, the crow's-nest. I could see the crow's-nest. The water was intensely cold and one's natural instinct was to try and get out of the water. I do not know whether I swam to the foremast with the idea, but of course I soon realised it was rather foolish, so I turned to swim across clear of the ship to starboard. The next thing I knew I was up against that blower on the fore part of the funnel. There is a grating. . . . The water rushing down held me a while. . . . It held me against the blower. . . ."

This blower led down to the stokehold for ventilation, and after a few moments, while Lightoller was dragged under with the ship, a gust of hot air rushed up from below and blew him free. When he surfaced he found himself right alongside the collapsible which he had helped to get down from the top of the deckhouse, and from which Bride must just recently have freed himself. The sides were still lashed up. Lightoller clung to a piece of lashing.

Slightly further astern Colonel Archibald Gracie of the United States Army was swimming for some wreckage after having been drawn down in the vortex as the ship plunged. He also had been watching the men working on the starboard collapsible and it had been his knife which had allowed Edward Brown to cut the falls. As the water rose, he and his great friend Clint Smith had tried to get aft, but had been impeded by a sudden surge of people coming up from the decks below and completely blocking any passage. Colonel Grade had bent his knees, and as the tidal wave swept up the decks had jumped with it as if riding the surf, and been propelled up toward the railings around the deck above the officers' quarters. He had clung there until the ship slid further and this deck too went under.

Edward Brown, whirled round and round in the vortex as the bridge went down, was propelled to the surface by his life-jacket as Lightoller was being sucked under against the grating of the blower. He came up amongst dozens of other people, struggling and gasping in the clutch of the freezing water. There was no wreckage near—only people. Weikman, the barber, some distance away, was swimming in the direction of a bulky, dark object which he could see above the surface. Soon afterwards everyone swimming there and those in the nearer boats heard one or two sharp reports which they thought emanated from the boilers way down below the surface. Lightoller, as we have seen, was blown from the grating; Weikman was propelled by a wall of water on the surface directly towards the dark object he had been making for, which turned out to be a bundle of deck-chairs. After a while he managed to clamber on top of them.

Bride, having freed himself from underneath the collapsible, had lost all contact with it. Lightoller still clutched the side lashings.

"And then the forward funnel fell down. It fell within three or four inches of the boat. It lifted the boat bodily and threw her about twenty feet clear of the ship as near as I could judge."

To the people in the water over where it had been propelled it was a godsend. They clambered on to the slight curve of the upturned bottom, balancing above the now smooth water and heard all around from the night the cries and groans of others whom they could not see and were powerless to help. Lightoller, without knowing how he got there, eventually found himself alongside it again, and he too climbed on. More came swimming up.

To many of those in the water and watching from the boats and to some of those on the poop, the ship seemed to right herself shortly after the explosions as if the bow had dropped off and the stern section released from the tremendous weight of it, popped upwards like a cork. Patrick Dillon, the trimmer who was on the poop, thought he saw the after funnel fall towards him for a moment. Edward Brown in the water, thought she trembled in her pendulum movement and came back slightly; George Symons, master of emergency boat number 1, thought for an instant that the stern half was going to float by itself. None of the officers who were watching saw this. They only saw her counter angling upwards steadily and slowly. Lightoller, observing keenly from a position on his upturned boat somewhere abreast of the top of number 2 funnel, was perfectly certain that there was no righting action at any time.

Meanwhile, in that portion of the superstructure still above water, there was a wild scramble aft—aft along the climbing boat-deck and over the rails at the end, down to A deck, some throwing themselves over the side into the sea, most carrying on down to B deck, to the well-deck, and struggling towards the stern. In among them was Charles Joughin, Chief Baker. He had been below in his cabin earlier having a drop of liqueur after helping with the after port boats, then had ascended to the boat-deck to find that all the boats had gone. So he had returned below as far as B deck, and seeing all the deck-chairs in rows, had begun pitching them through the great square windows into the sea below. It was while he was cooling off from his exertions in the deck pantry that the ship had given her tilt down—he had heard a kind of crash overhead as if something had buckled, and then a rush—a rush of people on deck.

"When I got up on top I could see them clambering down from those decks. Of course I was in the tail of the rush."

When he arrived on the well-deck it seemed to him that the ship gave a great shudder to port and threw everyone in a bunch, but he picked himself up and, climbing still, reached the poop and went over the rail actually on to the side of the vessel which was tilting so much that the plates of the hull on which he stood seemed no less level than the deck. He crouched there and clung to the rail.

After what seemed a long period in the water Edward Brown made out the dark silhouette of the starboard collapsible from which he had been washed as the deck went under. He couldn't swim but he propelled himself forward in his life-jacket with a dog paddle until he reached it and was pulled aboard by some of the sixteen or so men who had already found it. The sides had not been erected properly and the bottom was over a foot deep in water. Later they pulled a woman on board.

A little way away Weikman knelt on his bundle of deck-chairs, and somewhere quite near, but invisible, Lightoller, Bride, Phillips, Colonel Gracie and a swelling number of other men were huddling together on the bottom of the other unlaunched collapsible; some thirty eventually found this precarious refuge.

Much further aft those of the crew and passengers who had not got away in the boats, or dived, or been swept off the midships section were crowded still on the poop, clutching at anything solid which would prevent them sliding down the steep slope of the deck towards the water—being raised higher and higher in the air as the bow plunged and the ship pivoted around her centre of buoyancy. The water inside her was working aft as she sank, pushing the buoyancy before it.

Lightoller: *"The third, if not the second funnel was still visible. The stern was then clear of the water. . . . She was gradually raising her stern out of the water. Even at that time I think the propellers were out of the water. . . ."*

Away to the west-south-west the *Mount Temple* was driving towards her—and the ice barrier. To the south-east and still more than 30 miles away, the *Carpathia* was steaming north-westwards at about 17 knots. The boilers were roaring and the whole engine-room pounding with the effort. Captain Rostron, himself on the bridge with his officers as they raced for the ice zone, had two men in the eyes of her on the stem head and one in the crow's-nest. He had already organised extensive preparations for the rescue. The Chief Engineer was diverting all steam from the boilers away from subsidiary heating purposes to the main engines. The Bosun had been instructed to call all hands, who were now clearing and swinging out the boats, working as silently as was possible with strict orders not to alarm the passengers who were asleep in their bunks. A steward had been posted to each gangway in case any passengers should hear the activity and wonder what was going on. They were to reassure them and get them back to their cabins. The English doctor had been ordered to take over the First Class diningroom, the Italian doctor, the Second Class dining-room, the Hungarian doctor, the Third Class dining-room—all to have supplies of stimulants, restoratives and first aid necessities. The Purser, Assistant Purser and Chief Steward had their instructions to receive the rescued at the various gangways with batches of stewards to take the survivors direct to the respective dining-rooms, also to take so far as possible the names of the survivors to be sent by wireless. The Inspector, steerage stewards and masters-at-arms to control the *Carpathia*'s steerage passengers, keeping them from going on deck or to the dining-room; all spare steerage berths to be prepared for the *Titanic*'s Third Class passengers. In addition the Chief Steward was to organise blankets for the saloons and public rooms, and others to be placed near the gangways and handy for the boats; coffee for the *Carpathia*'s crew as they worked, and soup, coffee and tea ready for the survivors.

The First Officer had been ordered to prepare and swing out all boats, open all gangway doors, have electric clusters (lights) at each gangway and over the side, a block and tackle hooked in at each gangway, a chair slung at each gangway for lifting aboard the sick and injured, pilot ladders over the side, cargo falls with both ends clear and the bights secured all along the ship's side on deck for boat ropes, lines, gaskets to be distributed about the decks to be handy as lashings, steam on the winches, forward derricks to be topped, oil handy to pour down the lavatories, canvas ash bags handy for the gangways to help up children or injured.

Individual deck officers had been instructed which boats they were to take away if necessary.

The Captain had done all he could. The crew were working swiftly, and as silently as was possible. But she was too far away still.

Way up over the horizon to the north-west the Second Officer on the bridge of the *Californian* was watching the strange steamer's lights intently. The *Californian* herself had swung around from an easterly heading through South to about WSW, and the other vessel was fine on the port bow bearing about SW by W, having steamed across from a southerly bearing. She had shut in her red sidelight and was showing what the Second Officer took to be her stern light.

He told the apprentice with him to go down and call Captain Lord, make sure he woke him, and tell him that they had seen altogether eight rockets from the steamer, that she was steaming off and disappearing to the south-west—and that the *Californian* herself was heading WSW. The apprentice was also to tell Captain Lord that they had called her up on the morse lamp repeatedly but had received no reply.

The boy went down to the chartroom just below and woke Lord and made his report. Lord said, "All right," and then asked him if there were any colours in the rockets.

"No, they were all white."

"What time is it?"

The boy told him and went out. As he closed the door he thought he heard the Captain say something but he didn't know what it was, and he went straight back to the bridge and reported the conversation to the Second Officer.

The Captain, however, was only conscious for the tail end of this visit. Fully-dressed still, lying on the settee in the steam-heated chartroom, the first he knew of Gibson's presence was when the door closed to behind the boy. He had woken, then, from his deep sleep and called out, "What is it?" Receiving no reply he had gone to sleep again.

***

Those watching the *Titanic* from the lifeboats and the collapsibles and in the water knew that she hadn't long to go now. George Symons in number 1 boat was staring at her, twisted around in his seat by the tiller, while the boat pointed away towards the northern stars.

"She suddenly took a top cant, her stern came well out of the water then . . . head down—and that is the time I saw her lights go out—all her lights. . . . There was a sound like a steady thunder as you hear on an ordinary night at a distance. . . .

One of the few photographs taken of the *Titanic* prior
to her maiden voyage, which was also her last

The *Californian,* alleged to have been lying stopped in the ice close to the
scene of the *Titanic* disaster and to have done nothing to assist survivors

Artist's impression of the *Titanic* sinking, drawn
from details supplied by eyewitnesses

Captain Smith of the *Titanic*

Survivors approaching the *Carpathia* in the one
adequately erected Englehardt collapsible lifeboat

Captain Stanley Lord, master of the *Californian*,
after his dismissal from the Leyland Line

J. Bruce Ismay giving evidence at the British Court of Inquiry

Lord Mersey, President of the Court,
on his way to the British Inquiry

Sir Rufus Isaacs, Attorney General of the British Court

"The next thing I saw was her poop. . . ."

She was just a great black, angled silhouette then, a long, dark shape against the dark night and the many bright stars.

Lightoller, abreast and only feet away from her funnels watched this finally lifeless afterbody rising up slowly for the final plunge.

"After she reached an angle of fifty or sixty degrees . . . there was this rumbling sound, which I attributed to the boilers leaving their beds and crashing down on or through the bulkheads. The ship was at that time becoming more and more perpendicular until she reached the absolute perpendicular . . . and then went slowly down. She went down very slowly until the end, and then after she got so far, the after part of the second cabin deck, she of course went down much quicker."

Small waves spread out from the point where she disappeared but they weren't strong enough to dislodge the men from the upturned collapsible, or even to upset Weikman on his deck-chairs.

Patrick Dillon slid into the water with the poop and was sucked downwards some 2 fathoms before the pull of the vessel released him and the buoyancy of his life-jacket propelled him fast to the surface. He was surrounded by hundreds of people. Some were numbed and silent, most were crying out, gasping, choking and yelling for help.

To the people watching in the boats dispersed at varying distances around the spot the voices mingled in one long, agonised wail.

"We do not want unnecessarily to prolong the discussion of it but they were the cries of people who were drowning?"

"Yes."

"Did it occur to you that with the room in your boat if you could get to these people you could save some?"

"It is difficult to say what occurred to me. Again I was minding my wife, and we were rather in an abnormal condition you know. There were many things to think about, but of course it quite well occurred to one that people in the water could be saved by boat, yes."

"And that there was room in your boat?"

"Yes, it is possible."

"And did you hear a suggestion made that you should go back to the place whence the cries came?"

"I heard no suggestion of going back."

Trimmer from the same boat: "I proposed going back and they would not hear of it."

"In the presence of those cries for help from the drowning were you the only one in your boat to propose to go back to the rescue?"

"I never heard anyone else."

Sailor in charge of the same boat: "There was no question raised about going back. . . . There was no conversation at all in the boat. They were all doing their work. . . ."

The passenger again: "I did not hear any of the ladies saying anything about the danger of being swamped."

"Did you hear any discussion about being swamped if you went back?"

"No, I did not hear the subject raised. The subject was not raised I think."

"Was any notice taken of those cries in your boat?"

"I think the men began to row again immediately."

"Did they get any orders to do that?"

"That I could not say."

"That would seem rather strange . . . to row away from the cries?"

"To row—I do not know which way they were rowing, but I think they began to row. In my opinion it was to stop the sound."

A steward in another boat: "When we heard the cries the man in charge of the boat asked the ladies if they should go back and they said no."

"Can you explain why it was, with an unfilled boat (twenty-five persons) he failed to go to the rescue of the drowning people?"

"I have answered the question."

"It was because the ladies protested?"

"Yes, I have answered the question."

"If you had had charge of that boat would you have gone back?"

"I do not suppose I would have done any more than he did. He acted as an Englishman."

The man in charge of another boat: "We heard the screams but we did not go back."

"What is your reason?"

"Well, there was such a mass of people in the water we should have been swamped."

Many of the boats, wary of suction, were too far away by that time to be of much assistance to those in the water, others were full to capacity, and one collapsible, the one which had been lowered last from the port side, was full of water and down to the canvas gunwales. Of all those boats, most of which were certified to carry sixty-five persons, and which had an average of thirty-six persons actually in them—some far more, some far less—only one was near enough and empty enough to be of any immediate use. This was number 4, which had returned, after being one of the last to be lowered, to pick up two firemen who had climbed down the falls from the after port side davits. This boat picked seven from among those struggling in the water, including Patrick Dillon.

Of the rest not one made any early attempt. Some rowed away from the terrible sounds, some just rowed, some tried singing so that they would not hear.

For the men in charge of the boats and particularly the officers in charge of the groups of boats it was an impossible decision they were called upon to make. Some of the boats were only half full and they could have gone back and pulled some of those 1,000 and more people from the water, but just as certainly it would only have taken a dozen of the desperate and drowning on the gunwales of each boat to capsize it and plunge all those already safe—most of whom were women—into the sea to drown or be frozen to death with them. It was an unbearable decision. The men in the boats were not inhuman monsters or cowards—they were human beings faced with impossible alternatives, and in the event they rowed in any direction except towards the centre of the cluster of people who were crying out for them.

The Fifth Officer, Lowe, an impetuous Welshman new to the White Star Line, had gathered together all those boats on the port side which he had helped to fill, and had taken charge of the group and kept them together. He had all the passengers taken from his boat and distributed among the others, and then taking only six crewmen, five on the oars and one as lookout right up in the bows, he lay off near the voices. When he thought a suitable time had elapsed and the voices were stilled he ordered them to row towards the last place they had seen the *Titanic*.

"Did you approach as soon as you thought you could do so with reasonable safety?"

"I did. I had to wait until I could be of some use. It was no good going back there to be swamped."

When they reached the spot they found nothing—no one, no bodies, no wreckage. Lowe ordered them to lash the boats together to present a larger target to any rescue ship—but as they were doing it they heard faint cries coming from another direction altogether. Immediately they pulled for them.

After a while they reached the bodies.

Joseph Scarrott, A.B., in the bows: *"It was still dark . . . and the wreckage and bodies seemed to be all hanging in one cluster. When we got up to it we got one man, and we got him in the stern of the boat—a passenger it was—and he died shortly after we got him into the boat. One of the stewards that was in the boat tried means to restore life to the man; he loosed him and worked his limbs about and rubbed him, but it was of no avail at all. . . . We got two others as we pushed our way towards the wreckage, and as we got towards the centre we saw one man there. I have since found out he was a storekeeper—he was on top of a staircase—it seemed to be a large piece of wreckage anyhow—it was wood anyhow. He was kneeling there as if he was praying and at the same time he was calling for help. When we saw him we were about from here to that wall away from him, and the bodies, the wreckage were that thick—and I am sorry to say there were more bodies than there was wreckage—it took us a good half-hour to get that distance to that man to get through the bodies. We could not row the boat—we had to push them out of the way and force our boat up to this man."*

Lowe: ". . . . it was awkward to get in amongst it, because you could not row—because of the bodies. You had to push your way through."

Lowe picked up four in his boat; number 4 picked up seven; others had clambered on the upturned collapsible and the starboard half-rigged collapsible; a few, a very few, had found other pieces of small wreckage to cling to; many more than a thousand had faded out.

Lawrence Beesley had heard them.[1] "The cries which were loud and numerous at first, died away gradually one by one, but the night was clear,

---

1 *The Loss of the Titanic,* by Lawrence Beesley.

frosty and still, the water smooth, and the sounds must have carried on its level surface free from any obstruction for miles, certainly much further from the ship than we were situated. I think the last of them must have been heard nearly forty minutes after the *Titanic* sank. Lifebelts would keep the survivors afloat for hours; but the cold water was what stopped the cries."

The man in charge of another starboard side boat: "After we rowed a little way, as we were going for this self-same light of my first story, we stopped, we laid on our oars. Then I gave the order to pull back, and told the men in the boat we would pull back to the boats. I was going on my way back then as near as I possibly could to the scene of the disaster after we met with the other boat. I strained my ears to hear whether I could hear anybody—any person whatever making a cry."

"And you heard no one?"

"I heard no one"

"They were all drowned by that time, is that not so?"

"I could not say that sir. . . ."

Where there had been a great ship and a pampered, living body of people there was only darkness and silence and the cold stars—and then hails across the water as the scattered boats tried to establish contact.

CHAPTER SIX

For those in the new, sturdily constructed timber lifeboats, standing huddled together for warmth, or sitting on the thwarts and side benches or even down on the bottom boards, many with rugs and warm clothing, those long, early hours of the morning of the 15th were physically bearable. And while it must have been a time of agonising apprehension for those who had been parted from their husbands or families there was no certainty that they were dead. The starboard side boats had been filling with men when women were no longer available, and it was impossible to take a roll call of all who had been saved. Few of the lifeboats could see each other even, and by the morning they were all scattered for a radius of 4 or 5 miles. The cries in the dark may not have been from their own.

Lawrence Beesley records that gratitude was the dominant note in his feelings, gratitude that he had been spared and was safe in a boat on the still sea where so many had gone down with the ship. And after gratitude the cold—bitter cold—which had settled down on them like a garment and wrapped them closely around although they stamped their feet on the bottom boards and rubbed their limbs vigorously to keep the circulation going.

Some of the stokers especially had only thin trousers and singlets and a hurriedly-thrown jacket over their shoulders, and they probably suffered most from the icy conditions. One lay huddled beneath the tiller all morning in Beesley's boat.

For those who were dry it was bearable; but it is difficult to imagine without experiencing it, the agony of those who had scrambled from the water on to the last two collapsibles which had been washed from the ship. The starboard collapsible, A, was right side up, but most of the canvas gunwales were drooping and it was hardly more than a raft beneath the weight of the people forcing the air-pocketed bottom under the water. Collapsible B was upside down with some standing upright, some, like Bride the wireless operator, lying or sitting on it—Bride's legs were actually held on by the weight of people sitting on him—and others clinging to the ropes around the edge. More came up all the time, but there was no room. Probably some were turned away for the greater good of those already on board, for undoubtedly with the thirty-six that it supported by morning, a few more clambering on could have upset them all into the water.

Lightoller was in charge of this collapsible and he has tried to describe what must surely be impossible to convey adequately.[1] "However anyone that had sought refuge on that upturned Englehardt survived the night is nothing short of miraculous. If ever human endurance was taxed to the limit, surely it was during those long hours of exposure in a temperature below freezing, standing motionless in our wet clothes. . . . Hour by hour the compartments in this collapsible boat were surely filling with water, no doubt due to the rough and ready treatment she had received when dumped incontinently from the top of our quarters with a crash on to the boat-deck. . . . The fact remains that we were painfully conscious of that icy cold water slowly creeping up. Some quietly lost consciousness, subsided into the water and slipped overboard. There being nothing on the flat, smooth bottom of the boat to hold them. No one was in a condition to help and the fact that a slight but distinct swell had started to roll up rendered help from the still living an impossibility. . .

Phillips, the senior operator, was standing next to Lightoller and Bride was at the other end, so that while they shouted back and forth about the other ships they had been speaking to, all on board knew that the *Carpathia* was making full speed towards them, and was the nearest ship. Lightoller worked out from the position given that she should be up to them by daybreak. They had to keep alive until then.

Not far away, but unknown to them, Lowe was still searching among the bodies and the drifting deck-chairs for any signs of life. Further out

---

1 *Titanic and Other Ships,* by Charles Lightoller.

other lifeboats were rowing aimlessly, and some were lashed together. Way over to the East the amateurs in Boxhall's boat were still rowing while he himself was lighting up the company's green flares at intervals to try and gather other boats in towards him, and to point the way for the rescue ships.

Captain Rostron, staring ahead from the *Carpathia*'s bridge, first saw one of these lights at about 2.40. He was talking with the Doctor at the time, after the man had reported that all was in readiness for the reception of the survivors.

"There's her light!" Rostron exclaimed. "She must be still afloat."

Some moments later the Second Officer reported an iceberg a point on the port bow, and the Captain saw it too, betrayed by a pin-point reflection from a star on its surface.

"Port your helm!"

Rostron moved with quick, agile motions. He was known as "The Electric Spark". Quite the reverse of the popular conception of the bluff old seadog, he was a total abstainer from strong drink, smoking and swearing—but a fine sailor none the less who had at one time been mate of the clipper, *Cedric the Saxon,* and who was destined in later years to become Commodore of the Cunard fleet. He was slightly built, wiry, with sharp, keen features and piercing blue eyes, a strict disciplinarian, a believer in the power of prayer, and with it all a man of quick decision, who once embarked on a course of action, stuck to it.

Not the least extraordinary of all the happenings on that night and early morning was the way his ship led a charmed life through the zone of danger. As Rostron later described it, "More and more we were all keyed up. Icebergs loomed up and fell astern; we never slackened, though sometimes we altered course suddenly to avoid them. It was an anxious time with the *Titanic*'s fateful experience very close in our minds. There were seven hundred souls on the *Carpathia;* these lives as well as the survivors of the *Titanic* herself depended upon a sudden turn of the wheel."[2]

"Will you allow me, Captain, at the very earliest opportunity to express to you on behalf of His Majesty's government how deeply grateful we are to you for your conduct and the very great number of lives which you were instrumental in saving?"

---

2 *Home from the Sea,* by Arthur Rostron.

"Thank you very much."

The *Carpathia* fired off rockets every quarter of an hour to let those in the liner—they still hoped she might be afloat—know they were near.

The rockets had an electrifying effect in the boats, as they flashed up briefly from below the horizon with a sound, reaching them later, like distant gunfire.

Sometime after 3.20 the apprentice on watch on the bridge of the *Californian* saw a faint light in the sky two points before the port beam of his ship which had swung through South to a south-westerly heading. He was to see two more before his watch ended.

At about this time Captain Moore of the *Mount Temple,* which was still steaming eastwards in company with an unknown vessel ahead of him, and was now some 15 miles from the *Titanic's* broadcast position, saw the green sidelight of a sailing vessel which he had to avoid suddenly, and shortly afterwards reached pack ice.

And at much the same time on the *Carpathia* Captain Rostron could see the masthead lights of a steamer two points on the starboard bow between him and the *Titanic's* position; one of his officers also made out the port sidelight of the stranger.

CARPATHIA CALLING MGY. IF YOU ARE THERE WE ARE FIRING ROCKETS.

Besides the mystery ships in the vicinity, and the *Californian* lying stopped, and the *Carpathia* and the *Mount Temple* approaching very close under all steam, there were the Russian *Birma,* the German *Frankfurt,* the Allan liner, *Virginian,* and the White Star *Baltic* and *Olympic* making towards the spot, and many others listening in, the *Celtic,* the *Asian,* the *Caronia, the La Provence,* the *Ypiranga,* all relaying messages, and maybe also heading for the last position of the *Titanic.*

Those in the lifeboats who had been alerted by the rockets gazed towards the horizon from whence they had come. Even the stoker who had been huddled under the tiller in Beesley's boat had leapt up and was standing, shivering with the cold and watching with the rest.

"With every sense alert, eyes gazing intently at the horizon and ears open for the least sound, we waited in absolute silence in the quiet night. And then, creeping over the edge of the sea where the flash had been, we saw a single light, and presently a second below it, and in a few minutes they were well above the horizon and they remained in line! But we had been deceived before, and we waited a little longer before we allowed ourselves to say we were safe. The lights came up rapidly: so rapidly it seemed only a few minutes (though it must have been longer) between first seeing them and finding them well above the horizon and bearing down rapidly upon us. We did not know what sort of a vessel was coming, but we knew she was coming quickly, and we searched for paper, rags—anything that would burn. . . . A hasty paper torch was twisted out of letters found in someone's pocket, lighted, and held aloft by the stoker standing on the tiller platform. The little light shone in flickers on the faces of the occupants of the boat, ran in broken lines for a few yards along the black, oily sea (where for the first time I saw the presence of that awful thing which had caused the whole terrible disaster—ice—in little chunks the size of one's fist, bobbing harmlessly up and down), and spluttered away to blackness again as the stoker threw the burning remnants of the paper overboard."[3]

The men on the upturned bottom of the port collapsible had their time occupied in just keeping aboard. Lightoller had already organised them into two lines, standing close to each other on the slippery planks which were now well under the water, and they swayed in unison as he ordered them, so that their combined weight counteracted the effect of the swell. "Lean to the left men—steady—lean to the right——"

Boxhall was still firing his green flares, and the *Carpathia* was answering with Cunard roman candles, although all hope that the *Titanic* was still afloat had left them. They were almost up to the position and would surely have seen her had she been there. Rostron realised the green lights must be from her boats; he was steering now on bearings from the flares. At 3.16 he was some 12 miles from the *Titanic*'s position[4] and at 3.30, bumping occasional small ice and amongst numerous bergs, he rang the engines to "Half Ahead" and then to "Slow".

At four o'clock he thought he must have run his distance despite the detours around icebergs and he put the engines on stand by. Shortly afterwards he gave the order to stop.

---

3 *The Loss of the Titanic*, by Laurence Beesley.
4 *Tramps and Ladies,* by Sir James Bisset (then Second Officer, *Carpathia*).

"As if in corroboration of that judgement I saw a green light just ahead of us low down. That must be a boat I knew, and just as we were planning to come alongside her I saw a big berg immediately in front of us—the Second Officer reported it at the same moment. . . ."[5]

He had meant to make a lee for the boat on the port side, but as the berg loomed up he starboarded the wheel and passed her to port, carrying his way ahead of her.

Boxhall's hail came up to them on the bridge. "We have only one seaman in the boat and cannot work very well."

Rostron waved his hand in acknowledgement and prepared to back his ship down towards her.

In boat number 13 to the West of this first contact Beesley and his companions had their eyes fixed on the *Carpathia*'s mast lights.

"With our torch burnt and in darkness again, we saw the headlights stop, and realised that the rescuer had hove to. . . . We waited, and she slowly swung round and revealed herself to us as a large steamer with all her port-holes alight. I think the way those lights came slowly into view was one of the most wonderful things we shall ever see. It meant deliverance at once. . . . It seemed almost too good to be true, and I think everyone's eyes filled with tears, men's as well as women's, as they saw again the rows of lights, one above the other shining kindly to them across the water. . . .

"The boat swung round and the crew began their long row to the steamer; the captain (of the boat) called for a song and led off with 'Pull for the shore boys'. The crew took it up quaveringly and the passengers joined in, but I think one verse was all they sang. It was too early yet, gratitude was too deep and sudden in its overwhelming intensity for us to sing very steadily. Presently, finding the song had not gone very well we tried a cheer, and that went better."[6]

The sky was pale in the East as the first survivors came aboard the *Carpathia* and with the twilight a breeze stirred over the water, and became stronger every minute.

Over at the western edge of the icefield the *Mount Temple*'s Commander was obeying the Company's instructions *never* to enter ice; to the North

5 *Home from the Sea,* by Sir Arthur Rostron.
6 *The Loss of the Titanic,* by Laurence Beesley.

the *Californian* swung at the whim of the current and shortly after eight bells were struck the Chief Officer, Stewart, relieved the Second on the bridge and heard from him the story of the strange rockets he had seen during the night from the ship which had steamed off to the south-west.

Stewart took his binoculars over to the port wing and scanned the horizon. "There she is," he said after a few moments. "There is that steamer. She's all right."

Stone took the glasses from him and looked himself.

"No. That's not the same one." He could see a ship just abaft the beam showing two masthead lights and apparently heading in much the same direction as themselves. "No, that's not her. She has two lights." He then handed over the watch and he and the apprentice retired below, leaving the Chief Officer on the bridge.

As the light grew stronger the officers on the bridge of the *Carpathia* began to see the shapes of the bergs and field ice which they had negotiated through the last dark hours. To starboard, about a third of a mile away was the large one which they had altered around at the last moment as they had seen the green light from Boxhall's lifeboat, and 200 yards on the port quarter lay a growler which they had not seen—barely 10 feet high and 20 feet long. The coming day revealed them as far as the eye could see, spreading in every direction, all sizes and fantastic shapes and heights. Rostron sent one of his junior officers up to the monkey island to count them. When he came down he reported twenty-five large ones—in the region of 200 feet high or over—and dozens more of varying sizes downwards, at which he had stopped counting.

"Had you seen anything of that icefield before it became daylight?"

"Oh no—nothing—it was quite daylight before we saw the icefield." Standing on the top of the collapsible, half dead with the cold which the morning breeze was now driving through their sodden clothes, the thirty-five or so who still lived sighted another lifeboat in the distance, and another close behind it. Lightoller remembered he had his officer's whistle in his pocket and he reached in for it, placed it to his numbed lips and blew. Heads turned in the boats and slowly they pulled around and towards them.

Charles Joughin, the Chief Baker, who had gone down with the ship while standing on the hull plates outside the rails of the poop was now clinging to the outside of the collapsible. He had been the last arrival. There was no room up on top for him and his legs hung down in the water as he held on to the side with one hand and with the other to the arm of a friend, Maynard, whom he had luckily spotted as he paddled around. It was a mystery how he survived in the cold water. He watched the boats approaching.

"A lifeboat came along—it got within about fifty yards and they sung out they could only take ten. So I said to this Maynard, let go my hand, and I swum to meet it, so that I would be one of the ten. . . . Yes, I was taken in."

"I do not want to be harrowing about it, but was the water very cold?"

"I felt colder in the lifeboat—after I got in the lifeboat."

All the men on the collapsible were, in the event, taken in and squeezed down among the occupants of the boat, all except the wireless operator, Phillips who had died before it reached them, and he was left. Lightoller took charge and pointed the boat's head around to where they could see the *Carpathia* stationary against the eastern horizon. Rowing was almost impossible with the crowd in the boat; it had already taken off the people from the other port side collapsible which had become mysteriously waterlogged, and Lightoller counted seventy-five in her, beside any who may have been sitting down in the bottom. The breeze was freshening all the time and he judged it might soon become difficult to keep the sea out.

The collapsible from the starboard side which had been washed off the deck at the same time as Lightoller's, and which had been later found by a number of people in the same way, had already been seen by Lowe, after he had finished his search among the bodies. He erected the mast of his own boat, hoisted the sail and beat towards it with his crew of six and the four rescued on the bottom boards. It looked to be in a bad way.

"I reckon it had been pierced, but I do not know. She was right sides up and all that. . . . The sides had dropped somehow or other."

"How many people were on her?"

"I do not know. I do not want to appear sarcastic or anything like that, but you do not count people in a case like this. I should say roughly about twenty men and one woman."

They had taken the woman off first, and then the men, one by one. Three bodies had been left when they cast it off.

"I made the men on that collapsible turn those bodies over before I took them into my boat. I said, 'before you come on board here you turn those bodies over and make sure they are dead', and they did so."

Then Lowe set sail for the *Carpathia*, taking in tow the other collapsible.

All the boats were making for the ship now, and there were shouts and cheers across the water as some of the crews indulged in friendly rivalry. A soft golden glow around the horizon was giving way to faint pink, and in the far distance fleecy, wafer-thin fillets of cloud stretched in bands horizontally down almost to the water's edge, tinged pink with the rising sun. The stars died slowly, all except one which remained long after the others just above the horizon—and near by a pale crescent moon.

Beesley, looking towards the liner in this early light "saw what seemed to be two large, fully-rigged sailing ships near the horizon, with all sails set, standing up near her. . . . But in a few minutes more the light shone on them and they stood revealed as huge icebergs, peaked in a way that readily suggested a ship. When the sun rose higher it turned them pink, and sinister as they looked towering like rugged white peaks of rock out of the sea, and terrible as was the disaster one of them had caused, there was an awful beauty about them which could not be overlooked. Later, when the sun came above the horizon, they sparkled and glittered in its rays; deadly white, like frozen snow. . . .

"As the dawn crept towards us there lay another almost directly in the line between our boat and the *Carpathia*, and a few minutes later, another on her port quarter, and more again on the southern and western horizons, as far as the eye could reach: all differing in shape and size and tones of colour according as the sun shone through them or was reflected directly or obliquely from them.

"We drew near our rescuer and presently could discern the bands on her funnel, by which the crew could tell she was a Cunarder; and already some boats were at her side and passengers climbing up her ladders. . . .

"We could read the Cunarder's name—CARPATHIA—a name we are not likely ever to forget. We shall see her sometimes, perhaps in the shipping lists—as I have done already once when she left Genoa on her return voyage—and the way her lights climbed up over the horizon in the darkness, the way she swung and showed her lighted portholes, and the moment when we read her name on her side will all come back in a flash; we shall live again the scene of rescue, and feel the same thrill of gratitude for all she brought us that night."[7]

04.28. LA PROVENCE TO CELTIC. NOBODY HAS HEARD THE TITANIC FOR ABOUT 2 HOURS.

* * *

At 04.30 *Californian* time, Stewart, the Chief Officer, went down the ladder from the bridge and into the chartroom beneath, where Captain Lord still slept on the settee. He woke him as he had been instructed and told him it was breaking day. Then he told him about the strange ship the Second Officer had seen to the southward, and the rockets the man had seen during the watch.

"Oh, yes I know," Lord replied. "He has been telling me."

Stewart returned to the bridge, and some minutes later Lord joined him and they discussed the advisability of trying to push through the ice-field, which now lay revealed as far as the eye could see, or whether they should try and skirt around to the south-eastwards, looking for a clearer channel.

Eventually they decided to try and push their way through the loose ice ahead of them, and Lord told Stewart to put the engines on stand by. He did so, and then came back.

"Will you go down to look at this steamer to the southward?"

"What's wrong with it?" Lord asked.

"He might have lost his rudder—or something like that."

"She hasn't got any signals up has she?"

The Chief Officer examined her through the glasses again, and made her out as a four-master with a yellow funnel. "No, she hasn't." But he was still doubtful and repeated what the Second Officer had told him about the rockets.

"Call the wireless operator then."

---

7 *The Loss of the Titanic*, by Laurence Beesley.

Stewart went below and roused Evans out of his bunk and asked him to find out what the ship was to the southward; he waited while the operator adjusted the set and settled himself at the ear-phones, and began tapping out CQ CQ CQ; this was the general call to any ships in the vicinity.

At 05.20 (*Californian* time) the *Mount Temple* heard him and replied back at once with the news that the *Titanic* had sunk, although this was pure guesswork on his part, proceeding from the fact that he had not heard from her for so long. He then gave the *Titanic's* signalled position and Evans, in the *Californian*, hurriedly scribbled it down on a piece of paper and handed it to Stewart. Almost immediately the *Frankfurt* jumped in and told him the same thing.

Stewart was hurrying back up the ladder to the bridge, where he imparted the shattering news to Lord.

All hands were called, the boats swung out, the officers roused up from their watches below, and by the time they received the official message from the *Virginian,* they were under way, pushing through the ice on various courses and speeds, making a general southerly direction.[8]

06.00 From: Commander Gambell (*Virginian*) to: Captain:

TITANIC STRUCK BERG WANTS ASSISTANCE URGENT. SHIP SINKING PASSENGERS IN BOATS. HIS POSITION LAT 41 46 LONG 50 14.

At about 06.30 Lord found himself clear of the field ice and increased engine revolutions to 70—full speed—which he estimated as 13 knots.

Sometime about 07.30, all officers up on the bridge, the crew buzzing with excitement, all boats cleared and swung out and inspected and a lookout man hoisted to the truck in a basket, they passed the *Mount Temple* stopped in about the *Titanic's* reported position. They continued on to the South at full speed, having received a message that the *Carpathia* was at the scene of the disaster and rescuing passengers, and shortly after passing the *Mount Temple,* passed a four-masted, pink funnel steamer, the *Almerian*, bound North. There was another, smaller vessel in the vicinity with a black funnel and some device on it. Soon afterwards the *Carpathia* was sighted to the eastward of the ice barrier they were skirting; she was stopped with her flags at half mast. They continued south until she was nearly abeam, and then altered round to head straight for her, still at full speed, through the field ice.

---

8 Trying to make S 16W (19½ miles) to the CQD position.

Rostron first saw her coming at eight o'clock, which would be approximately 07.45, *Californian* time. She was steaming straight for him from a direction WSW true. He was then in a position very close to the main cluster of wreckage, having moved over all the immediate area picking up the scattered boats during the previous three and a half hours, and nearly all the survivors were now aboard his ship. They had come up chattering with cold and a mingled sense of thankfulness for their safety and knowledge of their loss. In Rostron's cabin below were three women, each bereaved; their husbands, all millionaires, had perished, and in addition one had lost her son. One thing which stood out in Rostron's memory afterwards was the quietness of it all. "There was no noise, no hurry." "The *Carpathia* had stopped in mid-Atlantic. It was a beautiful morning, a clear sun burning on sea and glistening on the icebergs. On every side there were dozens of these monsters, so wonderful to look at, so dreadful to touch."[9]

Not all of them were clear, sparkling white though. One of the *Carpathia*'s passengers, waking up that morning, was astounded to see that the ship was stopped, and not far off was a great rock standing up out of the sea. She wondered what islands they could possibly have come to in the middle of the Atlantic.

By the time the *Californian* arrived Rostron had decided that there was no more to be done. All the boats, with the exception of a damaged one, had been hauled aboard and stowed on deck after being emptied of passengers, and he had cruised all around to see if there were any survivors on other rafts or wreckage. But there had been none. In fact there was very little wreckage, only scattered deck-chairs and small stuff and patches of broken-up cork from lifebelts which resembled drifts of seaweed—and one body lying on its side, head half submerged. That was all.

So he left the search to the *Californian* and set course westwards through the ice.

"There surely never was so much ice in that latitude. All we could see was that it stretched to the horizon—a remarkable and awesome sight with great bergs up to two hundred feet in height standing out of the

---

9 *Home from the Sea*, by Sir Arthur Rostron.

general field, which itself was six to twelve feet above the waterline. These little mountains were just catching the morning sun which made them take on all manner of wonderful aspects. Minarets like cathedral towers turned to gold in the distances and, here and there, some seemed to shape themselves like argosies under full sail."[10]

CARPATHIA HAS PASSENGERS FROM LIFEBOATS.

CARPATHIA RESCUED 20 BOAT LOADS.

BALTIC TO CARPATHIA. CAN I BE OF ASSISTANCE TO YOU AS REGARDS TAKING SOME OF THE PASSENGERS FROM YOU. WILL BE IN POSITION ABOUT 4.30. LET ME KNOW IF YOU ALTER YOUR POSITION.

Ismay, shattered by the disaster, refusing food in the Doctor's cabin aboard the Cunarder, was consulted by Rostron. Then the reply was sent.

CARPATHIA TO BALTIC. PROCEED ON YOUR COURSE TO LIVERPOOL.

The *Baltic*, having steamed 134 miles west towards the *Titanic*, turned around and headed back on her original course.

MPA (*Carpathia*) CQ NO NEED TO STAND BY ME.

The *Mount Temple,* still cruising slowly around the western edge of the icefield, turned and headed west again.

FROM OLYMPIC TO OWNERS NEW YORK VIA SABLE ISLAND. HAVE NOT COMMUNICATED WITH TITANIC SINCE MIDNIGHT.

CARPATHIA TO BALTIC. AM PROCEEDING TO HALIFAX OR NEW YORK FULL SPEED. YOU HAD BETTER PROCEED TO LIVERPOOL. HAVE ABOUT 800 PASSENGERS ON BOARD.

CARPATHIA TO VIRGINIAN. WE ARE LEAVING HERE WITH ALL ON BOARD ABOUT 800 PASSENGERS. PLEASE RETURN TO YOUR NORTHERN COURSE.

About 652 people out of 2,201 on board the *Titanic* had got away in the boats, a further 60 had afterwards made the collapsibles, or small wreckage, or been rescued from the water, making about 712 to be taken on board the *Carpathia*. One had subsequently died.

In total,[11] 1,490 people perished—Just over thirty-two per cent of her complement survived. The largest passenger liner the world had ever

---

10 *Home from the Sea,* by Sir Arthur Rostron.
11 British Inquiry figures.

known, the most extravagantly and opulently furnished ship ever conceived, one of the safest vessels to be produced by the foremost maritime and engineering nation in an age of virtually unchecked scientific advance had been ripped apart and left to founder slowly like a tin, toy boat in a pond.

J. Bruce Ismay:[12] "In the presence and under the shadow of a catastrophe so overwhelming my feelings are too deep for expression in words. I can only say that the White Star Line, its officers and employees will do everything humanly possible to alleviate the suffering and sorrow of the survivors and of the relatives of those who have perished. The *Titanic* was the last word in shipbuilding. Every regulation prescribed by the British Board of Trade had been strictly complied with, the master, officers and crew were the most experienced and skilful in the British service."

AUTHOR'S NOTE TO THE PRECEDING CHAPTERS

I make no claims to the absolute accuracy and authenticity of Part 1, which you have just read, other than this: I have done my utmost to check as many of the facts stated as is possible, and further that every fact stated comes from evidence at either the British or American Inquiries, or, for the background details from eyewitness books published afterwards. No newspaper reports have been used.

The picture thus painted of the actual disaster is as it appeared to those listening to the witnesses at the British Inquiry. Where certain key witnesses were not called at the British Inquiry I have had to seek their testimony at the American Inquiry. All italicised passages are from the British Inquiry with the single exception of Weikman's. The three points where the picture thus given differs from the picture given by the British Report after the Inquiry are, first Murdoch's order to port the helm after striking the berg. This is nowhere given in evidence at either Inquiry. My reasons for including it are given later. Second, the timing of the lowering of the first lifeboats, and thus the firing of the first rocket. There is good reason to believe that these events happened before the times stated in the British

---

12 After arrival in New York.

Report, although again the evidence is so confused that it is difficult to place any times. This again is dealt with later, as is the third major point of difference—Captain Rostron's engine orders while the *Carpathia* raced to the scene. The inference in both Inquiries and in Captain Rostron's book is that the engines were left at full ahead. The only hints to the contrary are from the probable range of visibility of Boxhall's green flares in the life-boat, and Sir James Bisset's autobiography, which has been mentioned in footnotes. Rostron was not directly asked this question at either Inquiry.

I hope this is a reasonably accurate picture, but I make no other claims.

PART 2

THE UNITED STATES SENATORIAL
INVESTIGATION

CHAPTER SEVEN

"**S**tunned by the terrific impact, the dazed passengers rushed from their staterooms into the main saloon amid the crash of splintering steel, rending of plates, and shattering of girders, while the boom of falling pinnacles of ice upon the broken deck of the great vessel added to the horror. . . . In a wild, ungovernable mob they poured out of the saloons to witness one of the most appalling scenes possible to conceive. . . . For a hundred feet the bow was a shapeless mass of bent, broken and splintered steel and iron. . . ."

There was more hysteria ashore than there had been on the decks of the *Titanic*. This extract was from a New York evening paper. Others followed with equally sensational "eyewitness" accounts, crew as well as passengers. Bride, the junior wireless operator, described how he had re-entered the wireless room towards the last moments and found a stoker tearing the lifejacket from Phillips' back, and had fought him, and the two of them, Phillips and he, had left the man motionless on the floor as they went out of the door for the last time. Minutes later the sea swept in.

Lady Duff Gordon told how panic had begun to seize some of the passengers by the time her boat had been ready for lowering.

"A few men who crowded in were turned back at the point of Captain Smith's revolver, and several of them were felled before order was restored. I recall being pushed towards one of the boats and being helped in. Just as we were about to clear the ship a man made a rush to get aboard our lifeboat.

"He was shot and apparently killed instantly. His body fell in the boat at our feet. No one made any effort to move him, and his body remained in the boat until we were picked up."

To try and establish the facts from among the rumours, speculation, exaggeration and downright nonsense which, inseparable from any great disaster, were given added impetus by the intensely dramatic and as yet unexplained loss of the great liner, the United States Senate set up a sub-committee of the Committee on Commerce to investigate all the circumstances of her loss. To head the committee they chose Senator William Alden Smith of Michigan—a sad mistake, as they must quickly have realised.

Smith was a self-made man—not that this disqualified him—who had started his working life, in the tradition of self-made men, selling popcorn and newspapers on the street. Afterwards he became a messenger boy for the Western Union Telegraph Company, and made his first acquaintance with politics when he was appointed page to the Michigan House of Representatives. Later he began studying for the Law, and it says much for his perseverance and diligence—because it stands out from his handling of the *Titanic* case that he was not overburdened with intelligence—that after four years, in 1883, he was admitted to the Bar. He developed a good practice remarkably quickly and six years later organised his own firm, Smiley, Smith and Steven. In 1895 he was elected to Congress and in 1907 to the Senate.

During his time in the two Houses he became noted for his air of solemnity and self-importance, and it is recorded that he never lost an opportunity of shouting his opinions during debate. ". . . No matter what the subject is under discussion," said the *Daily Mail*, "whether he knows anything about it or not, Mr Smith is sure to be found on the list of speakers." He was caricatured as a wild gesticulator, and all his speeches were delivered in stentorian tones amidst a spate of coloured invective.

With it all, he was a transparent seeker after fame, and was regarded for the most part with amused tolerance. Occasionally he went too far—as when he brought on himself in the Senate the angry rebuke that he knew nothing whatever of the subject under discussion. This, alas, was true time and again during the course of his *Titanic* investigation.

But there can be no criticism of his diligence. From the start he was raring to go and the Inquiry opened only one day after the arrival in New York of the *Carpathia* with her 711 survivors—at 10.30 on the morning of April 19th.

The first witness was the senior surviving officer from the *Titanic,* Charles Lightoller, to take the brunt of the attack. "Why had the *Titanic* been speeding? Why had she paid no attention to the ice messages? Why did she not have sufficient lifeboat accommodation? Why were some of the boats half empty anyway? Had she been structurally sound?" And in among the pertinent questions others, many others, of inconceivable irrelevance, and others in which Senator Smith, unschooled in the sailor's craft or idiom, struggled hard to understand. There is one celebrated passage in which he questioned Lightoller about the possibility of any passengers having been aware of the existence of watertight compartments in the ship.

"Are you able to say whether any of the crew or passengers took to these upper watertight compartments as a final last resort? I mean as a place to die?"

By this time Lightoller was resigned to the man's ignorance. "I could not say, sir."

"Is that at all likely?"

"No, sir—very unlikely."

"As for yourself—you preferred to take your chance in the open sea?"

"Undoubtedly."

The Senator's incompetence to understand, let along judge the nautical aspects of the case was established on the first day. Senator Smith himself was thereafter "Watertight" Smith.

Meanwhile one of the newspapers in Boston, where the *Californian* had berthed on the day that Lightoller's interrogation began, published the donkeyman Gill's story about the large ship he had seen about midnight, and later rockets from the sea. And despite the confused cross swell of slander and rumour swaying the nation, this eruption generated a tidal wave of emotion which threatened to equal the other two great scandals— the escapes of Bruce Ismay and Sir Cosmo Duff Gordon.

But it didn't reach the Senators before they had finished with Lightoller, or if it did they paid no attention, for he was not asked about any ship he may have seen from the decks of the *Titanic*. And he didn't volunteer the information. In contrast to his answers later to the British Inquiry, which he respected, his replies to the Senators were non-committal, disinterested—even terse. He wrote later, "With all the good will in the world the Inquiry could be called nothing but a complete farce, wherein all the traditions and customs of the sea were continuously and persistently flouted."

However that may be, he was not asked about any ships' lights visible while he was lowering the boats. The Third Officer, Pitman, who followed him, was asked, but replied that he knew nothing of his own knowledge, although he had heard about it. So it was left to the Fourth Officer, Boxhall, to introduce the first positive reference to 'mystery' lights on the third day.

"I was around the bridge most of the time, sending off distress signals and endeavouring to signal to a ship that was ahead of us."

Smith interjected, "Taking the signals from the Captain?"

"No, sir.

"Carrying them yourself to the operator?"

"No. Distress signals—rockets."

After more discursive questions Boxhall was returned to the subject, ". . . But my attention until the time I left the ship was mostly taken up with firing off distress rockets and trying to signal a steamer that was almost ahead of us."

"How far ahead of you?"

"It is hard to say. I saw his masthead light and I saw his sidelight." "In what direction?"

"Almost ahead of us . . . by the way she was heading she seemed to be meeting us."

"You say you fired three rockets and otherwise attempted to signal her?"

"Yes, sir, she got close enough, as I thought, to read our electric morse signal, and I signalled to her—I told her to come at once, we were sinking—and the Captain was standing——"

"This was the signal?"

"Yes, sir . . . I told the Captain about this ship and he was with me most of the time when we were signalling."

"Did he also see it?"

"Yes, sir."

Thus was the legend of the *Californian* given its first real authority. The donkeyman had said that rockets had been seen from his ship and that the crew was abuzz with speculation about them all the way to Boston; now the Fourth Officer of the *Titanic*, a well-spoken, upstanding young man, had testified to the lights of a steamer within clear morsing distance. And the Captain of the *Titanic* had also seen these lights.

Boxhall described how he had signalled repeatedly to this vessel whatever she was, in the morse code.

"And did you get any reply?"

"I cannot say I saw any reply. Some people say she replied to our rockets and our signals, but I did not see them."

"Did you see any signals from this ship at all?"

"No, I cannot say that I saw any signals except her ordinary steaming light. Some people say they saw signals, but I could not."

"From what you saw of that vessel, how far would you think she was from the *Titanic*?"

"I should say approximately the ship would be about five miles." Boxhall had seen her two masthead lights first. "And then as she got closer she showed her sidelights, her red light."

"So you were quite sure she was coming in your direction?"

"Quite sure."

"How long was that before the boat sank?"

"It is hard, to tell. I had no idea of the time then, I do not know what time it was then."

"Can you recall how long it was after the collision?"

"No."

"You busied yourself with the morse signals?"

"I would signal with the morse and then go ahead and send off a rocket, and then go back and have a look at the ship until I was finally sent away."

There are several points here that are worth noting. The most important is that the ship whose lights Boxhall saw was undoubtedly moving towards them. To start with he could not see her sidelights at all, but later he saw her red sidelight and judged her to be about 5 miles off, certainly within morsing distance. Secondly, the inference from Smith's question, "How long was that after the collision?" is that the lights were not visible at the time of the collision. Thirdly Boxhall saw the lights ahead, but no attempt was made to ask him in which direction the *Titanic's* head pointed as she lay sinking. Ahead could have meant literally any point of the compass.

The next mention of the mystery ship was on the following day when Frederick Fleet, one of the lookouts in the crow's-nest at the time of the collision, was being examined.

He was an unco-operative witness.

"How long before the collision or accident did you report ice ahead?"

"I have no idea."

"About how long?"

"I could not say at the rate she was going."

"Would you be willing to say that you reported the presence of ice an hour before the collision?"

"No, sir."

"Forty-five minutes?"

"No, sir."

"A half hour before?"

"No, sir."

"Fifteen minutes before?"

"No, sir."

"How far away was this black mass when you first saw it?"

"I have no idea, sir."

After interminable question and non-commital answer the story gradually unfolded that it was he who had seen the ice first, although he thought his mate, Lee, had seen it just as soon, and that there was just a slight grinding noise as they struck, which made him think it was a narrow shave. He had remained in the crow's-nest until relieved. It was not apparent from his answers what time that was as the clocks were to have gone back that night and he was expecting to do two hours twenty minutes on watch instead of two hours. Whether he was relieved at 12, then, or 12.30 (old time) was not apparent. He and his mate had gone below to find the quarters deserted and a quartermaster had appeared and said they were wanted on the bridge. They had made their way up to the boat-deck and he had helped to lower number 6 boat on the port side, and to hand the women in over the rails. They half filled her with about thirty women, besides three men and he and the quartermaster, Hitchins, had been ordered in before she was lowered down to the water.

"And what did you do then?"

"We got the oars and pulled for the light that was on the port bow." This is his first mention of any light.

"Did you see it?"

"Yes, sir. . . . We could not get up to it."

"When you found you could not get up to it what did you do?" "We kept on pulling—that is all. . . . We thought we could get up to this light, but we could not. It seemed to be getting away from us all the time."

"Did you see the *Titanic* go down?"

"No, sir. . . . The lights were out and we were too far away." "You could not see her when she disappeared?"

"No, sir.

"Were there lights of any other vessels in sight when you came down from the crow's-nest?"

"*There were no lights at all when we was up in the crow's-nest.* This is after we was down and on the boats—then I seen the lights."

"Where did you see it?"

"On the port bow. The other lookout reported it."

"How far ahead?"

"It was not ahead. It was on the bow—about four points."

"I am not speaking of that. I wanted to know whether you saw ahead, while you were on watch, on the lookout, Sunday night, after the collision occurred or before, any lights of any other ship?"

"No, sir.

"What colour were the lights toward which you were pulling when you were in the lifeboat?"

"A bright light . . . white."

"How many were there?"

There are several points here: the first and most important, which is vital to the question of whether the ship ahead on the port bow was the *Californian* or not, is that there was no light visible while he was in the crow's-nest, which was for some little while after the collision—how long exactly was not established. This supports Boxhall's evidence that the ship or boat showing the light must have been moving towards them. The other alternative is that the *Titanic* was still moving ahead. But it is unlikely that Boxhall would have drawn the inference that the other vessel was moving towards them had the *Titanic* actually been steaming at that time, and certainly the *Titanic* must have stopped moving before the first lifeboats were put down. There is ample evidence to prove that she had.

The second thing is that Fleet only saw one white light—not the two white and one red which Boxhall eventually saw.

The third thing about his evidence, and this is the only time in either Inquiry that this point comes up, is that "the other lookout reported it". He did not mention which other lookout he was referring to. If he meant the two men who had relieved them in the crow's-nest they certainly did not mention it in their evidence, and no one else specifies anyone as being the first to see the light. It would only be important if a specific time was fixed to it.

The fourth point is that this light appeared to move away as they pulled towards it. That the ship eventually moved away was implied in Boxhall's evidence, for when he had taken one of the last of the lifeboats away he had not bothered to pull towards this ship which he had been signalling. This implication was later confirmed by Boxhall in evidence when he was recalled.

The following day Fleet was still in the witness-box being subjected to repeated examination about how well he could see and which colours he could distinguish best. Eventually the questioning returned to the strange ship.

"You saw some light on the horizon that night?"

"Not on the lookout, sir."

"Not on the lookout?"

"The only thing we saw was the iceberg. We had no lights on that watch."

"You did not see this light of which mention has been made until you got into the lifeboat?"

"No, sir."

"Are you sure it was a light?"

"It was a light all right, because Mr Lightoller, when I got into the boat, made us pull straight for it."

"What did you think it was?"

"It might have been a fisher sail, or something—it was only just one bright light. I could not say what it was . . . Mr Lightoller made us pull towards it. He seen it as well as us."

"You saw it before you got off the *Titanic*?"

"Yes, sir."

"What became of the light?"

"We did not know. We pulled for it, but we did not seem to get any nearer to it."

"Did it finally disappear?"

"Well, it disappeared by daybreak."

Does this sound as if it could possibly have belonged to a 6,000-ton steamer lying stopped in the water?

After Fleet stood down, Senator Smith felt compelled to make an announcement about what he and his fellow members of the Committee were about. The terms of this announcement are a good pointer to the public feeling the proceedings had already aroused, although the Inquiry had only been sitting five days.

"I desire to make an announcement. First, I want to meet the inquiry, so often heard, as to our purpose in this Inquiry, and I want to say that it is to get all the facts bearing upon this unfortunate catastrophe that we are able to obtain. . . .

"The committee will not tolerate any further attempt on the part of anyone to shape its course. We shall proceed in our own way, completing the official record, and the judgement of our efforts may very appropriately be witheld until those who are disposed to question its wisdom have the actual official reports."

The next witness was Robert Hitchins, the Quartermaster who had been at the wheel at time of the collision.

"All went along very well until twenty minutes to twelve, when three gongs came from the lookout and immediately afterwards a report on the telephone, 'Iceberg right ahead'. The Chief Officer rushed from the wing of the bridge, or I imagine so, sir. Certainly I am enclosed in the wheelhouse and cannot see—only my compass. He rushed to the engines. I heard the telegraph bell ring—also gave the order hard a-starboard, with the Sixth Officer standing by me to see the duty carried out and the quartermaster standing by my left side repeated the order, 'Hard a-starboard!' The helm is hard over, sir. . . . But during this time she was crushing the ice, or we would hear the grinding noise along the ship's bottom. I heard the telegraph ring, sir. The skipper came rushing out of his room—Captain Smith—and asked 'What is that?' Mr Murdoch said 'An iceberg'. . . . He also came back to the wheelhouse and looked at the commutator (clinometer) in front of the compass, which is a little instrument like a clock to tell you how the ship is listing. The ship had a list of five degrees to starboard."

"How long after the impact or collision?"

"I could hardly tell you, sir. Judging roughly about five minutes—about five to ten minutes. I stayed to the wheel then, sir, until twenty-three minutes past twelve. I do not know whether they put the clock back or not.[1] The clock was to go back that night forty-seven minutes, twenty-three minutes in one watch and twenty-four in the other."

"Had the clock been set back up to the time you left the wheel?"

"I do not know, sir. I did not notice it . . . I left the wheel at twenty-three minutes past twelve. . . ."

If the clocks were to go back at midnight, which is the usual practice, it is unlikely that anyone bothered about them that night; it is almost certain they remained on the previous noon's time.

". . . I think the First Officer, or one of the officers said, 'That will do the wheel—get the boats out.' I went out to get the boats out on the port side. I think I got in number 6 boat, sir, put in charge of her by the Second Officer, Mr Lightoller. We lowered away from the ship, sir, and were told to 'pull towards that light', which we started to do, to pull for that light. I

---

1 Pitman's reply to a question whether the clocks had been put back was, "We had other things to think about that night."

had 38 women in the boat, sir, one seaman (Frederick Fleet) and myself, with two male passengers, one Italian boy and a Canadian major."

"Were you in charge of the boat?"

"I was, yes, sir . . . and I told them somebody would have to pull—there was no use stopping there alongside of the ship, and the ship gradually going by the head. We were in a dangerous place, so I told them to man the oars, ladies and all. . . . We got away about a mile, I suppose, from the ship, going after this light, which we expected to be a cod banker, a schooner that comes out on the Banks."

"A fisherman's boat?"

"Yes, sir—we expected her to be that, sir—but we did not get any nearer the light. . . . There were several other boats around us. . . . We stopped there until we saw the *Carpathia* heave in sight about daybreak. The wind had sprung up a bit then and it got very choppy. I relieved one of the young ladies with the oar, and told her to take the tiller. . . ."

"Do you know what that woman was?"

"I do not, sir. They were all entire strangers to me, sir. But the lady I refer to, Mrs Mayer, she was rather vexed with me in the boat and I spoke rather straight to her, and she accused me of wrapping myself up in the blankets in the boat, using bad language and drinking all the whisky, which I deny, sir. I was standing to attention, exposed, steering the boat all night, which is a very cold billet. . . ."

After some while describing his experiences with women of breeding in the lifeboat, Hitchens was brought back to his recollection of the light.

"When you left the *Titanic* in the lifeboat did anyone tell you to take that load off and come back to the *Titanic*?"

"I think it was the First Officer or the Second Officer . . . one of them, I am not sure which."

"You did not carry out that order?"

"Yes I did, sir."

"What did you do?"

"I pulled for that light—this imaginary light. We were pulling for it all the time."

"You pulled for this imaginary light?"

"Yes, sir.

Hitchin's evidence thus bears out Fleet's, or at least does nothing to contradict Fleet's. Hitchins gave no intimation that he was aware of the light while on the bridge until 12.23—although he was not specifically asked—but saw it from his lifeboat on the port side, and was told to make for it by Lightoller. Whereas Fleet thought it had been one bright white light, Hitchins hinted it might have been an imaginary light. Both he and Fleet thought that, if it was a light it was a fisherman. Both testified they could not seem to get near it as they pulled.

On the following day, April 25th, George Rowe, the quartermaster who had been stationed down aft at the time of the collision, was called to give evidence. And his testimony is interesting, both because he seems to have been one of the few men observing times during the emergency, and because his recollection of those times differs from the American to the British Inquiry.

"You were located practically right on the stern of the boat?" "Right on the stern, sir—the poop."

"And the iceberg, when the boat rubbed against it, was right near, was it?" This is a Senator Burton asking the questions.

"It was so near that I thought it was going to strike the bridge." "Only ten or twenty feet away?"

"Not that far, sir."

"Could you hear the ice scraping along the boat where you were?"

"No, sir."

"Do you not think that if the helm had been hard a-starboard the stern would have been up against the berg?"

"It stands to reason it would, sir, if the helm had been hard a- starboard."

"How long did the rubbing or grinding against the ice last?"

"I never heard anything except the first contact—the first jar was all I knew about. I never heard any rubbing at all."

"Do you not think the propeller would have hit the ice if the helm had been hard a-starboard?"

"Yes, sir.

These very pertinent questions by Senator Burton are the only ones in either Inquiry which imply that the wheel was not kept hard over all the time. The only other evidence of a similar nature came from the stand-by quartermaster of the watch who said he remembered the order "hard a-port" and the wheel being put over—in other words he remembered a reverse order to that which all the other witnesses had testified. But, like the questions to Rowe about the swing of the stem, this was not followed up.

After the collision Rowe had stayed on the after bridge.

"No orders came down, and I remained until twenty-five minutes past twelve, when I saw a boat on the starboard beam . . . I telephoned to the fore bridge to know if they knew there was a boat being lowered. They replied asking me if I was the Third Officer. I replied, 'No, I am the quartermaster.' They told me to bring over detonators which are used in firing distress signals. . . ."

This, then, is the first mention of a specific time for any event subsequent to the actual collision. It is important because, if Rowe's recollection here is correct, the first boat had left the *Titanic* by 12.25 (and not 12.45, as found later in the British Inquiry) and this places the firing of the first rocket at about 12.25 (and again not 12.45, as found by Lord Mersey). The connection between the first boat being lowered and the first rocket fired came in the previous evidence of the Third and Fifth Officers,[2] and was to come again in the Fourth Officer's evidence to the British Inquiry.

Rowe took the detonators up to the fore bridge and helped Boxhall firing rockets and morsing the ship to port until 01.25—again he remembers the time precisely—when he was ordered away in starboard emergency boat number 1, the boat into which Ismay finally stepped. He remembered the boat scraping down the side slowly as it was lowered against the list to port. It took them about five minutes to get down although the bows were so low that the well-deck was submerged by the time they reached the water.

"We pulled away for the light in sight, roughly five miles. We pulled away for about three-quarters of a mile, when the ship sank. We pulled through the night but seemed to get no nearer to the lights. So we altered course back to a boat that was carrying a green light. During that time daylight broke and the *Carpathia* was in sight."

Later he was examined in greater detail about the nature of the light towards which his boat had been pulling.

2 See Appendix.

"What do you conclude that light was?"

"A sailing ship."

"What sort of a light was it?"

"A white light."

"Did you get any nearer to it?"

"We did not seem to get nearer to it. . . . We kept on pulling for it because it was the only stationary light. . . . Towards daylight the wind sprung up and she sort of hauled off from us."

"Did you see her?"

"No, sir.

"Did you see any sidelights?"

"No, sir. I think there was a ship there. Indeed I am sure of it, and that she was a sailer."

"The light you saw was a white light?"

"Yes, sir. . . . I judged it to be a stem light."

"When did you first see her?"

"When I was on the bridge firing the rockets. I saw it myself and I worked the morse lamp at the port side of the ship to draw her attention."

This was the man who had been working with the Fourth Officer, Boxhall. While Boxhall had seen two masthead lights and the red side-light, Rowe had seen only one white light which he, in company with Fleet and Hitchins, had thought was the stern light of a sailer. And he had cor-roborated those two seamen's evidence that whatever it was, it had been moving away as they pulled towards it.

But on the same day, after Rowe, another seaman, John Buley, testified to having seen a *steamer*—definitely a steamer and not a fishing-boat.

"There was a ship of some description there when she struck and she passed right by us. We thought she was coming to us—and if she had come to us everyone would have boarded her. You could see she was a steamer. She had her steamer lights burning. . . .

"She was off our port bow when we struck, and we all started for the same light, and that is what kept the boats together. . . . She was stationary all night—I am very positive for about three hours she was stationary, and then she made tracks."

"How far away was she?"

"I should judge she was about three miles."

"Why could not she see your skyrockets?"

"She could not help seeing them. She was close enough to see our lights and to see the ship itself, and also the rockets. She was bound to see them."

"How many lights did you see?"

"I saw two masthead lights."

It was difficult to understand what John Buley was talking about, or where the steamer had been in relation to his boat or the sinking *Titanic*, and as if to confound anyone who might be trying to work it out, he added in answer to a question about whether she had approached bows on, "Yes, sir, bow on towards us, and then she stopped, and her lights seemed to go right by us. . . . She was stationary there for about three hours, I think, off our port there, and when we were in the boat we all made for her, and she went by us. The northern lights are just like a searchlight, but she disappeared. . . ."

If the words 'go away from us' are substituted for 'go by us', his testimony begins to make sense.

Another Able Seaman, George Moore, appeared on the same day. After lowering numbers 5 and 7 boats on the starboard side he had been ordered into number 3 boat by the First Officer. When they reached the water they had pulled away in the direction of "one bright light away on the starboard bow—two or three miles away . . ."

"What did you think that light was at the time?"

"I thought it was a fisherman. That is what I thought. It was just one single light."

"Did that light disappear?"

"We kept pulling for it until daylight and we could not see a thing of it then."

"You were sure that light was there?"

"Yes, sir.

"It was a genuine light you think?"

"Yes—one bright light."

And after George Moore came another Able Seaman, Frank Osman, who had helped in lowering the port side boats under Lightoller and was then sent away in the emergency boat number 2 with the Fourth Officer, Boxhall. Boxhall, Osman remembers, had just been firing rockets and signalling to a steamer which had come close enough to show her red sidelight. When Osman was asked whether his emergency boat had steered for this light on the bow, he replied, "No, sir, we saw a light, but the other boats were making for it, *and the officer was not sure whether it was a light or whether it was not,* and as he had the rockets he could repeat the signals."

"Did you see that light?"

"Yes, sir."

"What did you think it was?"

"I thought it was a sailing vessel from the Banks."

"What do you think about it? Did it sail away?"

"Yes, sir, she sailed right away."

"What was it, a stern light?"

"No, sir, a masthead light."

Here Frank Osman is contradicting himself because sailing vessels do not carry white—or any other coloured—masthead lights when under way unless they are under power as well.

"You are sure that light was not a star?"

"I am sure it was not a star."

CHAPTER EIGHT

On the eighth day of the Inquiry, Friday, April 26th, came the bombshell that sank Captain Lord. Ernest Gill was sworn.

Senator Smith: "I want to read to you the following statement and ask you whether it is true:

"'I, the undersigned, Ernest Gill, being employed as second donkeyman on the steamer *Californian,* Captain Lord, give the following statement of the incidents of the night of Sunday, April 14th.

"'On the night of April 14th I was on duty from 8 p.m. until 12 in the engine-room. At 11.56 I came on deck. The stars were shining brightly. It was very clear and I could see for a long distance. The ship's engines had been stopped since 10.30 and she was drifting amid floe ice. I looked over the rail on the starboard side and saw the lights of a very large steamer about 10 miles away. I could see her broadside lights. I watched her for fully a minute. They could not have helped but see her from the bridge and lookout.

"'It was now twelve o'clock and I went to my cabin. I woke my mate, William Thomas. He heard the ice crunching alongside the ship and asked, "Are we in the ice?" I replied, "Yes, but it must be clear off to starboard for I saw a big vessel going along at full speed. She looked as if she might be a big German."

"'I turned in but could not sleep. In half an hour I turned out, thinking to smoke a cigarette. Because of the cargo I could not smoke between decks, so I went on deck again.

" 'I had been on deck about ten minutes when I saw a white rocket about 10 miles away on the starboard side. I thought it must be a shooting star. In seven or eight minutes I saw distinctly a second rocket in the same place, and I said to myself, "That must be a vessel in distress."

" 'It was not my business to notify the bridge or the lookout but they could not have helped but see them.

" 'I turned in immediately after, supposing that the ship would pay attention to the rockets.

" 'I knew no more until I was awakened at 6.40 by the Chief Engineer who said, "Turn out and render assistance. The *Titanic* has gone down."

" 'I exclaimed and leaped from my bunk. I went on deck and found the vessel under way and proceeding at full speed. She was clear of the field ice, but there were plenty of bergs about.

" 'I went down on watch and heard the Second and Fourth Engineer in conversation. Mr J. C. Evans is the Second and Mr Wooten is the Fourth. The Second was telling the Fourth that the Third Officer had reported rockets had gone up in his watch. I knew then that it must have been the *Titanic* I had seen.

" 'The Second Engineer added that the Captain had been notified by the apprentice officer, whose name I think is Gibson, of the rockets. The skipper had told him to morse to the vessel in distress. Mr Stone, the Second Navigating Officer, was on the bridge at the time, said Mr Evans.

" 'I overheard Mr Evans say that more lights had been shown and more rockets went up. Then, according to Mr Evans, Mr Gibson went to the Captain again and reported more rockets. The skipper told him to continue to morse until he got a reply. No reply was received.

" 'The next remark I heard the Second pass was, "Why in the devil they didn't wake the wireless man up?" The entire crew of the steamer have been talking among themselves about the disregard of the rockets. I personally urged several to join me in protesting against the conduct of the Captain, but they refused, because they feared to lose their jobs.

" 'A day or two before the ship reached port the skipper called the quartermaster who was on duty at the time the rockets were discharged, into his cabin. They were in conversation about three-quarters of an hour. The quartermaster declared that he did not see the rockets.

" 'I am quite sure that the *Californian* was less than 20 miles from the *Titanic,* which the officers report to have been our position. I could not have seen her if she had been more than 10 miles distant, and I saw her very plainly.

" 'I have no ill will toward the Captain or any officer of the ship, and I am losing a profitable berth by making this statement. I am actuated by the desire that no captain who refuses or neglects to give aid to a vessel in distress should be able to hush up the men.

" 'signed Ernest Gill.

'Sworn and subscribed to before

me this fourth day of April, 1912.

'signed Samuel Putnam, Notary Public.' "

Senator Smith went on, "I will ask you, witness, whether this statement is true?"

"Yes, sir. That is correct," the Yorkshireman replied.

Senator Fletcher rose to question him. "What direction was the *Californian* going?"

"We were headed for Boston, sir."

"In what direction were the rockets from the *Californian* when you first saw them?"

"On the starboard side, forward."

"Was the *Californian* passed by the *Titanic,* her course being the same as the *Titanic's* course was originally?"

"The only way I can account for this, we were stopped in the ocean, and it is not natural for a ship to keep her head one way all the time. She must have been drifting."

What Gill meant was that his ship, being stopped, must have swung to face towards the direction from which she had been coming. Thus a ship like the *Titanic*, also bound westward, would make her appearance ahead. This was borne out by the Captain's evidence later.

"How long after the rockets were sent up was it before the *Californian* got under steam and proceeded?"

"I do not know what time she got under way, sir. It was somewhere about five o'clock, or in the vicinity of five o'clock."

"Was that about daylight?"

"Yes, sir."

"Up to about that time the *Californian* was drifting?"

"Yes, sir, with her engines stopped."

"And you saw the rockets along about two o'clock—or before two o'clock?"

"About 12.30. At one bell, sir."

"About 12.30 you began first to see the rockets."

"Yes, sir, at first when I saw it, it was not very plain."

"Off on your starboard bow?"

"Yes, sir."

"What kind of rockets were they? What did they look like?"

"They looked to me to be pale blue, or white."

"Which? Pale blue or white?"

"It would be apt to be a very clear blue—but I could not catch it when it was dying. I did not catch the exact tint, but I reckon it was white."

"Did it look as if the rocket had been sent up and the explosion had taken place in the air and the stars spangled out?"

"Yes, sir, the stars spangled out. I could not say about the stars. I say, I caught the tail end of the rocket."

"Did you see any lights on the steamer where the rockets were sent up?"

"No, sir—no sign of the steamer at the time."

"You could not see any lights at all?"

"No, sir."

"Did you hear any noise—escaping steam or anything of that sort?"

"No, sir."

"There was not much noise on the *Californian* at that time?"

"No, sir, not much noise on the ship."

"What sort of a night was it?"

"It was a fine night . . . a clear night—a very clear night."

"You estimate that the rockets went up not over 20 miles away from the *Californian*?"

"It could not be 20 miles away, sir. I could not see 20 miles away. I seen the ship, and she had not had time to get 20 miles away by the time I got on deck again."

"As I understand, you never did see the ship did you?"

"No, sir—not without the one I seen, the big ship that I told my mate was a German boat—not without that was the ship in question—the *Titanic*."

"You think it may have been the *Titanic*?"

"Yes, sir, I am of the general opinion that the crew is, that she was the *Titanic*."

"When did you first see her?"

"At four minutes after[1] twelve exactly."

"How do you know that?"

"Because at five minutes to twelve I was working with the Fourth Engineer at a pump that kicked, that would not work, and while we were interested in our work we forgot the time; and I looked up and I said, 'It is five minutes to twelve. I haven't called my mate, Mr Wooten. I will go call him,' and I got to the ladder to climb out of the engine-room and got on deck. That taken me one minute to get up there."

"Was this ship moving at that time?"

"I did not take particular notice of it, sir, with the rushing to call my mate. I went along the deck. It taken me about a minute, going along the deck, to get to the hatch I had to go down, and I could see her as I walked along the deck. Suppose I am going forward now, I could see her over there," he indicated, "a big ship and a couple of rows of lights; so that I knew it was not any small craft. It was no tramp. I did not suppose it would be a 'Star' boat. I reckoned she must be a German boat. So I dived down the hatch, and as I turned around in the hatch I could not see her,

1 He means "before".

so you can guess the latitude she was in. As I stood on the hatch with my back turned, I could not see the ship. Then I went and called my mate, and that is the last I saw of it."

"How long after that was it before you saw the rockets go up?"

"About thirty-five minutes, sir—a little over half an hour."

"Did you observe the rockets go up in the direction this ship was as you first saw her, from where the *Californian* was?"

"It was more abeam, sir—more broadside of the ship."

"In the meantime the *Californian* as I understand was drifting?"

"Yes, sir."

"She was not under way at all?"

"No, sir."

"Was the ship too far away, when you first saw the rockets going up, for you to see the lights on her?"

"Yes, sir—no sign of the ship."

"What time was it when you heard these officers discussing the matter that was mentioned in this statement?"

"Twenty minutes past eight on Monday morning."

"Have you been discharged or dismissed by the *Californian*?"

"No, sir. I belong to the ship now."

✳✳✳

The same afternoon Captain Stanley Lord was sworn.

He was taken by Senator Smith through his log-book positions and the icebergs he had sighted and the messages he had sent out during Sunday, 14th, up to the time, about eleven o'clock, that he had sent the message to the *Titanic* that he was stopped in ice.

"Do you know the *Titanic's* position on the sea when she sank?" Smith asked.

"I know the position given to me by the *Virginian* as the position where she struck an iceberg, 41° 46'N, and 50° 14'W."

"Figuring from the *Titanic's* position at the time she went down and your position at the time you sent this warning to the *Titanic*, how far were these vessels from one another?"

"From the position we stopped in to the position at which the *Titanic* is supposed to have hit the iceberg, 19½ to 19¾ miles—south 16° west, sir, was the course."

"What is the average speed of the *Californian* under fair conditions?"

"On our present consumption we average 11 in fine weather."

"In case of distress, I suppose it would be possible for you to exceed that considerably?"

"Oh, we made 13 and 13½ the day we were going down to the *Titanic*."

"Were you under full speed then?"

"We were driving all we could."

"When you notified the *Titanic* that you were in the ice how much ice were you in?"

"Well, we were surrounded by a lot of loose ice, and we were about a quarter of a mile off the edge of the field."

The following morning Lord had seen the field ice in an area about 25 miles long and from 1 to 2 miles wide ahead of him.

"When did you notify the *Titanic* of your situation? What was your purpose?"

"It was just a matter of courtesy. I thought he would be a long way from where we were. I did not think he was anywhere near the ice. By rights he ought to have been 18 or 19 miles to the southward of where I was. I never thought the ice was stretching that far down."

"You gave him this information?"

"Just as a matter of courtesy. We always pass the news around when we get hold of anything like that."

"Captain Lord, for the purpose of making it a little clearer, what did you say your position was at 10.50 p.m. Sunday, April 14th?" (When he had sent the message to the *Titanic.*)

"I did not say at all."

"Will you state."

"It was the same position I was in when I stopped at 10.21 and that I gave you before as 42° 5' and 50° 7'."

"You had stopped and your position did not change?"

"No."

"Substantially for how long a time?"

"We moved the engines first at 5.15 on the 15th of April, full ahead."

"Do you know anything regarding the *Titanic* disaster of your own knowledge? Did you see the ship on Sunday?"

"No, sir."

"Or any signals from her?"

"Not from the *Titanic*."

"Was the *Titanic* beyond your range of vision?"

"I should think so—19½ or 20 miles away."

"How long did it take you to reach the scene of the accident from the time you steamed up and got under way Monday morning?"

Lord read from his log-book, "Six o'clock, proceeded slow, pushing through the thick ice. 6.20 clear of thickest of ice; proceeded full speed, pushing the ice. 8.30 stopped close to steamship *Carpathia*."

"Was the *Carpathia* at that time on the scene of the wreck?"

"Yes, sir, she was taking the last of the people out of the boats."

"Then from six o'clock in the morning you were under steam in the direction of the *Titanic* for two and one half hours?"

"Yes, sir."

Arriving at the scene of the wreck he had seen several empty boats, some floating planks, a few deck-chairs, and cushions, "—but considering the size of the disaster, there was very little wreckage. It seemed more like an old fishing-boat that had sunk."

"Did you see any life preservers?"

"A few lifebelts floating around."

"Did you see any persons, dead or alive?"

"No, sir."

"How long did you remain in the vicinity of the wreck?"

He referred to his log again. "11.20 we proceeded on our course."

"And you reached there at what hour?"

"At 8.30, sir."

"During that time what did you do?"

"I talked to the *Carpathia* until nine o'clock. Then she left. Then we went at full speed in circles over a radius—that is I took a big circle and then came around and around and got back to the boats again, where I had left them."

"I will ask you whether you saw any icebergs while you were making that circle?"

"I was practically surrounded by icebergs."

After some discursive exchanges about the amount of an iceberg below water compared with that above, Lord was asked if he had given any special instructions to his wireless operator.

"No, sir."

"Are there any rules and regulations prescribing the conduct of the wireless operator or operators on your ship?"

"No. They are kept amenable to the discipline, just like the rest of the crew are."

"Do you recognise them as subordinate to your wishes while they are at sea?"

"To a certain extent I do, yes."

"Did you have any hours particularly prescribed for him by yourself or anyone else after you became aware of your proximity to ice?"

"No."

"Suppose your wireless operator had been at his post in the operating room when the CQD call of distress came out from the *Titanic,* which was received by the *Carpathia* and other ships, would your ship have been apprised of the distress of the *Titanic*? I mean, have you a wireless apparatus on that ship as would have in all probability caught that message?"

"Most certainly."

Senator Smith suggested at length that it might be better if single wireless operators kept their watches at night instead of by day, but made little impression. Senator Bourne asked if wireless operators had any regular hours or not.

"No, I do not think there are any regular hours. I understand they are usually around from seven in the morning to half-past two and I think they lie down, because I never, as a rule, receive any messages between half-past two and four. I presume they are asleep."

Senator Fletcher asked Lord, "If the wireless operator on the *Californian* had been on duty, he would have picked up this message from the *Titanic* giving the alarm?"

"Yes."

"Could you have gone to the relief of the *Titanic* at that time?"

"Most certainly."

"The engines were not running then?"

"The engines were ready. I gave instructions to the Chief Engineer and told him I had decided to stay there all night. I did not think it safe to go ahead. I said, 'We will keep steam handy in case some of these big fellows come crunching along and get into it.' "

"Did you keep lookout men on duty after your engines were stopped?"

"A man on the lookout—only one—a man in the crow's-nest."

Senator Smith returned to the questioning. "Captain, did you see any distress signals on Sunday night, either rockets or the morse signals?"

"No, sir, I did not. The officer on watch saw some signals, but he said they were not distress signals."

"They were not distress signals?"

"Not distress signals."

"But he reported them?"

"To me. I think you had better let me tell you that story."

"I wish you would."

"When I came off the bridge at half-past ten I pointed out to the officer that I thought I saw a light coming along, and it was a most peculiar light,[2] and we had been making mistakes all along with the stars, thinking they were signals. We could not distinguish where the sky ended and the water commenced. You understand it was a flat calm. He said he thought it was a star, and I did not say anything more. I went below. I was talking with the engineer about keeping the steam ready, and we saw these signals coming along, and I said, 'There is a steamer coming. Let us go to the wireless and see what the news is.' But on our way down I met the operator coming and I said, 'Do you know anything?' He said, 'The *Titanic.*' So then, I gave him instructions to let the *Titanic* know. I said, 'This is not the *Titanic*—there is no doubt about it.' She came and lay, at half-past eleven, alongside of us until, I suppose, a quarter past one, within 4 miles of us. We could see everything on her quite distinctly—see her lights. We signalled her at half-past eleven with the morse lamp. She did not take the slightest notice of it. That was between half-past eleven and twenty

---

2 This is mis-transcribed, and should be "night".

minutes to twelve. We signalled her again at ten minutes past twelve, half-past twelve, a quarter to one and one o'clock. We have a very powerful morse lamp. I suppose you can see that about 10 miles, and she was about 4 miles off, and she did not take the slightest notice of it. When the Second Officer came on the bridge, at twelve o'clock, or ten minutes past twelve, I told him to watch that steamer, which was stopped, and I pointed out the ice to him—told him we were surrounded by ice—to watch the steamer that she did not get any closer to her. At twenty minutes to one I whistled up the speaking tube and asked him if she was getting any nearer. He said, 'No, she is not taking any notice of us.' So I said, 'I will go and he down a bit.' At a quarter past one he said, 'I think she has fired a rocket.' He said, 'She did not answer the morse lamp and she has commenced to go away from us.' I said, 'Call her up and let me know at once what her name is.' So he put the whistle back, and apparently he was calling. I could hear him ticking over my head. Then I went to sleep."

"You heard nothing more about it?"

"Nothing more until about something between then and half-past four, I have a faint recollection of the apprentice opening the door—opening it and shutting it. I said, 'What is it?' He did not answer and I went to sleep again. I believe the boy came down to deliver the message that this steamer had steamed away from us to the South West, showing several of these flashes or white rockets—steamed away to the South West."

"Captain, these morse signals are a sort of language or method by which ships speak to one another?"

"Yes, sir. At night."

"The rockets that are used are for the same purpose and are understood are they, among mariners?"

"As being distress rockets?"

"Yes."

"Oh yes, you never mistake a distress rocket."

"Suppose the morse signals and the rockets were displayed and exploded on the *Titanic* continuously for half to three-quarters of an hour after she struck ice, would you, from the position of the ship on a night like Sunday night, have been able to see those signals?"

"From the position she was supposed to have been in?"

"Yes."

"We could not have seen her morse code—that is an utter impossibility."

"Could you have seen the rockets?"

"I do not think so. Nineteen and a half miles is a long way. It would have been way down on the horizon. It might have been mistaken for a shooting star or anything at all."

"Did you see anything of the *Frankfurt*?"

"I met him five or ten minutes past twelve after I was leaving the *Titanic,* the scene of the disaster. He was running along parallel with the ice, apparently trying to find an opening, and he saw me coming through, and he headed for the place I was coming out, and as we came out, he went in. He went through the same place to the scene of the disaster."

After Smith had finished his questions, Senator Fletcher rose, "Let me ask you a question with reference to that steamer you saw 4 miles away. What was her position in reference to your ship——"

"Pretty near South of us—4 miles to the South."

"As to being on the starboard or port side."

"Well, on our ordinary course, our ordinary course was about West, true—but on seeing the ice, we were so close we had to reverse the engine and put her full speed astern, and the action of reversing turned the ship to starboard, and we were heading about north-east true. When this man was coming along he was showing his green light on our starboard side, before midnight. After midnight we slowly blew around and showed him our red light."

"And he passed south-west?"

"He was stopped until one o'clock, and then he started going ahead again—and the Second Officer reported he changed from south- south-east to west-south-west, six and a half points—and if he was 4 miles off, the distance he travelled I estimated to be 7 or 7½ miles in that hour."

"Was he ever closer to you?"

"No, sir."

"Were you able to tell what kind of a ship it was?"

"The officer on watch and the apprentice there, and myself—I saw it before one o'clock, before I went to the chart room—were of the opinion that it was an ordinary cargo steamer."

"Did you see the funnels?"

"No, sir. It had one masthead light and a green light, which I saw first."

"You could not hear any escaping steam or the siren or the whistle?"

No, sir.

Senator Smith came back again. "Senator Fletcher asked you regarding this ship that stopped by you on Sunday night?"

Yes, sir.

"Have you any idea what steamer that was?"

"Not the faintest. At daylight we saw a yellow funnel steamer to the south-west of us, beyond where this man had left—about 8 miles away."

"Do you suppose that was the same one?"

"I should not like to say. I don't think so, because this one had only one masthead light that we saw at half-past eleven."

"From the log which you hold in your hand, and from your own knowledge, is there anything you can say further which will assist the committee in its inquiry as to the causes of this catastrophe?"

"No, sir, there is nothing—only that it was a very deceiving night. That is all that I can say about that. I only saw that ice a mile and a half off."

That was that. There had been no very searching questions about the rockets, or why he had not called the Marconi operator out; no questions about the accuracy of his positions, or his estimate of the accuracy of the *Titanic*'s position as he found it from the wreckage. There had been no hint at all of the wrath to come. Lord sailed home on the *Californian* and thought little further of it.

***

Any comparison of Lord's evidence with Gill's shows a number of discrepancies, one of which is so fundamental that it is impossible to accept both their stories. Taking them in chronological order, Lord thought that the steamer, whoever she was, had stopped at about 11.30 some 4 miles from his own ship, whereas Gill stated in affidavit that she was moving fast and was about 10 miles off. Were it not that Lord was under the shadow of having neglected his duty, Gill's evidence about the distance could be rejected as from a man entirely inexperienced in judging distances at sea—a donkeyman. But leaving that aside, we can in any case reject his evidence about the vessel moving fast on two counts: first, it would have been impossible for him to tell whether she was moving at all, let alone moving fast, while he was walking along the deck to call his mate and she was 10 miles off and viewed from a swinging ship—impossible without compass bearings—and secondly because he admitted during examination by the Senators that he had *not* noticed whether she was moving—thus contradicting his original statement. "I did not take particular notice of it, sir, with the rushing to call my mate."

The exaggeration in Gill's affidavit makes it clear that, whatever it was he did see that night, he was not above embellishing it for greater effect.

The next conflict was that Gill saw a large passenger steamer with "a couple of rows of lights", which he reckoned at the time was a big German boat. Lord, at the same time, saw a cargo boat, moreover a cargo boat not large enough to be carrying two masthead lights—only one.

But the really vital discrepancy in the evidence comes after the first sightings, at about half-past midnight. This was the time that Gill had come up from below *in his thin flannel nightclothes* to have a smoke on deck. It was bitterly cold out, as all the *Titanic* survivors testified, but Gill leaned on the starboard rail for some minutes, puffing away at a cigarette. He then saw a flash in the sky from somewhere over the horizon, and after it another one from the same direction which could only have been a rocket, with stars spangling out. This was the same direction in which he had seen the "big German", but at that time, 12.30 or so, there was no sign of her, *or any other ship.*

Now here is Lord's version of the stranger's position at this time: "We signalled her at half-past eleven with the morse lamp. She did not take the slightest notice of it. . . . We signalled her again at ten minutes past twelve, a quarter to one, and one o'clock. We have a very powerful morse lamp. I suppose you can see that about 10 miles off, *and she was about 4 miles off. . . ."* According to Lord the ship was still stopped close by; according to Gill she had disappeared and was throwing up rockets from over the horizon!

Reading on through Lord's evidence we find that the Second Officer called him at quarter past one and told him that the other vessel had fired a rocket, that she had not taken any notice of the morsing, and had started to steam away from them. This was three-quarters of an hour after Gill had seen the rockets, but no sign of any ship.

***

After Lord in the witness-box on that same afternoon came Cyril Furmstone Evans, his wireless operator—his only wireless operator. Smith: "What time did you communicate with the *Titanic*?"

"In the afternoon, sir. I was sending a message to the *Antillian* of our line. I was sending an ice report, handed in by the skipper, sir. I was sending to the *Antillian* and the *Titanic* called me up and we exchanged signals. . . I said, 'Here is a message, an ice report.' He said, 'It's all right, old man,' he said. 'I heard you send to the *Antillian*.' He said, 'Bi.' That is an expression used among ourselves."

"What does it mean?"

"It is an expression used. It means to say 'enough', 'finished.'"

"Through?"

"Yes."

"Do you know which operator you were communicating with on the *Titanic*?"

"No, sir."

"You do not recall which one it was you spoke with that night?" "You never know who is on watch unless the operator is inclined to talk and tell you his name. Then you get to know the name of the person operating at the other end."

"When that message was sent by you do you recall the time exactly?"

"It was sent at," consulting his memorandum, "5.30 p.m. New York time (approx. 7.30 p.m. *Titanic* time), on the 10th April, sir. I worked New York time."

"What did the message say?"

" 'Latitude 42° 3' N Longitude 49° 9' W. Three large bergs 5 miles to southward of us. Regards Lord'. . . . It was handed in on the 14th, sir. . . . The sent date was 5.35 p.m. New York time."

"When did you next communicate with the *Titanic*'?"

"9.05, New York time, sir, (11.05 *Titanic* time) on the 14th—the same evening New York time that is. I went outside of my room just before that, about five minutes before that, and we were stopped, and I went to the Captain and I asked him if there was anything the matter. The Captain told me he was going to stop because of the ice, and the Captain asked me if I had any boats, and I said, 'The *Titanic*.' He said, 'Better advise him we are surrounded by ice and stopped.' So I went to my cabin, and at 9.05 New York time I called him up. I said, 'Say old man, we are stopped and surrounded by ice.' He turned around and said, 'Shut up, shut up, I am busy; I am working Cape Race,' and at that I jammed him."

"What do you mean by that?"

"By jamming we mean when somebody is sending a message to somebody else and you start to send at the same time, you jam him. He does not get his message. I was stronger than Cape Race. Therefore my signals came in with a bang, and he could read me and he could not read Cape Race."

"Was that the last time you heard from the *Titanic* that night?" "The last time I exchanged signals with them. I heard them working at 11.25. . . . He was still calling Cape Race, sending messages."

"What time did you retire that night?"

"At 11.25 I still had the phones on my ears and heard him working Cape Race, about two or three minute's before the half hour ship's time, that was, and at 11.35 I put the phones down and took off my clothes and turned in."

This is the truly poignant part of the story. If the *Titanic* struck at 11.40, as Mersey found, and if her clocks were ten minutes ahead of the *Californian*'s Evans must have taken his headphones off literally within seconds of the collision.

"When were you awakened?"

"About 3.30 a.m. New York time." (Roughly 5.25 ship's time.) "And who awakened you?"

"The Chief Officer. He said 'There is a ship that has been firing rockets in the night. Please see if there is anything the matter.' "

"He said rockets had been fired during the night?"

"Yes, sir."

"What did you do?"

"I jumped out of bed, slipped on a pair of trousers and a pair of slippers, and I went at once to my key and started my motor and gave 'CQ'. About a second later I was answered by the *Frankfurt.* He told me the *Titanic* had sunk."

"You put the telephone on your head?"

Yes, sir.

"And received from the *Frankfurt*——"

Evans interrupted, "I started my motor first, and called. I called CQ. The DFT answered me. He said 'Do you know the *Titanic* has sunk during the night, collided with an iceberg?' I said, 'No—please give me the latest position.' He gave me the position. I put the position down on a slip of paper, and then I said, 'Thanks old man,' to the German operator, and then the *Virginian* started to call me, MGM. He started to call me up, and I told him to go. He said, 'Do you know the *Titanic* has sunk?" I said, 'Yes, the *Frankfurt* just told me.' I sent them a message of my own, what we call a service message, that an operator can always make up if he wants to find out something. I sent a service message and said, 'Please send official message regarding *Titanic* giving position.' "

"Then he gave you her position?"

"Yes, sir. The Chief Officer was in the room, and I said, 'Wait a moment—I will get an official message.' I got the official message and the positions were both the same. I sent that up to the skipper. I did not have time to date the message, but I did not get the name of the ship on either, or the date, or who it was addressed to, in my hurry." "Did you tell me what the Mate said when he woke you up?"

"He came into my room, and I did not wake up, and he caught hold of me. As soon as he touched me I woke up with a start, and he said, 'Wireless, there is a ship that has been firing rockets in the night. Will you come in and see if you can find out what is wrong—what is the matter.' I slipped on my trousers and called at once. Within five minutes I knew what had happened."

Senator Bourne: "Did you think it at all strange when you got 'Shut up' from the *Titanic* or is that customary when you break in to prevent jamming?"

"If he was working. He had a lot of messages to get off."

"Do you think he got your full message?"

"His signals came in with a bang—therefore my signals must have come into him very loudly."

"Can you take more than one message at a time?"

"No. But my signals were the loudest."

Senator Burton: "You think he must have received your message before he shut you off because you had the louder note?"

"He must have received my communication, yes, sir."

Senator Bourne: "You gave your location did you not?"

"No, sir, I was just giving that as a matter of courtesy, because the Captain requested me to."

"You expected a reply from him, or an inquiry as to what your location was, where the ice was, did you not?"

"No, sir. I thought he was very much south of me, because we were bound for Boston, and we were north of the track. We were following the track of the *Parisian*

Senator Fletcher: "Do you know Gill, who was a member of the crew of the *Californian*—Ernest Gill?"

"I think I have seen him, yes, sir."

"Did you ever have any conversation with him about that ship that was seen that night throwing up rockets?"

"I think so. Practically everybody on the ship—it has been common talk on the ship."

"From the talk on the ship do you know when the rockets were seen that night—from what direction?"

"No, sir, I had turned in."

"In a general way what was the talk with reference to that, that you heard on the ship?"

"Well, I could not say. It was just simply the usual talk about rockets."

"Were the rockets described?"

"Not to my knowledge, no, sir. I never heard them described." "Do you know whether they were distress rockets or some other kind of rockets?"

"No, sir, I do not know."

Senator Burton rose to continue the questioning.

"You say everybody was talking on board about these rockets?"

Yes, sir.

"Do you mean by that that they were saying that they themselves had seen the rockets, or that there was merely talk about it on the ship?"

"There was some talk about it, and some of them said they had seen it, and some said they had not."

"With how many did you talk who said they saw rockets that night?"

"Nobody."

"Can you tell anyone you talked with who said he had seen rockets that night?"

"No, sir."

The subject was changed to wave-lengths. Afterwards Senator Smith came back to the rockets.

"Do you know why you were not called when the rockets were first seen?"

No, sir.

"What did the First Mate or any other officer of the ship or member of the crew tell you about Captain Lord being notified three times that a vessel was sending up rockets?"

"Well, we have talked among ourselves, but——"

"One minute. I do not want any idle gossip. If you can recall anything that was said by any officer of your ship about the matter, I would like to have you state it—and if you cannot say so."

"I know that the Mate did not say anything to me, no."

"Did any other officer of the *Californian* say anything to you about having notified the Captain three times that a vessel was sending up rockets?"

"I think the apprentice did."

"What did he say to you?"

"Well, I think he said that the skipper was being called—called three times. I think that is all he said."

"Did you hear anyone else speak of it, any officer of your ship?"

"No. I think not."

"Now, witness, tell me if you heard anybody else say anything about the Captain having been called three times and informed that rockets were being sent up the night the *Titanic* sank?"

"Well, I do not remember any other special individual, but I know it was being talked about a lot."

"Collectively?"

"Yes, sir."

"Was there any talk of this kind after you left the scene of the sinking of the *Titanic*?"

"Yes, it has been talked about all the time since then."

"As an unusual and extraordinary occurrence?"

Yes, sir.

"Did anybody in the course of this conversation that you heard, say anything about having seen the morse signals used?"

"Oh no. I remember the apprentice told me that he got the morse lamp out and called up on that, sir. But he did not get any reply on that."

"He started to call up the *Titanic*?"

"I do not know whether it was the *Titanic*   "

"But the vessel from which the rockets were being fired—he tried to call her up with his morse signals?"

Yes, sir.

"And got no morse reply?"

"That is correct."

"Was it said that the rockets were those which had been sent up by the *Titanic*? Was that the talk on board ship?"

"Some of them seemed to think so, and some not, sir."

Senator Burton rose. "Has anyone told you that he was to receive $500 for a story in regard to these rockets—anyone on your boat?" "I think the donkeyman mentioned it "

"What did he say?"

"He said, 'I think I will make about $500 on this.' "

"Did he say that to you?"

Yes, sir.

"That is the man who was a witness here this morning?"

"Gill, the second donkeyman."

"Where were you then?"

"I had gone ashore, and I was outside the station, I think. I do not remember whether it was the north station or the south station."

"It was after you had landed?"

"It was after I had landed, yes, sir. He asked if I was not going back any more. He said he had been up and told the newspaper about the accident."

"And he said he would make $500 out of it?"

"He said, 'I think we will make $500 out of it.' "

* * *

These three were the only witnesses heard from the *Californian.*

Gill and Evans between them had presented what appeared on the surface to be a damning case against Lord. True it was hearsay for the most part—except for Gill's big ship and his two pale blue-white rockets—but Evans had been a reluctant witness, and all the more impressive for being so. His recollection of what the Chief Officer had said when he called him in the morning—"Wireless, there is a ship that has been firing rockets in the night. Will you come in and find out what is wrong—what is the matter,"—certainly implied that there had been anxiety on the part of some, at least, of the *Californian's* officers over the meaning of the rockets. But Evans hadn't voluntarily accused his Captain. He could not be called vindictive or accused of being actuated by desire for profit or notoriety. The fact that the rockets and the Captain's inactivity had been the talk of the ship all the way to Boston really had to be prised out of him.

What had Lord's story been—his defence to all this? Simply that, during the relevant time, the fateful hours after midnight, he had been asleep!

"Asleep?" We can almost hear the incredulous voices now. "While the *Titanic* was sinking—sending up rockets to the clear sky and morsing him? Asleep!"

On the surface it seemed that Lord was as guilty as it was possible to be.

But this was a Senatorial Inquiry. These were elder statesmen of supposedly mature judgement spending public money to probe this tragedy to its limits; they were not schoolboys ganging up emotionally on a junior who had violated a code, accepting the first hearsay evidence they were given at its face value. A man's reputation and even his professional livelihood might rest on their judgement. They had no right to be emotional. They had no right to be facile.

CHAPTER NINE

The *Californian* incident grew in popular imagination and became accepted as fact long before any legal or quasi-legal pronouncements. And meanwhile the Senators plugged on, hearing, among the welter of detail, more versions of "the light" from *Titanic* crewmen. The first after the *Californian* brigade was Arthur John Bright, a quartermaster, who had been sent away in one of the starboard side boats which Ismay had been loading up.

"As soon as we got away from the ship, we were told to keep together if possible, to keep as close to each other in the boats as possible. There was a light sighted away, I should say, possibly 4 or 5 miles away, off the port bow of the ship. It looked to me like a sailing ship—like a fishing boat. There were no lights to be seen about the hull of the ship, if it was a ship. We pulled towards that for a time."

Senator Bourne asked him the colour of the light that he thought he saw

"It was a white light, like the steaming light of a ship would be." That was all Bright had to say about it. But a First Class bedroom steward, Alfred Crawford, had seen the ship in rather more detail. Immediately after the impact he had rushed out on deck and seen the iceberg passing by the side, had then assisted in rousing the passengers and getting them to tie their lifebelts on, after which he had helped with the starboard side boats under Murdoch and Ismay, and had then gone to his allotted boat, number 8 on the port side. Captain Smith had come to the boat and asked how many men were in it. There were only two sailors, and the Captain told Crawford to get in.

"He gave me orders to ship the rowlocks and pull for the light. He directed me to a light over there. We were pulling for about six hours I should say, and there were four men in the boat and a lady at the tiller all night."

This boat number 8 is the one in which the Countess of Rothes took the tiller. Crawford was mistaken about the six hours, of course, as there is overwhelming evidence that the *Carpathia* was in sight as it became light and all the boats started pulling towards her.

Senator Smith: "Did you see the light?"

"Yes, sir; there were two lights."

"How far away?"

"I should say it was not further than 10 miles. . . . They were stationary masthead lights, one on the fore and one on the main. Everybody saw them—all the ladies in the boat. They asked me if we were drawing nearer to the steamer, but we could not seem to make any headway, and when day broke we saw another steamer coming up, which proved to be the *Carpathia*—and then we turned around and came back. We were the furthest boat away."

"And you got no nearer to that light?"

"We did not seem to be making any headway at all, sir."

"Tell the committee what you think that light was."

"I am sure it was a steamer because a sailing ship would not have masthead lights."

"Did you see any sidelights on this boat the Captain told you to pull for?"

"No, I could not say I saw any sidelights."

"Did you see any more of that light than you have now described?"

"No, at daybreak it seemed to disappear. We came around and came back."

"Did you see any rockets?"

"Yes, sir. Plenty of them went up from the *Titanic,* and the morse code was used."

"Did you see any rockets from any other ship?"

No, sir.

THE EVIDENCE FROM THE MOUNT TEMPLE

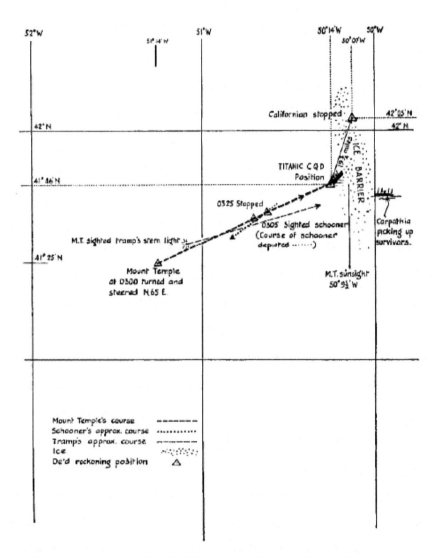

This was the point that the Senate seized upon. No one had seen any rockets from any ship other than the *Titanic,* and all had been looking anxiously for some sign. Crawford was examined at great length about these two steamer masthead lights which he had seen. He was positive he had seen them, and was under the impression that the ship was coming towards them in the lifeboat. Everyone saw it. "Sometimes she seemed to get closer; other times she seemed to be getting away from us."

Senator Burton: "Those lights remained visible until it became daybreak did they?"

Yes, sir.

The direction of the *Titanic's* head after she struck the berg was never established, and little attempt was made to establish it. But there is a good pointer to the Senator's thoughts on the matter in Crawford's evidence. Senator Fletcher asked, "If the *Titanic* was moving West, you moved South-West?"

"Probably so."

"Towards the light?"

Yes, sir.

There was only one more detailed description of the light to come and that was when the Fourth Officer, Boxhall, was recalled on the tenth day. In the meantime Captain James Henry Moore, master of the Canadian Pacific emigrant liner, *Mount Temple*, was called to give his account of the rescue attempt.

This was doubly interesting, both because it brought more unknown ships right into the heart of the disaster area that early morning, and because there had been stories from the *Mount Temple*, like those from the *Californian*, that rockets had been seen from her after midnight.

Captain Moore was an elderly man with thirty-two years of seagoing experience behind him, twenty-seven of them in the North Atlantic trade. It appeared he was a cautious man. He always altered course to avoid ice—for one thing his company's regulations forbade him from trying to make his way through.

At 00.30 ship's time on the morning of the 15th when he had received the CQD from the *Titanic* he had been in 41° 25'N, 51° 14'W, some way to the West of her and heading West. His clocks had been set at noon the previous day.

Senator Smith: "What did you do after receiving this message?"

"I immediately blew the whistle on the bridge. I have a pipe leading down from the bridge, and I blew the whistle at once, and told the Second

Officer to put the ship on North 45° East, sir, and to come down at once, and I informed him what was the matter, and told him to get the chart out. When I was sufficiently dressed I went up to my chart-room, and we computed where the ship was. . . . We turned her right round at once, sir, and then when he came down we took the chart out and found out where the *Titanic* was and steered her by the compass North 65° East true. . . . After I was sufficiently dressed I went down to the Chief Engineer and I told him that the *Titanic* was sending out messages for help, and I said, 'Go down and try to shake up the fireman, and if necessary even give him a tot of rum if you think he can do any more.' I believe this was carried out. . . .

"Before we had laid the course off I received another position, which read 41° 47'N, 50° 14'W—so that was 10 miles further to the eastward, and it was that position that I laid my course for."

"After satisfying yourself as to her position, how far was the *Titanic* from your vessel?"

"About 49 miles, sir."

"After you got well under way what speed were you making?"

"I should imagine perhaps 11½ knots. Of course, perhaps, she would have a little of the Gulf stream with her too, sir."

At about three o'clock they had begun to meet ice, passing it on their course, and Captain Moore put the engines on "stand by", doubled the lookout and sent the Fourth Officer up to the foc's'le head.

"At 3.25 by our time we stopped . . . I should say we were then about 14 miles off the *Titanic's* position."

"Can you tell me just what your position was—did you take it?" "I could not. I could not take any position. There was nothing—

I could not see——"

"You judged you were 14 miles from the *Titanic*?"

"That is what I estimate."

"Was it dark or was day breaking?"

"It was dark then, sir. I stopped the ship. Before that I want to say that I met a schooner or some small craft, and I had to get out of the way of that vessel, and the light of that vessel seemed to go out."

"The light of that schooner seemed to go out?"

"Yes, sir."

"And in your track?"

"She was a little off our bow and I immediately starboarded the helm and got the two lights green to green, sir . . . I was steering east and this green light was opening to me."

"Was he evidently coming from the direction in which the *Titanic* lay?"

"Somewhere from there, sir. Of course had he been coming straight he would have shown me his two lights, sir."

"You had no communication with any person, and did not see any person on that schooner yourself?"

"Oh no, sir, it was quite dark."

"How much nearer the *Titanic*'s position do you think that schooner was than your boat at the time you have——"

"I should say this light could not have been more than a mile or a mile and a half away, because I immediately put my helm hard a-starboard, because I saw the light, and after I got the light on my starboard bow then the light seemed to suddenly go out. I kept on and then the quartermaster must have let her come up towards the East again, because I heard the foghorn on this schooner. He blew his foghorn, and we immediately put the helm hard a-starboard, and I ordered full speed astern and took the way off the boat."

"You think the schooner was within a short distance of the *Titanic*?"

"I thought she was within a short distance of us because I put the engines full astern to avoid her."

"At 3.25 a.m. you think you were 14 miles away from the *Titanic*?"

"Yes, sir."

"At about that time you saw this schooner?"

"Oh no, it was just shortly after three o'clock when I saw the schooner, sir."

"That is what I say—about 3.25?"

"No. Just shortly after three o'clock I saw the schooner. That was before I stopped her on account of the ice getting so thick, sir. As a matter of fact I did not stop her altogether; I simply stopped the engines and let the way run off the ship and then proceeded slowly."

"One light you said was on the schooner?"

"One light. I just saw the one light. He would have his starboard side open to me."

"What did you do then, after the schooner passed and got out of the way?"

"I put her on her course again, sir."

"I want to be certain that the schooner was as near the *Titanic* as I thought I understood you to say it was."

"I should say the schooner, from the position of the *Titanic* would be, perhaps, 12½ to 13 miles."

"About how fast was the schooner moving?"

"He could not have been moving very fast. . . I dare say she would be making a couple of knots an hour. Some time after that the breeze sprang up until we had quite a fresh breeze."

"This schooner came from the direction of the *Titanic*'s position?"

"Fairly well, sir. You see, I was going North 65° East and he angled a bit to the south, because if he had come directly from the other, of course, he would have shown two lights, sir."

"What I am trying to get at is this. One or two of the ship's officers of the *Titanic* say that after the collision with the iceberg they used the morse signals and rockets for the purpose of attracting help, and that while they were using these rockets and displaying the morse signals they saw lights ahead, or saw lights, that could not have been over 5 miles from the *Titanic*. What I am seeking to develop is the question as to what light that was they saw."

"Well, it may have been the light of the tramp steamer that was ahead of us, because when I turned there was a steamer on my port bow."

"Going in the same direction?"

"Almost in the same direction. As he went ahead he gradually crossed our bow until he got on the starboard bow, sir—on our starboard bow."

"Did you see that ship yourself?"

"I saw it myself. I was on the bridge all the time."

"Did you communicate with him by wireless?"

"I do not think he had any wireless; I am sure he had no wireless because in the daylight I was close to him."

"How large a vessel was it?"

"I should say a ship of about 4,000 or 5,000 tons."

"How large a vessel is the *Mount Temple*?"

"6,661 tons register."

"Did you come close enough to that ship to which you have just referred to determine what she was?"

"No, I did not get her name. I think she was a foreign ship, sir. She was not English, because she did not show her ensign. We were trying to signal him because I think when I turned back after we both stopped, when he found the ice too heavy he followed me, because when I turned round, after finding the ice too heavy to the southward, after I went to the southward later on in the morning, when it got daylight, and I went down to where he was, thinking perhaps he had gotten into a thin spot, when I got there he had stopped, he had found the ice too heavy. I went a little farther, and I turned around because it was getting far too heavy to put the ship through. But that would be about five or perhaps half-past five in the morning, sir."

"Were you close enough to see whether her funnel was of any special colour?"

"If I can remember rightly it was black, with some device in a band near the top."

"Did you get any nearer the *Titanic*'s position than you have just mentioned?"

"At 3.25 I stopped the engines, and then went slowly to avoid the ice, because it was too dark to proceed full speed on account of the ice. . . . I reached the *Titanic*'s position, I reckon I was very close to that position, either that position or very close to it, at 4.30 in the morning, sir."

"Was there any other vessel there at that time?"

"None except the tramp, sir."

"Except the tramp that cut across——"

"That cut across my bow. I could see him then. He was a little to the southward of me, but ahead of me, sir."

"When you were at that point what did you do and what did you see?"

"I saw a large pack ice right to the east of me, sir—right in my course. . . . In consulting my officers as to the breadth of this, one said it was 5 miles and another said it was 6 miles . . . that was the width of it. Of course it extended as far as the eye could reach, north and south, sir."

"Twenty miles or more?"

"I should say 20 miles, perhaps more than that. It was field ice and bergs. . . I should say altogether, there must have been between forty and fifty I counted that morning."

"When you arrived at the *Titanic*'s position it was along after four in the morning?"

"Half-past four, sir—that is, I reckoned we were at that position at half-past four, sir."

"What did you see there, if anything?"

"I saw nothing whatever, sir."

"Any wreckage from the *Titanic*?"

"I saw nothing, but I saw this tramp steamer, sir."

"How long did you stay in that position?"

"We searched around to see if there was a clear place we could go through, because I feared the ice was too heavy for me to push through it. Of course I reckoned I was somewhere near, if not at, the *Titanic*'s position that he gave me, which afterwards proved correct, when I got observations in the morning, sir. I searched for a passage to get through this pack because I realised that the *Titanic* could not have been through that pack of ice, sir. . . ."

"Some passengers on your vessel, Sunday night about midnight, claim to have seen these rockets from the decks of the *Titanic*. Have you heard anything about that?"

"I have read it in the papers, sir, but as a matter of fact I do not believe there was a passenger on deck at twelve o'clock at night. I am positive, because they would not know anything at all about this, and you may be sure that they were in their beds. I know the steward tells me there was nobody on deck—that is the night watchman at the aft end. At the forward end there was nobody on deck. . ."

"Do you wish to be understood as saying that you did not see, on Sunday night or Monday morning, any signal lights from the *Titanic*?"

"I can solemnly swear that I saw no signal lights, nor did my officers on the bridge see any signal lights."

"What kind of wireless equipment has the *Mount Temple*?" "Marconi, sir."

"How many operators?"

"Only one, sir."

"What are his hours?"

"He has no special hours."

"How did he happen to be on duty at 12.30 midnight, Sunday night?"

"I don't know, sir. I think it was just about the time he was turning in. He just picked up the instrument just to see if there was anything coming along. It was just purely and simply an accident that he got the ship's message."

Captain Moore was taken at great length through all the messages his wireless operator had recorded in his log that night until they came to the *Carpathia*'s message at 1.40 New York time, 'IF YOU ARE THERE WE ARE FIRING ROCKETS'.

Senator Smith: "Let me ask you right there, did you see the rockets from the *Carpathia*?"

"I never saw any rockets whatever, sir."

"Is it possible that this passenger from Toronto, who claims to have seen rockets, may have seen the rockets from the *Carpathia* at that time?"

"I do not think it possible, sir, because if the *Carpathia* was farther away it is not likely you would see her rockets. But you see, this ship says she is sending rockets up, so it is possible that other ships may have seen them. I do not know. I thought of sending rockets up, but I thought it far better to let it alone, because if other ships—they thought they saw them—might be coming to me, and I had not seen anything of the *Titanic,* and did not know exactly where she was—because I think after all the *Titanic* was further east than she gave her position, sir. In fact I am certain she was."

"What makes you think so?"

"Because when I got the position in the morning I got a prime vertical sight—that is a sight taken when the sun is bearing due east. That position gave me 50° 9½´ W. I got two observations. I took one before the prime vertical and also on the prime vertical. . . and they both came to within a quarter of a mile of each other—so that the *Titanic* must have been on the other side of the field ice, and then her position was not right which she gave."

Elaborating on this, Captain Moore said, "My observation was this—my Fourth Officer took two observations, and of course he is a navigator, and also an Extra Master's Certificate is held by him, which is a better certificate than mine, and he took those observations both times and both of them tallied. One came to 50° 9|'W and the other came to 50° 9f'W. Of course it proved afterwards when, after coming southward and trying to find some place I could get through—I suppose at about six o'clock in the morning—that I sighted the *Carpathia* on the other side of this great ice pack, and there is where I understand he picked up the boats. *So this great pack of ice was between us and the* Titanic's *position.*"

"On which side of the ice pack was the *Californian*?"

"The *Californian* was to the north, sir. She was to the north of the *Carpathia* and steaming to the westward, because after I had come away and after giving up my attempt to get through that pack, I came back again and steered back, thinking I might pick up some soft place to the north. As I was going to the north the *Californian* was passing from east to west."

The only ship, Captain Moore reiterated, which had been in sight when he arrived at the *Titanic's* wirelessed position first had been the tramp steamer and then at about eight o'clock they had sighted the yellow funnel steamer which proved to be the Russian *Birma*.

In view of the doubt this evidence cast upon the accuracy of the *Titanic's* dead reckoning position as broadcast with the CQD, it is interesting to refer to Captain Rostron's evidence as given before the committee. He had received the message at 12.35 apparent ship's time when 58 miles to the south-east of the position given, and had immediately set course at forced full speed—which he estimated at 17 knots—and had not stopped until 4 a.m. He had been firing rockets every quarter of an hour from 2.45 a.m. He had picked up the first boat at 4.10, and the last at 8.30. He had seen the *Californian* first at eight o'clock coming directly towards him from the WSW.

In his view the *Titanic's* wirelessed position was completely accurate. And there is no doubt that had he been travelling at 17 knots without a break between 12.35 and 4.0 a.m. he would indeed have covered the 58 miles.

***

Afterwards Lightoller was recalled and asked about any light he had seen from the *Titanic*. But he was not able to describe it in more detail than "a white light off the port bow". Then on April 29th Boxhall was recalled.

"At first I saw two masthead lights of a steamer, just slightly opened, and later she got closer to us, until, eventually I could see her sidelights *with my naked eye*. . . . I considered she was about 5 miles away . . . just about half a point off our port bow."

"And apparently coming towards you?"

"Yes."

"How soon after the collision?"

"I cannot say about that. It was shortly after the order was given to clear the boats . . . I saw that light, saw all the lights of course before I got into my boat, and just before I got into the boat she seemed as if she had turned round. I saw just one single bright light then, which I took to be her stern light."

"She apparently turned round within 5 miles of you?"

"Yes, sir."

"Had the rockets then gone off on the *Titanic*?"

"Yes, sir. I had been firing off rockets before I saw her side lights. I fired off the rockets and then she got so close I could see her sidelights and starboard lights."

This is interesting. The *Titanic* was motionless in the water while the boats were being lowered—there is no doubt about this; if she had any movement at all it was downwards—yet the mystery ship, whose mast lights only were visible at the first rocket (and the first boat down) moved in closer to show her coloured sidelights *to the naked eye* while the rockets were being fired. This proved—if the Senators accepted Boxhall's evidence—that the vessel *had* moved her engines and *had* steamed towards the *Titanic* while she was sinking.

But all the evidence that the Senators had heard from the Californian, *from Gill, from Lord and from Evans was that she had been stopped in the water from 10.30 p.m. until 5 a.m.*

Next, Boxhall went into even greater detail and said that the white lights he had seen had been on masts which were fairly close together. "She might have been a four-mast ship, or might have been a three- mast ship, but she certainly was not a two-mast ship."

The reasoning here is that the masts of a two-master are further apart relatively than those of a three- or four-master, and so consequently are the lights.

He had entered the lifeboat and been lowered to the water. ". . . I saw it (the light) for a little while and then lost it. When we pulled around the ship I could not see it any more, and did not see it any more."

"Apparently that ship came within 4 or 5 miles of the *Titanic* and then turned and went away in what direction? Westward or southward?"

"I do not know whether it was southward or westward. I should say it was westward."

Again, the assumption that the *Titanic* lay stopped pointing along her original track westward, but again no questions as to what prompted Boxhall to think that, and no indication volunteered by Boxhall himself.

Examined about the statement of the Captain of the *Mount Temple* that the *Titanic's* position (which Boxhall had worked out) was wrong, he answered, "I do not know what to say. I know our position, because I worked the position out, and I know that it is correct. One of the first things that Captain Rostron said after I met him was 'What a splendid position that was you gave us.' "

"And you are satisfied that was correct?"

"Perfectly."

"You computed it yourself, did you?"

"I computed it myself, and computed it by star observations that had been taken by Mr Lightoller that same evening—and they were beautiful observations."

No questions as to whether he had allowed for any set against him or even what time the star position had been taken, or in fact what speed he had worked his distance up on, whether he computed the distance run and then pricked the position off with dividers on the chart, or whether he actually computed the position from tables knowing the course and distance.[1] If the Gulf Stream set against him had been as much as 1 knot he could have been 5 miles to the East of his calculations. Five miles was

---

1 At the British Inquiry Boxhall stated that he had not seen the charted position but had worked his position with traverse tables, using 22 knots.

Captain Moore's estimate of the width of the ice pack, on the westward side of which, in what he thought was the *Titanic's* position, no wreckage had been visible. The *Carpathia* was working from dead reckoning from her last star sight, was dodging about among bergs, and might also have been set to the eastward.

The *Mount Temple* had taken one sight with the sun almost due East, and one due East on a perfect morning; both had agreed and placed her about 4 miles *East* of the *Titanic's* wirelessed position and yet she was still to the *West* of the *Carpathia* and the wreckage. There is no doubt that any sailor would believe sun sights with a due East bearing for longitude in preference to dead reckoning. And although some of the discrepancy may have been caused by the easterly Gulf Stream drift it is unlikely that it was as much as 10 miles in about six hours.

Captain Lord was never asked his view, and the matter was never probed.

Boxhall's final words on the lights: "I saw the masthead lights first, the two steaming lights—and then as she drew closer I saw her sidelights through the glasses, and eventually I saw her red light. I had seen the green, but I saw the red most of the time. I saw the red light with my naked eye."

Senator Burton: "She kept on a general course towards the east, and then bore away from or what?"

Again the assumption that the *Titanic* lay pointing westward.

"I do not think she was doing much steaming. I do not think the ship was steaming very much, because after I first saw the masthead lights she must have been still steaming, but by the time I saw her red light with my naked eye she was not steaming very much. She had probably gotten into the ice and turned around."

"What do you think happened after she turned around? Do you think she went away to avoid the ice?"

"I do not know whether she stayed there all night, or what she did. I lost the light. I did not see her after we pulled around to the starboard side of the *Titanic.*"

Those were the seamen who described having seen the light. Towards the latter half of the Inquiry the passengers gave their evidence and amongst it came more descriptions. They accorded markedly with the majority verdict of those members of the crew who had been asked.

On April 30th Colonel Archibald Gracie, U.S. Army, the man who had leapt for the roof of the officers' quarters by the second funnel as the water rose, told how he had awakened in his cabin about midnight and heard the blowing off of steam and felt a decrease in the vibration which told him the machinery had stopped. He went on deck partly dressed, walked around trying to find out what the trouble was, went back to his cabin after a while, packed a few things as a precautionary measure and went out on deck again. He was given a life preserver and made his way up to A deck. And it was from there while standing with a group of women that he first saw the light on the bow.

"These ladies were Mrs E. D. Appleton, Mrs Cornel and Mrs Murray Brown, the publisher's wife from Boston, and Miss Evans. They were somewhat disturbed of course. I reassured them and pointed out to them the light of what I thought was a ship or a steamer in the distance.

"Mr Astor came up and he leaned over the side of the deck which was an enclosed deck, and there were windows and the glass could be let down. I pointed towards the bow, and there were distinctly seen these lights—or a light, rather one single light. It did not seem to be a star, and that is what we all thought it was, the light of some steamer. . . I should say it could not have been more than 6 miles away."

"Was it ahead?"

"Ahead towards the bow, because I had to lean over, and here was this lifeboat down by the side at that time, and I pointed right ahead and showed Mr Astor so he could see and he had to lean way over."

One white light only seen by the Colonel, but he has fixed it accurately in relation to the head of the liner: they leaned over the side to see it so it must have been nearly ahead—very fine on the bow as Boxhall had said. This is not early in the proceedings either for a lifeboat is already in the water.

On May 2nd Mrs J. Stuart White gave her testimony. She had been lowered in boat number 8 from the port side.

". . . Before we cut loose from the ship two of the seamen with us— the men I should say—I do not call them seamen—I think they were dining-room stewards—before we cut loose from the ship they took out cigarettes and lighted them—on an occasion like that! That was one thing we saw. All those men escaped under the pretence of being oarsmen. The man who rowed me took his oar and rowed all over the boat, in every direction. I said to him, 'Why don't you put your oar in the oarlock?' He said, 'Do you put it in that hole?' I said 'Certainly'. He said, 'I never had an oar in my hand before!' These were the men that we put to sea with at night. . . ."

"I wish you would describe as nearly as you can, just what took place after your lifeboat got away from the *Titanic*."

"We simply rowed away. We had the order, on leaving the ship, to do that. The officer who put us in the boat—I do not know who he was—gave strict orders to the seamen—or the men—to make for the light opposite and land the passengers and get back just as soon as possible. That was the light that everybody saw in the distance."

"Did you see it?"

"Yes, I saw it distinctly. . . . It was a boat of some kind."

"How far away was it?"

"Oh it was 10 miles away but we could see it distinctly. There was no doubt but that it was a boat. But we rowed and rowed and rowed, and then we all suggested that it was simply impossible for us to get back to it.

"We did what we were ordered to do. We went towards the light. That seemed to be the verdict of everybody in the boat. We had strict orders from the officer . . . to row as fast as possible for that boat, land the passengers and come right back for the others. We all supposed the boat was coming towards us, on account of all the rockets we had sent up.

"As I have said before, the men in our boat were anything but seamen with the exception of one man. The women all rowed, every one of them. Miss Young rowed every minute. The men could not row. Miss Swift from Brooklyn rowed every minute from the steamer to the *Carpathia*. Miss Young rowed every minute also, except when she was throwing up, which she did six or seven times. Countess Rothes stood at the tiller . . . but we could not get there. . . . It was evidently impossible to reach it. It seemed to be going in the same direction in which we were going, and we made no headway towards it at all."

Another passenger, Major Arthur Peuchen, who had been ordered aboard one of the port forward boats told how the quartermaster in his boat, "imagined that he saw a light away from the vessel, and insisted on rowing towards it".

***

On the penultimate day of the investigation Captain John J. Knapp, U.S.N., hydrographer to the Navy Department came to lend the weight of his professional authority to the popular indignation against Lord. This day can be called the turning-point in the *Californian* incident. Had Captain Knapp who had been present at the Inquiry and had heard and read the evidence, seen it for what it was, inadequate to prove that *any* specific ship was the mystery ship—had he realised this and testified to that effect it is difficult to see how the Senators could have brought in their adverse findings against Lord. And had they not done so it may well have been that Mersey at the British Investigation would have paused in his headlong attempt to prove Lord guilty. It only needed one man to pause, to think a little, to expose the whole outcry as a false alarm. But no one paused. Or at least, if they did, they thought better of it.

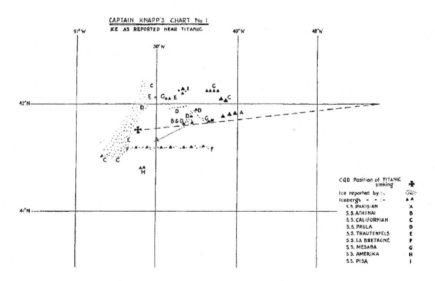

Captain Knapp gave the snowball which Ernest Gill had started rolling a great heave down easy slopes towards the meadows of exculpation of public conscience. A sacrifice had been found. It merely remained for Knapp to rationalise the choice.

"From being present at the hearings of your committee and from reading the printed testimony of witnesses examined by the committee I am led to the conclusion that if there was any vessel between the *Californian* and the *Titanic* at the time referred to she does not seem to have been seen by any of the ships near there on the following morning nor have there been any reports submitted to the Hydro- graphic office which would indicate that there was any such steamer in that locality.

"The evidence does not indicate to me that there was any such third steamer in those waters, especially in view of the fact that no such steamer was seen by other steamers or by those in the lifeboats the following morning, and as the ice barrier, from all reports, between the reported position of the *Californian* and that of the *Titanic* was impassable to a vessel proceeding to the westward and there is no testimony to show that if such a steamer was between the *Californian* and the *Titanic* she proceeded to the eastward, the Captain of the *Californian* having testified that he last saw the said steamer proceeding to the westward and being on a bearing to the westward of the *Californian*. Nothing appears in the testimony to show that the steamer so soon reversed its course and proceeded to the eastward."

So, with a spate of negatives, Knapp rejected Lord's navigational evidence, and, by inference, accepted that of Captain Moore of the *Mount Temple,* from which ship there had also been reports of rockets. He also rejected or forgot the steamer which Lord had seen when he came on the bridge after being called at dawn on the 15 th.

"At daylight we saw a yellow funnel steamer to the south-west of us, beyond where this man (the one firing rockets) had left—about 8 miles away."

"Do you suppose that was the same one?" he was asked.

"I should not like to say. I don't think so, because this one had only one masthead light that we saw at half-past eleven."

Now the whole of the rest of Captain Knapp's evidence about the *Californian,* and he spoke for some considerable time, is simply a statement of the obvious proposition that if the *Californian* was the ship the *Titanic* saw, the *Titanic* was the ship the *Californian* saw. His chart No. 2, his "hypothetical position", his involved reasoning came to no more than this.[2] He worked out radii of visibility with the object of proving that Boxhall was correct in seeing the *sidelights* of the steamer, and all the people in the boats were correct in only seeing the *mast lights,* the sidelights being shut out by the curve of the earth from their lower position. This meant, although Knapp didn't say so, that Boxhall saw those sidelights *with a naked eye* at between 7 and 10 miles (where Captain Knapp's hypothetical position lies) and not at 5 miles as he himself testified. Now Board of Trade regulations stipulated that a vessel's sidelights should be visible for 2 miles; in practice they are nowadays visible for perhaps 5 miles. Is it likely that anyone would have seen the sidelights of a vessel at 8 or 9 miles with the naked eye, even if, as Boxhall said, "that vessel had beautiful lights"?

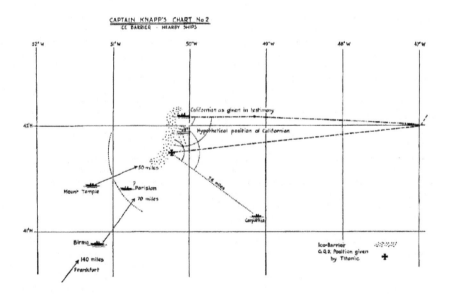

2 *See* Appendix F.

But Captain Knapp was a nautical man.

Another sentence from his extraordinary explanation of chart No. 2 runs thus: "In the case of the *Californian*, if the steamer which in the testimony given by members of the crew of the *Californian*, including the Captain and donkey-engine man and others is said to have been seen by them was the *Titanic*, she must have been somewhere inside of the circle with the 16-mile radius. . . ."

This is misleading. Gill's evidence and Lord's and Evans' evidence were mutually exclusive. You either take Gill's or you take the other two. You cannot have both because Gill's ship was not visible while it was firing rockets whereas Lord's ship was about 4 miles distant and Evans' ship was visible and within morsing distance. Yet Knapp has both the Captain and the donkey-engine man and other members of the crew—these from hearsay only—seeing *the same ship*.

But Knapp was a nautical man.

The sentence following this one ends, "then the *Titanic* must have been outside of the circle drawn with the 7-mile radius around the *Californian*."

Again and again, Boxhall, the star witness for the steamship theory said 5 miles—5 miles. He was the only officer asked. He was a man accustomed to judging distances from his everyday work. He was the only reliable witness to support the steamship theory. Boxhall stated 5 miles and the other sailors said 3, 4, 5 miles—someone said 10 but that was Crawford, a steward. All the sailors said 5 or under and the officer said 5. There is a great difference between 5 and 8 because 8 is on the line of the horizon and 5 is not. Ten miles is hull down. So besides disregarding the evidence from the *Californian* Captain Knapp disregarded every piece of evidence from the *Titanic*—except that of Alfred Crawford, steward, First Class.

He also must have assumed that the *Titanic* foundered pointing in a north-easterly direction against the trend of the evidence and even the questioning.

Is it possible to believe that Captain Knapp, a nautical man, was Uninfluenced by pressure from outside or by the general hysteria?

CHAPTER TEN

"In our imagination we can see again the proud ship, instinct with life and energy, with active figures again swarming its decks: musicians, teachers, artists and authors—soldiers and sailors and men of large affairs—brave men and noble women of every land." This is Senator Smith making his closing address on May 28th. "We can see the unpretentious and the lowly, progenitors of the great and strong, turning their back upon the old world where endurance is to them no longer a virtue, and looking hopefully to the new. At the very moment of their greatest joy the ship suddenly reels, mutilated and groaning. With splendid courage the musicians fill the last moments with sympathetic melody. The ship wearily gives up the unequal battle. Only a vestige remains of the men and women that, but a moment before, quickened her spacious apartments with human hopes and passions, sorrows and joys. Upon that broken hull new vows were taken, new fealty expressed, old love renewed and those who had been devoted in friendship and companions in life went proudly and defiantly on their last pilgrimage together. In such a heritage we must feel ourselves more intimately related to the sea than ever before, and henceforth it will send back to us on its rising tide the cheering salutations from those we have lost."

With such splendid oratory Smith clothed the appalling scenes as the passengers, finally realising their danger, rushed to the poop or the upper decks as any group of people would, and leaped off or clung where they could until they were swept off into the water as she went down and then screamed and choked and cried out for help until they died.

Oh God! Oh Washington!

"Ernest Gill," said the Senator during a lengthy reference to the *Californian* incident, "a member of the crew of the *Californian,* says that he came on deck from the engine-room at 11.56 ship's time, and just before the accident that fatal Sunday evening,[1] and saw plainly over the starboard side 'the lights of a very large steamer about 10 miles away' and that he could see 'her port sidelights'—that he then went to his cabin and said to his mate William Thomas that it was clear off to starboard, 'for I saw a big vessel going along at full speed', that he went on deck again and saw a white rocket about 10 miles away on the starboard side and in seven or eight minutes saw distinctly a second rocket in the same place, saying to himself 'that must be a vessel in distress.' "

It is worth noting here that had that large vessel been the *Titanic* and had the *Californian* been in Captain Knapp's hypothetical position Gill would have seen her starboard sidelights, not her port side if she was still steaming, as he said, "at full speed" on her westerly course—if in fact she had not already struck the berg.

"Why did the *Californian* display its morse signal lamp from the moment of the collision continuously for nearly two hours if they saw nothing? And the signals which were visible to Mr Gill at 12.30 and afterwards and which were also seen by the Captain and officer of the watch should have excited more solicitude than was displayed by the officers of that vessel."

In fact Captain Lord never said he had seen any rockets either in this or the British Inquiry. He had been in the chartroom, on the settee, asleep.

"The failure of Captain Lord to arouse the wireless operator on his ship, who could easily have ascertained the name of the vessel in distress and reached her in time to avert loss of Life places a tremendous responsibility upon this officer from which it will be very difficult for him to escape.

"I am well aware from the testimony of the Captain of the *Californian* that he deluded himself with the idea that there was a ship between the *Titanic* and the *Californian,* but there was no ship seen there at daybreak."

There was—and in any case all this depends upon where the *Titanic* actually foundered.

---

1 According to Lord Mersey at the British Inquiry between fifteen and twenty minutes after the accident.

"The ice floe held but two ships," thundered Smith, "the *Titanic* and the *Californian*. The conduct of the Captain of the *Californian* calls for drastic action by the government of England and by the owners of that vessel, who were the same owners as those of the ill-fated ship."

There is no room for doubt in all this. The Senator is quite sure of his facts; there is not one single expression of misgiving that perhaps some of the evidence might not point so strongly to Lord's guilt. It is all black and white, and Lord is black.

Equally so with the official Report drawn up by the Committee.

"Steamship light seen from steamship Titanic.

"Sixteen witnesses from the *Titanic,* including officers and experienced seamen and passengers of sound judgement, testified to seeing the light of a ship in the distance, and some of the lifeboats were directed to pull for that light, to leave the passengers and to return to the side of the *Titanic.* The *Titanic* fired distress rockets and attempted to signal by electric lamp and morse code to this vessel. At about the same time the officers of the *Californian* admit seeing rockets in the general direction of the *Titanic,* and say that they immediately displayed a powerful morse lamp, which could be easily seen a distance of ten miles, while several of the crew of the *Californian* testify that the sidelights of a large vessel going at full speed were plainly visible from the lower deck of the *Californian* at 11.30 p.m. ship's time, just before the accident. There is no evidence that any rockets were fired by any vessel between the *Californian* and the *Titanic* although every eye on the *Titanic* was searching the horizon for possible assistance."

" *The steamship* Californian's *responsibility.*

"The Committee is forced to the inevitable conclusion that the *Californian,* controlled by the same company, was nearer the *Titanic* than the nineteen miles reported by her Captain, and that her officers and crew saw the distress signals of the *Titanic* and failed to respond to them in accordance with the dictates of humanity, international usage and the requirement of law. The only reply to the distress signals was a counter signal from a large white light which was flashed for nearly two hours from the mast of the *Californian.* In our opinion such conduct, whether arising from indifference or gross carelessness, is most reprehensible, and places upon the commander of the *Californian* a grave responsibility. . . . Had assistance been promptly proffered, or had the wireless operator of the *Californian* remained a few minutes longer at his post on Sunday evening, that ship must have had the proud distinction of rescuing the lives of the passengers and crew of the *Titanic*."

Strong language! But most of it was nonsense.

Take the first section. The initial sentences appear to be supported by the evidence: there *was* some sort of light seen on the bow of the *Titanic*; the *Titanic did* fire rockets and *did* morse. Then: "At about the same time the officers of the *Californian* admit seeing rockets in the general direction of the *Titanic,* and say that they immediately displayed a powerful morse lamp, which could be easily seen a distance of ten miles. . ." No officer from the *Californian* except Captain Lord came before the Committee and what Lord said was that a rocket was reported to him by the Second Officer. This is vastly different. If the Committee wanted to establish what sort of rocket or rockets they were the Second Officer should have been called. The Committee have taken Captain Lord's judgement that the morse light could be easily seen for 10 miles as it appears in the statement. Yet Boxhall said that he was examining the ship which he thought was 5 miles away *through glasses* and could not see any morse signalling from her. Whatever distance the light was that Boxhall saw, the inference in the report is that Boxhall could see sidelights with the naked eye but not the morse lamp even with glasses—which is plainly ridiculous. There was no evidence from anyone on the *Titanic* except hearsay that the vessel they saw displayed any morse lamp.

". . . While several of the crew of the *Californian*", the report continued, "testify that the sidelights of a large vessel going at full speed were plainly visible from the lower deck of the *Californian* at 11.30 p.m. ship's time, just before the accident. . . ." All this is fabrication unsupported by any evidence whatever. Captain Lord saw a medium-sized tramp steamer coming up before this time and stopping 4 miles away at about this time. Evans did not mention seeing anything. Gill, by his own statement, was in the engine-room, from which he did not emerge until 11.56. Even Senator Smith had this time right in his address.

Assuming that the Committee inadvertently mistook the time Gill gave in his statement and his subsequent testimony as 11.30, before or about the time that the *Titanic* struck, instead of 11.56, after the *Titanic* struck,[2] if it be assumed that they inadvertently made this mistake then the sentence becomes clearer, because Gill did say that the large steamer was going at full speed in his original affidavit. And the Committee chose to take this version rather than his later denial during examination, though it is quite impossible for anyone to gauge the speed of a ship between 5 and 10 miles away without taking compass bearings.

The Report continued, "There is no evidence that any rockets were fired by any vessel between the *Californian* and the *Titanic*—although every eye on the *Titanic* was searching the horizon for possible assistance." Agreed there was no direct evidence because only three men from the *Californian* were called, but as we have seen even their evidence suggests two ships, one which Gill saw, and which he couldn't see half an hour later when rockets were coming from the same direction, and one which was throwing up rockets or flares while in sight and within morsing distance.

Finally, from the few crumbs of positive evidence available, from fabricated evidence, from hearsay, and with the help of their own loose thinking, "The Committee is forced to the *inevitable* conclusion (author's italics) that the *Californian* . . . was nearer the *Titanic* than the nineteen miles reported by her captain, and that her officers and crew saw the distress signals of the *Titanic* and failed to respond to them....."

***

Despite these apparently authorative pronouncements and the dogmatic way they were made, it is not necessary to probe far below the surface to realise that whoever or whatever the strange ship was, she could not, on the evidence heard before the Committee have been the *Californian*. This is clear from whichever angle the evidence is viewed—from the *Titanic* or from the *Californian*.

So far as the *Titanic* is concerned the first stumbling block in any assessment of the testimony of her various crew members is that no

---

2 Taking Lord Mersey's finding about the time of the accident.

attempt was made to establish her heading at any time after she struck, or what was done with the wheel. She must have carried her way for some distance after the collision even without the engines moving—and there is evidence that the engines were going ahead after the emergency full astern; had the wheel been held at hard a-starboard she would have described a complete circle—and perhaps hit the iceberg again! It is impossible to believe that this would have been allowed to happen. But no one asked the quartermaster, Hitchins, what he had done with the wheel after the hard a-starboard emergency helm.

The point was touched upon in a most interesting exchange between Senator Burton and Rowe, the quartermaster who had been stationed right aft when the berg came rushing past very close without touching the hull.

The Senator had been sceptical about the rudder being hard over.

"Do you not think that if the helm had been hard a-starboard the stem would have been up against the berg?"

"It stands to reason it would, sir, if the helm were hard a-starboard."

When the rudder of a ship is put over the vessel continues her forward course and begins to pivot about a point roughly on the centre line and about one-third of the ship's length from the stem. This position naturally varies with the size of rudder and the shape of the underwater form but for practical purposes it is generally taken as one-third. This means that the stern swings twice as much as the bow while the ship continues plunging forwards. In the case of the *Titanic* the effect of the ice right forward would also tend to push the bows off to port—if it had any effect at all besides a cutting one—and thus enhance the stem's swing. The ice gashed the ship from almost the extreme starboard bow to about *one-third* of the length from forward—in other words all of that part of the ship before the centre of turn on the starboard side. If she had indeed been swinging hard over it is impossible to imagine how the stern could have escaped dealing the berg a most terrible thump as the ice passed the pivoting point.

There are only two things which might have happened to prevent this without the rudder being moved: the actual cutting part of the berg was a spur below the waterline and this may have been broken off to a considerable extent by the first 300 feet of the hull and allowed the stern to escape.

Against this is the fact that the upper part of the berg also struck the ship (actually *vice versa* of course) and deposited ice on the fore-deck. The spur could not therefore have protruded very much, and its breaking off would probably not have allowed the 500 odd feet of the stern two-thirds of the ship to swing clear. The other possibility is that the sheer force of the blow which the *Titanic* struck moved the berg bodily out of the way. To what extent this would happen would depend on the size of the berg, and this was not established.

It is hard to believe that an officer with Murdoch's speed of reaction would not quickly have reversed the helm order directly the bow struck, knowing that the stern would swing into it. There is plenty of evidence that he intended to port around the berg. Surely he must have done so. But no witness mentioned the fact, and no witness was asked.

The trend during the Senate Inquiry was to assume that the *Titanic* was heading more or less on her previous course as she foundered. Senator Fletcher said to Crawford, "If the *Titanic* was moving west you moved south-west," when he tried to get from him the direction of the light which had been seen on the port bow. Boxhall said that when the steamer he was watching turned and showed her stem light she was heading westerly, and no comment was made on that.

Yet if Captain Knapp's chart is to be accepted as the basis of the "scientific proof" of the *Californian's* position, as Senator Smith had it in his closing address, the *Titanic* must have been heading about northeast to bring the *Californian's* lights on to her port bow. Had she been heading westerly those lights must have been very broad on the starboard beam.

And if that reasoning was too involved for Captain Knapp there were other very simple points that conclusively torpedoed his "hypothetical position". The *Californian* was stopped. There was no evidence to suggest anything else. Even Ernest Gill, the star "witness for the prosecution", said that her engines had not been moving after 10.30 that night, and he had been on watch in the engine-room. Yet neither the lookouts on the *Titanic*, nor the quartermaster on the poop of the liner, nor, so far as we know, any of the officers of the watch saw her at any time during their watch—in fact when Gill was seeing what he took at first to be a large German. Rowe was quite definite he saw no lights in his watch; Fleet, the lookout, was equally certain. He repeated it again and again.

All six lookout men were saved, and if it was felt necessary to fix the blame on some ship, the other three men, Lee who was on watch with Fleet, and the two who relieved them in the crow's-nest after the collision, could have been called and asked questions to try and fix the time of sighting the mystery ship more accurately.

While still aboard the *Titanic,* what about the nature of the light or lights on the bow? Leaving the passengers out as being untrained observers—although Colonel Gracie, a military man, should have known what he was talking about when he described one single white light—and taking only the evidence from members of the crew, the following statistics emerge: three men saw the two white masthead lights of a steamer; one of them, Boxhall, saw both green and red sidelights; of the other two men, one, Buley, was an Able Seaman and the other was a First Class steward. Then there were seven men, an officer and six sailors, who were either quite sure they only saw one light, or wondered if it was a light at all. Of these, Quartermaster Hitchins and Able Seamen Fleet and Moore thought the light was a cod banker and Quartermasters Rowe and Bright and Able Seaman Osman thought it was a sailer of some description. Seven against three. The strongest evidence for the existence of two mast headlights is Boxhall, who is an officer. Yet Rowe, who was firing rockets with him and helping him to morse the vessel, is quite positive there was only one light. He is an ex-Royal Navy man, a quartermaster and experienced sailor, and while Boxhall is seeing with the *naked eye* the red sidelight of this vessel ahead, Rowe can only see *one* white light—not the two that Boxhall is seeing. This is not impossible, but is certainly strange, for it is difficult to believe that Boxhall, having seen these sidelights would not have communicated it to someone—probably in some excitement. Yet no one else, not even the man he was working with, remembered this at the Inquiry. And with this must be put Able Seaman Osman's evidence that the officer in charge of his boat, Boxhall, did not seem to know whether this light ahead was a ship or not. Surely not the attitude of a man who has just seen a ship steam towards him within 5 miles and then turn away in the face of all his rockets and morsing. And Boxhall, who had been watching this was in charge of one of the few boats which did not try and pull for the light, although he said that the vessel did not do much steaming after she turned around.

The preponderance of evidence, then, is that the mystery ship was a sailer, and from some of the descriptions from experienced seamen it could have been so far away it was barely visible even though it was a beautiful night. Here is Quartermaster Hitchins: "I pulled for that light, this imaginary light. We were pulling for it all the time." "You pulled for this imaginary light?"

"Yes, sir."

And Quartermaster Bright: "It looked to me like a sailing ship—like a fishing boat. There was no lights to be seen about the hull of the ship, if it was a ship. We pulled towards that for a time."

We do not know when the light was first sighted. It was not while Fleet was in the crow's-nest, but we cannot be certain what time he was relieved. He should have been relieved at 12.23 as the clocks were going back forty-seven minutes, but he thought it was only about a quarter of an hour after the collision that his mates came up to the crow's-nest. Hitchins was not relieved at the wheel until twenty-three minutes past, and Rowe was still on the poop at twenty-five minutes past. Were the lookouts relieved at midnight? Rowe saw the light soon after he reached the bridge with the detonators, which must have been about 12.27 to 12.30. Hitchins didn't mention anything about hearing of a light while he was still at the wheel—but he wasn't asked. All we can say is that the light was probably first seen between midnight and 12.30 with the strong probability that it was about 12.20.

But assuming now that the six sailormen who thought this light belonged to a cod banker were wrong and Boxhall *did* see two masthead lights and two sidelights, here is his description: "I do not think she was doing much steaming. I do not think the ship was steaming very much, because after I first saw the masthead lights she must have been still steaming, but by the time I saw her red light with my naked eye she was not steaming very much. She had probably gotten into the ice and turned around."

That description seems more appropriate to Captain Moore's movements with the *Mount Temple* than the *Californian's* if she was stopped.

On Captain Moore's evidence of times and distances it could not have been the *Mount Temple*, but it is at least as likely as the *Californian* theory because Moore admits he was moving that night. A light cannot suddenly appear if the ship showing it and the ship it is viewed from are both stopped—certainly not on such a beautiful night as this.

Had the *Californian*, or indeed any ship been in sight after the collision and *before the first boat was lowered* there is little doubt that Captain Smith would have steamed towards it once he knew the extent of the damage to his own ship. His after boiler-rooms were in perfect working order, his engineers were working down below, his ship had only a fractional dip by the head and was still capable of moving at 20 knots or so. Had the *Californian* been in sight even as far as 10 miles away he could have been alongside her in half an hour. By accusing Lord of gross indifference the Senate also accused Smith of imbecility. Only an imbecile would lower boats and order them to row towards a light if he could steam towards it himself at six, ten times the speed. The only explanation is that there was no light visible until at least one boat—and probably more—were in the water. This is borne out by Rowe's evidence that he telephoned to the bridge at 12.25 to report that there was a boat in the water on the starboard side.

If there was no light visible until considerably after she struck, the light could not conceivably on the evidence have belonged to the *Californian*.

Now the same absolute doubt applies to the evidence from the *Californian*. Gill saw a large steamer just before midnight with rows of lights. Half an hour later she was not there but there was a rocket, and then another rocket from where she had been. At this time the *Titanic* had barely begun to sink by the head so if the large steamer which Gill thought he saw was the *Titanic* she must have moved a considerable distance between 11.56 and 12.30 or thereabouts to have put all her rows of lights, which Gill had seen, below the line of the horizon—not even leaving her steaming lights above. We do not know how far she moved after striking the berg or if indeed she moved an appreciable distance at all, but we can be quite certain that she did not steam *away from the Californians* lights, which she must have been able to see if the *Californian* could see hers. Of course no light was in fact visible at 11.56 from the *Titanic and there is not one person's evidence to suggest that there was.*

This argument only needs to be taken one step further to reveal the real lunacy behind the Senators' accusation. Assume that Gill *did* see the *Titanic* at 11.56—the Senators assumed it; assume that the white light fine on the bow which was seen from the *Titanic was* the *Californian* at approximately the same time—the Senators assumed it. Half an hour later Gill saw the rockets and no liner. But the *Californian* lay stopped in the water. Ergo, the *Titanic* steamed away from her stern first!

The evidence from the other two *Californian* witnesses suggests, in fact demands, that there was a vessel in sight when Gill claimed to have seen the rockets. Captain Lord said that his Second Officer kept telling him about her, that she had been about 4 miles away when he left the bridge at about 1.10, that she had been stopped, and that she was in his opinion, a tramp steamer. The Second Officer had subsequently reported rockets *from her* as she moved off towards the south-west. He had been morsing her almost continuously and received no reply. The hearsay evidence from the wireless operator confirms this: "I remember the apprentice told me that he had got the morse lamp out and called up on that, sir. But he did not get any reply on that."

"He started to call up the *Titanic*?"

"I do not know whether it was the *Titanic*."

"But the vessel from which the rockets were being fired—he tried to call her up with his morse signals?"

"Yes, sir."

Now here is Gill being questioned: "Did you see any lights on the steamer where the rockets were sent up?"

"No, sir—no sign of the steamer at the time."

Were two steamers sending up rockets that night then—one about 4 or 5 miles from the *Californian,* stationary for a time, that the Second Officer and apprentice were trying to signal by morse? And another which had been a large liner and which had popped down below the horizon before sending up her rockets? Or was Captain Lord's evidence a tissue of lies, and Evans' reported conversation with the apprentice incorrect? Or was Gill's evidence a tissue of lies? They cannot all be correct unless there were two ships sending up rockets because the Second Officer saw the rockets from his ship *after* Gill, according to Captain Lord's evidence.

It is worth noting now what Senator Smith was at pains to point out: none of the anxious searchers from the *Titanic* saw any other vessel firing rockets that night until the *Carpathia* came up.

It is also worth noting that Gill remarked to Evans, the wireless operator, that he was going to make $500 from his story.

Temporarily discarding Gill's account then—although neither Captain Knapp nor the Senators did so—and concentrating on the apparently far more damning evidence from the mouth of Captain Lord himself it appears that the vessel had been only 4 or 5 miles away, and had sent up rockets, whereupon the Second Officer had called him and he had done nothing apart from ordering the man to call her up by morse light. Stated baldly it looks bad.

The first thing to remember though is that from 5 miles away on a night like April 14th the *Titanic* broadside (and she must have been broadside at some stage while getting to Captain Knapp's position) would have been absolutely unmistakable. The *Titanic* would almost certainly have been unmistakable as a large passenger liner at *10* miles broadside. It is inconceivable that if that ship had been the *Titanic* with all her lights blazing there would have been the slightest doubt who she was on the part of *anyone* on board the *Californian*—and least of all from the wireless operator, Evans, who knew she was in the vicinity. According to Lord's evidence he had met the wireless operator out on deck while the stranger was still approaching them, had asked him what he knew and had got the reply, "Only the *Titanic*." He had said, "That is not the *Titanic*." If that vessel had been a passenger liner Evans would surely have said so in the witness stand.

Then there are the rockets. The detonators for distress rockets make a fearful noise. The people in the lifeboats from the *Titanic* had heard the *Carpathia*'s rockets like cannon from over the horizon *before* they saw the vessel herself. Is there any doubt that even the watch below on the *Californian* would have been wakened by distress signals with detonators from a ship *within morsing distance* on a perfectly clear, still night when the engines on their own ship were not moving? And the officer on watch could not have failed both to see and hear them. However, the officer of the watch was not called. Captain Lord was censured from the evidence of his donkeyman, or from the hearsay evidence of Evans, the wireless operator, about what the *apprentice*—not any of the officers, but the *apprentice*—had said to him, and of what was apparently the general talk in the ship. The crystal clarity and complete frankness of Lord's own evidence—during which he had been asked no embarrassing questions about navigation or distress rockets from the *Titanic*—must have been discounted.

As to what these signals from the ship near the *Californian* may have been, it was established practice in the North Atlantic for ships to carry their own recognition flares, or roman candles. Lord would have been quite justified in assuming that this is what these rockets were when his Second Officer reported them. He had ordered the Second Officer to call her up by morse after it had been reported that the steamer was *moving away*. A steamer in distress does not move away from the ship it is trying to contact. The morse lamp had been ticking as he went to sleep. At no time had he seen these rockets. He had trusted his officer of the watch to know whether the flares were in fact signals of distress. And if a commander cannot trust his senior officers he must lead an impossible life.

Why didn't he call out his wireless operator then while this vessel steamed away exhibiting some form of noiseless flare? To start with he had no reason to suppose she was in distress, and secondly he had previously asked his operator what ships he had—and had been told 'Only the *Titanic*'. In those days by no means all ships had wireless, and obviously the vessel he had seen approaching, and which was then steaming away, didn't have wireless or Evans would have known about her. Equally obviously she was not the *Titanic*—she was in his estimation a medium-sized tramp.

So far as Captain Lord's own evidence is concerned, then, he did all that the ordinary practice of seamen would recommend. He warned his Second Officer about a near-by steamer, told him to see that she did not come too close, and on later being told that she was steaming away firing rockets he had instructed him to morse her and let him know directly her name had been ascertained.

So the evidence from the *Californian* is in no sense as damning as it must have appeared at first sight. When examined in detail Captain Lord's actions cannot be faulted. That he had no extra-sensory perception must be regretted, and was surely regretted by him, but was hardly sufficient to justify the harsh words used in the Senator's report.

Now take the *Mount Temple*: to start with she had nearly run into the starboard side of a schooner on a direct line of bearing from the *Titanic's* reported position, and coming away from that position. According to Captain Moore he was doing 11½ knots plus about half a knot's help from the Gulf Stream—12 knots. He sighted the schooner just after three o'clock when he had been travelling roughly two and a half hours, and that placed him some 20 miles from the *Titanic's* position, and the schooner 18 or 19. However, the *Mount Temple's* speed according to Lloyd's Register was 12½ not 11½. The *Carpathia's* speed at Lloyd's had been 15 knots and she had done 16½—the *Californian's* 13 and she had done 13 or 13½ the following morning. Imagine the *Mount Temple* then, the firemen breathing fire and rum, making 13½ knots—or one knot above Lloyd's—and with the half knot set cracking along at 14. This would put her 15 miles from the *Titanic's* wirelessed position and the schooner 13 or 14, travelling "at a couple of knots" away from the *Titanic*. That would put the schooner 10 miles from the *Titanic* at about one o'clock. Give her 1 knot more and she is only 8 miles away at one o'clock. At about that distance she might well seem to be an imaginary light even on a clear, dark night.

Remember, Captain Moore actually thought the schooner was "perhaps 12½ to 13 miles" from the *Titanic* position. Now, if you give the schooner an auxiliary motor you can easily put him within 5 miles of the *Titanic's* position at one o'clock, and by giving him the motor you also give him a white masthead light while he is using it, under the International Regulations. Is this less likely than the *Californian* theory? On the evidence it is not impossible, whereas the latter is.

Take the navigational evidence from the *Californian*: this was completely disregarded for no stated reason, presumably because Gill and the rest of the crew had been talking about the rockets and the number of times during the night that the Captain had been called. One passenger whom the Committee knew about had reported the same thing from the *Mount Temple*. Why not equally disregard the navigational evidence from the *Mount Temple*? And once this evidence from Captain Moore is questioned you can place that schooner coming away from the *Titanic*'s position literally at any distance from the *Titanic* at any time you like and you can then move her away at 1½ to 2 knots and make her disappear just before dawn, leaving the *Mount Temple* hunting around on the opposite side of the ice pack to the wreckage. If you are going to disregard the log book positions of the ships in the vicinity, why only disregard the *Californian*'s?

And what about the tramp steamer some miles ahead of the *Mount Temple* all night, which also turned back on reaching the ice pack? Place the *Mount Temple* to the East of Captain Moore's position and you can bring the tramp steamer up to the ice in much the fashion described by Boxhall. Of course it is difficult to know why the *Mount Temple* wasn't also seen if it was either the tramp or the schooner which was seen from the *Titanic,* but then we don't know how far ahead of her the tramp was, or how far she steamed after seeing the schooner, by which time she was in amongst the ice.

So anyone playing games with log-book positions as the Senators did can fit any theory they wish. Carrying this to its logical conclusion it can be said that the theory which the Senate Committee wished to fit was the *Californian* theory.

Now where did Captain Knapp come in?

***

The evidence from this Inquiry examined in the cold light of fifty years afterwards brings out only one undoubted fact about "the *Californian* incident": Captain Lord was "framed".

He was "framed" either consciously or subconsciously for one of three reasons. Either all the leading actors in the construction of the Report were natural idiots, or the edict had gone out that a scapegoat had to be found and they were doing the best they could to make it plausible, or the very magnitude and shock of the tragedy so unhinged them that they were incapable of examining the evidence with clear minds. Perhaps the last theory is most likely because exactly the same sort of mistakes were made by very eminent men and technically qualified men on the other side of the Atlantic at the British Court of Inquiry.

PART 3

THE BRITISH FORMAL
INVESTIGATION

CHAPTER ELEVEN

Meanwhile in England the initial traumatic shock occasioned by the loss gave way to the same speculation, rumours and scandals which had swept America, and the gossip was fed by the daily reports of the Senatorial investigation which appeared in the Press. There were other reminders too. The cable ship, *Mackay Bennett,* which had been out in the Adantic searching for bodies found 306 of them. When first sighted they had seemed like a great flock of gulls on the water, bobbing gently in the swell. They were all floating in an upright position as if treading water, most of them in a great cluster in amongst and surrounded by small debris, many with faces distorted by terror, so the reports went, clutching clothes or objects which they had grasped at in their agony—others with their legs or bodies mangled as if by an explosion. It was noticed that practically all the men's watches had stopped at 2.10 a.m. Other vessels recovered bodies in the normal course of their trading voyages. The White Star *Oceanic* found one of the collapsibles almost a month after the disaster still afloat and containing the bodies of three men—two members of the crew, and one passenger in evening dress, and with them a fur rug, a ring and a lady's comb. The Press reports had the ship's surgeon stating that they had died from hunger and had eaten cork before succumbing, but this was denied later. The three men had died of exposure. They were almost certainly the dead whom the Fifth Officer, Lowe, left in the collapsible when he transferred the rest of the passengers to his own boat at dawn.

There was unrest in the shipping lines. Lifeboats and rafts were hastily added to passenger ships which were sailing up to Board of Trade standards but short of capacity for all souls on board. And on the *Olympic* the firemen successfully stopped her voyage to New York by walking off on to a waiting tug while the liner's Captain, the redoubtable Herbert Haddock—friend of Admiral Lord Fisher, and later to perform sterling service in the war—ordered them to return, appealed to them and finally told them that they were taking a very serious step—mutiny—before he strode from the rails back towards his bridge.

There was, quite understandably, widespread and angry criticism of the Board of Trade. Many practical seamen and seamen's associations could say with truth that they had been agitating for a more rational life-saving policy for passenger liners for years. The Imperial Merchant Service Guild said "The *Titanic* disaster is an example on a colossal scale of the pernicious and supine system of the officials as represented by the Board of Trade." Not that the *Titanic* was the only disaster for which they were under fire. The P & O liner *Oceana* had just previously been sunk in collision in the Channel, and one of the lifeboats had overturned while being lowered and occasioned a small loss of Life among the passengers. The Board were on the defensive about this too, both for their allegedly casual inspection only a day previously of the lifeboats and lowering gear, and for their acceptance of a large proportion of native seamen on British vessels. However ill-informed this latter criticism, it was taken extremely seriously at the time.

Much more remarkable than the seamen's complaints was an article written by the editor of *John Bull* which described an almost prophetic passage in his December 24th issue. "Just then the *Pericles*, belonging to the Aberdeen White Star line, had gone down in a calm sea and fair weather. Fortunately she possessed sufficient lifeboat accommodation to take off every soul on board, 'but,' said we, 'supposing the *Olympic* (or the *Titanic*) with 16 boats only, had been in the same position, and had had 3,400 souls on board? Loaded to the water's edge, these boats could only have taken off less than a thousand passengers; *2,400 souls must have gone to the bottom of the Ocean.*' But for the fact that the *Olympic* sailed a few days before the *Titanic* there would undoubtedly have been the full complement on board the ill-fated vessel, in which case our figures would have been literally justified."

This was the hostile atmosphere in which the Board of Trade found itself when the Formal Investigation was ordered into the loss of the liner. It began in London on Thursday, May 2nd, 1912—long before the Senatorial Inquiry published its findings, long before it had finished taking evidence even—under the presidency of the Rt. Hon. Lord Mersey of Toxteth, Q.C., a Wreck Commissioner of the United Kingdom. Sitting with him were five skilled and practical assessors, and the Court thus composed was, on the face of it, and in marked contrast to the United States Committee, quite competent to deal with all the questions before it. It is worth noting here that all the questions on this May 2nd and for many weeks afterwards concerned the *Titanic,* her navigation and her loss. None of them touched the *Californian* or any other vessel in any way.

The Scottish Drill Hall, Westminster, was taken over for the Inquiry. Rows of seats faced the dais on which Lord Mersey sat, flanked on either side by his assessors; almost overshadowing them along the left wall a great chart of the North Atlantic showed shipping routes and ice locations and next to it, immediately behind the witness table on the right of the dais, an enormous picture of the liner herself provided a dramatic backdrop for the men who had sailed her as they came up one by one to tell their stories. The front rows before the dais were filled with counsel, the big names of the day, and for the Board of Trade itself the two principal law officers of the Crown, the Attorney-General, Sir Rufus Isaacs, who before his appointment had been receiving the highest fees ever paid to an advocate, and the Solicitor-General, Sir John Simon.

To assist Lord Mersey with the technical considerations were Rear Admiral the Hon. Somerset Gough-Calthorpe, C.V.O., R.N., Captain A. W. Clarke, an Elder Brother of Trinity House, Commander F. C. A. Lyon, R.N.R., Professor J. H. Biles, LL.D., D.Sc., and Mr. E. C. Chaston, senior engineer assessor to the Board of Trade. It was a formidable bench.

The Admiral was only forty-two years old and had risen from lieutenant in 1886 to commander in 1896 to captain in 1902. Between 1902 and 1905 he had been Naval Attache to Russia, Norway and Sweden, and from 1909 to 1910 had been Captain of the Fleet in the Home Fleet.

Captain Clarke had been retired from sea life for some years, but was credited with having kept himself closely in touch with everything in connection with the modem merchant marine in his capacity as one of the Elder Brethren.

Commander Lyon had been in command in the P & O company, and was a well-known nautical assessor, who had served previously on many wreck inquiries.

Professor Biles was the senior professor of naval architecture in the country. He had served his apprenticeship in Portsmouth dockyard and had been selected from there to study at the Royal School of Naval Architecture, South Kensington. He had afterwards joined the naval construction department at the Admiralty and from there moved to G and J. Thompson, Clydebank. He had been involved in the design of the liners *City of New York* and *City of Paris,* was a frequent contributor to the Journal of the Institute of Naval Architects, sat on many boards and committees and had written a book on marine steam turbines.

Mr Chaston had been to sea at the age of twenty-one as an engineer on the Glasgow to New York run, and had subsequently been a chief engineer in the Prince Line, and then head engineer superintendent of the Venus Steam Shipping Company, which ran a fleet of some fifteen steamers. He had a senior engineer's commission in the Naval Reserve and was a senior engineer assessor on the Admiralty list for appointment to the Board of Trade inquiries.

These were all practical men. Three were experienced sailors, one a marine engineer who had served afloat, and one a top flight naval architect. Between them they could answer any practical questions on design, navigation and engines that might come up. Examined in greater detail, though, the sailors were certainly not picked for their knowledge of up-to-date conditions in the Atlantic passenger trade. The Admiral was a Royal Navy man, Captain Clarke had been retired for some years, and Captain Lyon had also been ashore for some years, and as a P & O officer was extremely unlikely ever to have sailed regularly across the North Atlantic.

Just as these maritime qualifications, although certainly adequate, were not the best possible, so the President's official title—Wreck Commissioner of the United Kingdom—was misleading. Lord Mersey knew little about practical sailoring. True he had been one-time President of the Probate Divorce and Admiralty Division, but this had only lasted for a year before he had retired on account of ill health. Since that time, two years before the *Titanic* Inquiry, he had been principally concerned in diminishing the difficulties of suitors in divorce cases—this although his biographer states that during his time as President of Probate, Divorce and Admiralty, he had not found the divorce work congenial—and also in seeking to protect newspaper proprietors from irresponsible people who brought libel actions against them. He believed British juries fickle, and reasoned that any gambler, banking on this fickleness, could bring an action against a newspaper—to prevent which he canvassed that security of costs should be guaranteed by the plaintiff in such an action.

These were his interests in the time immediately preceding the loss of the *Titanic*. His previous experience had been equally unconnected with practical seafaring.

He was born in 1840, the second son of a wealthy Liverpool merchant named Bigham, and after schooling at the Liverpool Institute, then London University, he continued his further education at the Sorbonne and in Berlin. He was called to the Bar at the age of twenty- nine by the Middle Temple and joined the Northern Circuit, where his learning, industry and tremendous confidence brought him a large share of commercial business. Besides his success on the Circuit he had a private income, and in 1883 he took silk.[1] Now, he had an intimate knowledge of business from his family background and his time as a junior, and in combination with a nimble mind and great powers of lucid expression this—despite an unimpressive physical appearance and a somewhat weak speaking voice—soon brought him pre-eminence.

Two years after taking silk he stood as Liberal candidate for the Toxteth Division of Liverpool, but was defeated; he was defeated again seven years later when he stood for the Exchange Division, but succeeded at his third attempt, in 1895, as Liberal Unionist candidate. However, his interest in political questions was not great and he made no real impression in the Commons. In 1897 he was knighted and raised to the Bench, being placed upon the rota of judges in charge of the commercial list. Twelve years later, at the age of sixty-eight, came his appointment as president of the Probate, Divorce and Admiralty Division—and we can assume his first detailed contact with naval matters—which lasted until his retirement the following year.

---

1 Was appointed a councilor by the Lord Chancellor.

This briefly was the rise of John Charles Bigham, now Baron Mersey of Toxteth in the County of Lancaster. "He was a pleasant companion," wrote his biographer, "and enjoyed all the social entertainments, both as host and guest. As a judge, he showed the ability that was expected of him, though he was inclined to the failings of those whose minds work quickly. Disliking tedious arguments, and full of robust common sense, he often took a short cut or forced the parties into a settlement."[2]

He had a reputation for jokes on the Bench, and, to paraphrase his biographer, took a delight in cutting through a mass of detailed evidence right into the heart of the matter. "He often took a short cut. . .

The great weight of the evidence in the *Titanic* case was proportionate to the size of the vessel herself, and the time taken to hear it must have been galling indeed to a man of Mersey's temperament. And it is a sad fact that in too many respects the Formal Investigation under his presidency was conducted with a lack of the thoroughness which was due in such an important Inquiry. To take an instance unconnected with the *Californian*, the Court was able to report at the end of their mammoth sitting, ". . . there appears to be no truth in these suggestions [that the Third Class, or steerage, passengers had been kept below while the First and Second Class entered the boats]" without hearing a single Third Class passenger, or indeed one Second Class passenger. The only passengers heard throughout the entire Inquiry were three First Class passengers whose conduct in entering the boats, or in preventing their own lifeboat from returning to the scene after the liner went down, were in question. By today's standards, and in view of the questions before the Court, this is almost incredible.

The points which concern us are that the navigational evidence about where the *Titanic* actually foundered was never thoroughly probed despite evidence heard against the official view from two of the ships in the area, and despite a report from the Russian liner *Birma* which occupied a whole page of the *Daily Telegraph* while the Court was sitting, and which also questioned the official position; equally lamentable, the correct time which the *Titanic* was keeping was never probed. The *Californian* was convicted of having been the ship in sight of the *Titanic* on a series of

---

2 *Dictionary of National Biography.*

coincidences which depend entirely on the time they happened, and yet no conclusion was reached as to how far ahead of New York the *Titanic's* clocks were set.

At the end of all the evidence we have this extraordinary exchange between Mersey and the Attorney-General, Sir Rufus Isaacs, who was presenting the case for the Board of Trade.

Isaacs: ". . . It is said for example that this white rocket, this distress signal, was not seen till a quarter past one. It is very difficult to explain that in view of the evidence of the *Titanic* which is that they were sending up these rockets from 12.45. I should have thought upon this evidence and the evidence which follows it that the estimate of time must be quite wrong."

Mersey: "There might be some difference in the clocks of the two vessels."

"Yes, certainly there might be."

"That might partly account for it."

"Yes, it might. . ."

This in the *final* address! Any difference in time there *might* have been would undoubtedly have acted the *other way*, though, for *Titanic* time must have been *later* than *Californian* time.

It is worth looking briefly now at Sir Rufus Isaacs, for he was instrumental in confirming Mersey in his early belief that Lord was guilty, and later, in his closing address on behalf of the Board of Trade, in swaying Mersey's judgement about the legal position of the Court in relation to Captain Lord, and by skilful advocacy, which in this instance was also sophistry, again confirming Mersey in his judgement on Lord as a man who had plainly heard of the rockets from the *Titanic* during the night and equally plainly not gone to the rescue. Unfortunately this is not all. He went far beyond the bounds of advocacy or decency or truth in accusing Lord, by innuendo and inference of being drunk and in a stupor on the night in question. In fact Lord made it a habit never to touch any liquor at sea.

Like Mersey, Rufus Isaacs was born the second son of a wealthy tradesman. He grew up in a large, devoted Jewish family, the members of which were all gifted and enterprising, and he shone in their company.

"Rufus . . . was one of those singular personalities of which there are only a few in each generation, who seem to be born at double strength. He had, in addition to a brilliant brain, unusual physical strength, vast energy and . . . an exceptional memory. . . "[3] When young he and his brothers were so wild and ungovernable that the headmaster of the school which two of them attended refused to keep both—"either Rufus or Harry," he said, "but in no circumstances, both." Later, Rufus' headmaster suggested to his parents that he ought to stay at school until of university age, and then study for the Bar. His father thought otherwise and put him to the family business, but it was not a success and after a while it was decided he should go to sea. He was due to be indentured as an apprentice, but gave early evidence of his independence and strength of mind by refusing to sign the indenture once he learned that it would bind him for four years. Instead he sailed as ship's boy. After seven weeks at sea he had had enough and "jumped ship" in Rio de Janeiro, where he stayed, penniless for a while until he was caught and returned to the vessel. On the return voyage, still only fifteen years old, he fought and laid out the Bosun who had been bullying him. Returned to London, he paid off finally and started a second time in the family business.

This was no more successful than his first attempt, for the routine of an office, although broken by trips abroad for the firm, did not suit his temperament. So he tried stockbroking, and for a while was both successful and happy, leading a gay, even wild life, confident that at last he had found his niche. Alas, a slump struck the markets and in his inexperience he was left with debts he could not meet. He left the Stock Exchange owing about -£8,000, which he intended to repay. To his credit he eventually did so with interest.

At last, at the age of twenty-four, his headmaster's original advice was taken, mainly due to the determination of his mother, and he began reading for the law. At this point a change seems to have come over the young Rufus. From a wild youth addicted to theatres, expensive clothes, girls, and amateur boxing, he schooled himself into a quiet, studious young man, and his profession became his life. He married early even though he was still studying, and after being called to the Bar by the Middle Temple

---

3 *The Marconi Scandal,* by Frances Donaldson.

developed a successful practice at which he worked for a number of years so hard and for such long hours that his health gave out. He was told by his doctor that he could not keep the pressure up any longer, and consequently thought about taking silk as one way of easing the work. It is interesting to note that, although he had misgivings about the step on account of his relatively short time of call, a mere ten years, he was finally persuaded by the encouragement of the then Mr Justice Bigham, who also wrote on his behalf to the Lord Chancellor, begging him to "save Rufus Isaacs' life" by including him in the next list of silks. The Lord Chancellor was pleased to do so, and in 1898 Isaacs became the youngest silk in terms of length of call ever created—a record, however, which was soon broken by John Simon.

Rufus Isaacs, whatever his reasons for taking silk, was not a man to give up his régime of hard work. He had a burning ambition and the attributes of diligence and memory which had served him so well as a junior, together with his good looks and personality quickly set him on the way to success. Within a very few years he was one of the leading advocates of the day, his name spoken in the same breath as Edward Carson, Lawson Walton, or Marshall Hall, his fees higher than any which had ever before been charged at the Bar. And he also found time to become interested in politics, eventually winning a seat in the House as the Liberal member for Reading.

The next step came in 1910, when Mr Justice Bigham, President of the Probate, Divorce and Admiralty Division, was elevated to the peerage. The Solicitor-General was appointed to succeed him, and in the natural order of things Rufus Isaacs, K.C., M.P., became Solicitor- General. That was two years before the *Titanic* disaster, almost to the month.

By 1912 Sir Rufus Isaacs, G.C.V.O., was Attorney-General, and during the course of the Inquiry, in June, he was appointed a member of the Cabinet in Asquith's government.

As he steps into the pages of this book he is an elegant and powerful figure with a fine presence and handsome features, an alert glance and a voice of such exceptional quality that it was compared favourably with that of many actors—a polished, quiet man, not addicted to the bullying, power advocacy which had been fashionable before his day, but none the less dangerous—scrupulously fair, but incisive and ruthless. His last trial had been the Seddon case, in which, leading for the Crown he had successfully shown Seddon up to the jury during examination as a man capable of the grasping depravity of which he was accused, had shown this with methods so scrupulously fair that they earned the praise of even the defending counsel. This makes his subsequent attack on Captain Stanley Lord even more remarkable than it might have appeared from a lesser man.

Sir Rufus was not addicted to speculation. His method at the Bar, similar to Mersey's, was to seize upon the striking points in his case, the points which were liable to sway the jury, to impress the judge, and to build on these, casting aside other considerations which would not have the same impact. It is easy to see how this eliminating process, carried to extremes, would indeed have damned Lord in his eyes, for the evidence in the *Titanic* case needs very careful study from all angles before it can be seen as conclusive circumstantial proof that Lord was innocent. If only the striking points are extracted we have the gist of Isaacs' incredibly one-sided closing address for the Board of Trade.

That is looking forward. At the time the Inquiry started Sir Rufus—successful, popular, the confidant of the Chancellor of the Exchequer, David Lloyd George, and other Cabinet Ministers—was about to begin the most agonising period of his life, a period during which he openly wondered whether all his ambitions were after all to end in ruins, his name to become a synonym for corruption in the highest places. The loss of the *Titanic* coincided within days with his purchase of shares in the American Marconi company; the first hints of scandal, the first lobby gossiping about ministers of the Crown speculating in the shares of a company in contractual relations with the government started and grew and then appeared in print during the course of the *Titanic* Inquiry while he led for the Board of Trade, and while in the process he appointed himself "counsel for the prosecution" of Captain Stanley Lord. Perhaps this is putting it too high; presumably he was instructed in this as well by the Board of Trade.

***

Before Lord or anyone from the *Californian* gave evidence Mersey, Isaacs and the Court had heard five accounts of the "mystery" light or lights seen by members of the crew of the *Titanic*. The first was from Hitchins, the quartermaster who had been at the wheel at the time of the collision.

"There was a light about two points on the port bow about 5 miles away I should judge."

"When had you first seen this light?"

"During the time I was standing in the lifeboat, taking the passengers into the lifeboat, my Lord."

This is an interesting answer, for we know from the U.S. Inquiry and Lord Mersey soon finds out, that Hitchins was relieved at the wheel at 12.23. Admittedly he could not see ahead from the wheelhouse, but it is likely he could hear what was going on, and extremely likely that when he was relieved he went out to his boat through the open bridge. So while it is not explicit in his statement that there was no one looking at the light from the bridge before he left, it is a very likely interpretation. If accepted it places the first sighting of the light some time after 12.23.

"When you looked and saw this light, could you tell what it was at all?"

"No, we surmised it to be a steamboat."

Hitchins' boat had been lowered and they rowed towards the light. "The light was moving, gradually disappearing. We did not seem to get any nearer to it. It seemed to get further away." He did not see any rockets from the vessel which carried it. Examined by Sir Rufus Isaacs, Hitchins agreed that in New York he had said that he had started for the light which he had expected to be a fishing schooner.

The next man to say anything about it was an A.B., William Lucas, who had got away in the last correctly launched boat, the collapsible, from the port side. He testified to seeing the red sidelight and one mast light of a vessel which he judged to be 8 or 9 miles off. His report of the light indicated that it was abaft the beam to port.

Next was Fleet's companion in the crow's-nest at the time of the collision, Reginald Robinson Lee, who had been lowered in boat number 13.

2564 Q. "When the steamer struck was there any light of any other vessel to be seen?" A. "No."

2565 Q. "And after leaving the steamer did you see the lights of any other steamer before the *Carpathia*?" A. "There was a ship apparently ahead of the *Titanic* as she was then, but the ship was supposed to have disappeared. Anyway we did not see her in the morning."

2566 Q. "But did you see the lights after you left the steamer?" A. "We saw a light, yes, but we did not know what it was. It might have been one of our own boats that was showing a light. I could not say that it was a steamer."

Pressed, all he could say about the light was that he had not seen it before he left the *Titanic* but he had seen it before the *Titanic* went down.

Following him was another A.B., John Poingdestre, who had got away in one of the port after boats, number 12.

"I saw an imaginary light which kept showing for about ten minutes."

Mersey saw an opportunity for some gentle humour. "How do you see an imaginary light?"

"Well, what we thought was a light. There is such a thing at sea as seeing imaginary lights."

"Oh, is there?"

"Yes."

Butler Aspinall for the Board of Trade continued the questioning. "When did you see this imaginary light? Was it while you were on the *Titanic* or after you had left the *Titanic*?"

"When I had left the *Titanic*."

But Mersey was irrepressible. "I do not understand it. Did you imagine that you saw a light?"

"Yes."

"Or did you see a light that you imagined? Which?"

"Well, one way or the other."

Aspinall went on, "Where was it that you saw what you call this imaginary light?"

"Off my port bow."

"Have you ever seen imaginary lights at sea before?"

"Yes."

"Are they frequent things?"

"Yes. I have been on the lookout on ships, on the foc's'le head, and reported a light, and it has been an imaginary light—as soon as you see it it has gone again." He went on to say that the one from the *Titanic* seemed low down, "a matter of 5 miles."

"Might it have been a star do you think?"

"Well, it might have been that."

"You saw no red sidelight did you?"

"No."

The next man who had seen it was James Johnson who had been night watchman on duty that night. He had been lowered in number 2 emergency boat—Boxhall's.

"Did you see the light from the deck of the *Titanic*?"

"I should think we saw it for about twenty minutes on the port bow."

Assuming (as the Court eventually did) that number 2 boat left at approximately 1.45, this indicated the time of first sighting as around 1.25.

"Was it nearly right ahead?"

"No, something like an angle."

"A right angle?"

"A left angle—from the port bow rather."

"Was somebody steering?"

"Sometimes there was a girl steering and sometimes an officer steering. He was telling her what to do and he was helping the foreigner at the other oar to pull. He was pulling a stroke oar."

"Did the officer direct you to steer to the light?"

"We took a star and got this star underneath us and kept it in front of us, and tried not to get away from it."

"What coloured light was it?"

"I think it was red. I think there were two lights in fact—a red and a white light."

"Are you sure?"

"I am certain."

***

Meanwhile the *Californian* had docked in Liverpool. Gill was not with the ship—he had been subpoenaed by the Senatorial Committee—but statements were taken by the Board of Trade from Captain Lord and his officers, two apprentices, an A.B. and some of the engine- room staff, as a result of which the Captain, Chief, Second and Third Officers, the apprentice, Gibson, and the wireless operator were required to attend the Court of Inquiry as witnesses.[4]

The first to be called, on May 14th, was Captain Lord. At this juncture, counsel, Robertson Dunlop, for the Leyland Line, rose and asked to be made a party to the proceedings on behalf of the *Californian* and her master. Sir Rufus Isaacs could not agree that this was proper and explained that although the evidence showed that the *Titanic* and the *Californian* were not far apart at the time of the disaster, it was very difficult to say that the evidence from the *Californian* had any bearing on the questions Mersey had to decide. Which was true. There were no questions before the Court which affected the *Californian* in any way. Dunlop's plea was rejected.

So when Lord was sworn he appeared, as he had at the Senatorial Inquiry, as a witness only; there were no charges against him; he was not a party to the proceedings. So far as he was concerned, and so far as anyone else should have been concerned, he was there to help the Court in their investigation into the circumstances surrounding the loss of the *Titanic*— not to defend himself. The Senate sub-committee was still sitting and he had no reason to suppose that they would indict him in any way. There was nothing to defend himself against—only irresponsible allegations in the Press.

The Court thought otherwise.

Not that this was immediately apparent. The examination started quietly enough—a repeat performance of the mild questioning in the United States. He was taken through a description of the ice report he had sent out on the evening of the 14th, and gently through his movements when he stopped his ship in 42° 5'N, 49° 9'W at 10.21 ship's time that evening. The field ice had stretched ahead to the North and South and he had been surrounded by small ice. The ship had swung under the action of the reversing propeller to head ENE by compass—approximately NE true. And then at about eleven o'clock he had seen a steamer's lights approach from the eastwards.

---

4 See page *204.*

From the eastwards. . . . Immediately the courtroom was electric.

"How did it bear?"

"I did not get the bearing of it. I was just watching casually from the deck."

"Where was it? On your quarter?"

"It was just on the starboard side . . . I just saw a white light to commence with. . . I went to his room (the wireless operator) and asked him what ships he had."

"What did he say?"

"Nothing. Only the *Titanic*."

6724 Q. "Did you think that the vessel approaching you was the *Titanic*?" A. "No, I remarked at the time that was not the *Titanic*."

6725 Q. "How could you tell that?" A. "You can never mistake those ships—by the blaze of light."

He had seen the green light afterwards and a few deck lights, getting closer all the time. At about eleven o'clock he had said to the wireless operator "Let the *Titanic* know we are stopped surrounded by ice." He had heard the next morning the operator had been told to keep out. He had seen the green light at about 11.30. The Third Officer (on watch) was trying to contact her with the morse light with no result. Lord estimated the steamer to be about the same size as themselves, and he thought she was about 5 miles away. He was up and down off the bridge until about twelve o'clock when the Second Officer relieved the Third. He told the Second to "watch that steamer", that she was stopped.

"She was stopped?"

"The other steamer was stopped."

"When did you notice the other steamer was stopped?"

"About half-past eleven."

(This was significant. The *Titanic* had struck at 11.40 and Lord had just admitted that the strange vessel which approached, as the *Titanic* must have done, from the eastwards, had stopped at *about* 11.30. Here was the first of the coincidences.)

Lord continued his story. There was ice running North and South and the *Californian* was stopped in loose ice which they had run into before being able to stop.

"There was ice between you and this vessel?"

"Yes."

The ship, whoever she was, was heading to the westward and bearing from his ship (he had heard it since) SSE by compass (SE true).

He had gone into his chartroom at 12.15, called the Second Officer up by speaking tube at 12.40 and asked him if the steamer was the same. The Second replied that he had called her up once but could get no reply from her. Lord told the Second he was going to he down in the chartroom.

At 1.15 the Second had whistled down to say the ship was altering her bearing towards the SW. He had seen a white rocket from her.

The Court stirred. Mersey held a consultation over his chart, then turned to Sir Rufus, "Is it right Mr Attorney that at this time the *Titanic* would be bearing to the SW of where the *Californian* was?"

Sir Rufus replied that it was.

"Is it also true, as this witness is telling us, that the vessel of which we do not know the name was also bearing SW?"

"I understand him to say so."

Mersey turned to Captain Lord. "Is that so? Did you hear him?"

"I did, my Lord. The steamer was heading SSE by compass till ten minutes to one."

"Yes, I know it was, but at the particular time we are talking about it was heading SW."

"Towards the SW," Lord corrected him.

"I do not know what that means. Does it mean not SW? What does towards SW mean? Does it mean SW or does it not?"

"It does not mean exactly SW—she was heading towards the SW," Lord explained.

Here Mersey seemed confused by the word "heading" which merely meant "moving towards". He took it to mean "bearing" which is vastly different. "Well, near enough," he went on without understanding. "Is it the fact—am I right in supposing that this vessel, the name of which you apparently do not know, from which a rocket appeared, was at the time that the rocket was sent up in the position in which probably the *Titanic* was?"

"No."

"How did this rocket bear to you?"

"I have never heard the exact bearing of it."

Further questioning revealed that the Second Officer told Lord the ship was heading between SSW and SW a distance of at least 5 miles, and going slowly between these bearings.

Mersey turned to the front benches. "This mysterious vessel would be between the *Californian* and the *Titanic,* and must have been well within sight of the *Titanic."*

Sir Rufus replied, "Yes."

"We have heard about the mysterious light that was seen, the imaginary light as it was called, that was seen from the *Titanic,* but dismissing that light was there any light or any vessel seen by any witness on the *Titanic* at this time?"

"There is some evidence of a light having been seen."

"I know. I say dismissing that imaginary light, is there any evidence of any ship having been seen at this time or about this time by the *Titanic*?"

"No, I do not think so."

"What is in my brain at the present time," Mersey continued, "is this—that what they saw was the *Titanic."*

Isaacs replied. "I know."

"That is in my brain and I want to see if I am right or not."

"It certainly must have been very close," the Attorney-General agreed.

The disease had crossed the Atlantic. Here again were two very eminent men talking nonsense. How could one ship have been seen by the others and not herself have seen the other—especially as Lord said 5 miles as the distance, and the *Titanic*'s lookout man Lee had already testified that no lights were visible while he was in the crow's- nest. Remember this was a perfect night, the most beautifully clear, dark night many witnesses had ever seen.

Afterwards Lord was questioned about the number of masthead lights he had seen on the ship approaching from eleven o'clock. He replied, "One."

"You only saw one?"

"The Third Officer said he saw two."

Lord said this. The *Titanic* would have shown two masthead lights, a small tramp probably only one. Lord himself told the Court that the Third Officer saw two lights. The only theories it is possible to hold about this statement are either that it was from a perfectly honest man with a clear conscience, or a highly intelligent man who knew that his Third Officer was going into the witness-box afterwards and was going to say he thought there were two lights.

Whichever way it was Sir Rufus jumped in. "Now that is important."

And Mersey followed. "That is very important because the *Titanic* would have two."

It is difficult to escape the conclusion even at this early stage that Lord Mersey's mind was made up. There is nothing which follows throughout the whole Inquiry to dispel it.

Sir Rufus went on, "Yes, that is it—two masthead lights." He turned to Lord. "You only saw one but the Third Officer said he saw two?"

"And the Second Officer said he saw one," Lord replied shortly. Sir Rufus was going to leave it but Mersey was not satisfied, and asked when it was that the Third Officer saw two lights, so Sir Rufus asked Lord, "I must put this to you. Do you remember about a quarter past eleven on that night his telling you that he had noticed a steamer—that is the Third Officer, Mr Groves?"

"No, I do not."

"A steamer about three points abaft the starboard beam—10 to 12 miles away?"

"No, I do not."

"Did he say to you that she was evidently a passenger steamer?" "No."

"And did you say to him 'the only passenger steamer near us is the *Titanic*'?"

"I might have said that with regard to the steamer, but he did not say the steamer was a passenger steamer."

There followed a most confused series of exchanges in which both Mersey and Isaacs tried to get Lord to admit that he *had* said in Court a few moments ago that the *Titanic* was the only passenger steamer near them. They may have been meaning his answer that he *might* have said that, or they might have confused it with a remark made to or by the wireless operator, but nowhere in the transcript is the remark evident, and at no time did Lord admit that he said it.

Finally Mersey remarked, "You do not give answers that please me at present. You said just now as plainly as possible that you answered the Third Officer, I think it was, and said, 'The only passenger steamer near us is the *Titanic*.' You now suggest that you do not remember whether you said that or not?"

"I do not recollect saying anything to him about it, my Lord."

"Could you have forgotten such a thing?"

"Well, I have heard so many stories about the *Titanic* since that I really do not know what I heard that night."[5]

This remark of Lord's may explain many of the things heard in both the British and American Inquiries.

After more examination of how he had first heard of the rockets which had been fired that night, the Attorney-General said, "My Lord, I think it very desirable that the other witnesses from the *Californian* should be out of Court while this witness is giving evidence."

"By all means," Mersey replied, after which the *Californian* officers were told to stand up, and they left the courtroom.

There followed for Lord a rigorous and searching examination about how many rockets the Second Officer had reported to him, or how many he had heard of that night and he repeated again and again that he knew of only one rocket until the Chief Officer called him in the morning at daybreak.

Questioned on why he had not taken any action when first hearing of the rocket he explained that he had been trying to get in touch with the steamer by morse since 11.30, that she was stopped and could not therefore be in danger from the ice, and he thought she might answer his morse. Of course she may not have been fitted with a lamp.

He then went to sleep. He did not receive any message from the apprentice, Gibson.

---

5 Compare this with Captain the Hon. Maurice Bourke's evidence when he was standing Court Martial after the disastrous collision and loss of H.M.S. *Victoria* in 1893. "It is very difficult to know what one's impressions were at the moment. One has thought about it so much and so much has been said since as to what might and ought to have happened, that at last I am in that position that I could not swear what my impressions really were."

"You do not expect at sea, where you were, to see a rocket unless it is a distress signal do you?"

"We sometimes get these company's signals which resemble rockets—they do not shoot as high and they do not explode."

This was the invariable practice on the North Atlantic before the *Titanic* disaster. It was proved by the disaster to have been a bad practice, but it was nevertheless the custom of ships to show their roman candles as recognition signals at night. These were generally coloured and they went off without the cannon-shot explosions of distress rockets. On a night like that of April 14th, 1912, from 5 miles distance there would have been no mistaking which was which.

When asked about the apprentice, Gibson, giving him the message about further rockets seen from the ship he admitted only to having heard the door open and bang shut, whereupon he had come out of his sleep and said, "What is it?" But the apprentice had gone.

This is the most difficult part of Lord's evidence to understand—indeed the most difficult part of the evidence from the *Californian*. It was too difficult for Mersey, Sir Rufus or the Board of Trade to swallow, and Lord's answers under rigorous examination despite his transparent and touching honesty, quite obviously didn't satisfy the Court—they actually deepened the suspicions the Court already held. Which is understandable. For Mersey was already convinced of Lord's guilt and the proposition Lord asked him to accept was not such as would appeal to the reason of an already sceptical landsman. It is doubtful, indeed, if anyone but a seaman can appreciate this part of the evidence. And we shall never know what Mersey's three, or actually four, seamen assessors advised him.

Jumping a few hours in time, then, this is his story as brought out in examination by Sir Rufus Isaacs:

"Did the boy (Gibson) deliver a message to you and did not you inquire whether they were all white rockets?"

"I do not know. I was asleep."

"Think. You know, it is a very important matter."

"He came to the door, I understand—I have inquired very closely of him since—and reported rockets, and I asked whether there were any colours in the lights."

Mersey was impatient to get to the bottom of it. "Well, is he telling the truth?"

"I do not doubt it for a moment."

"That means the boy *did* go to the chartroom—he *did* tell you about the rockets, and you asked whether they were white rockets, and told him to report if anything further occurred?"

"That is what he says."

"Did you say this in your sleep?" Mersey was incredulous.

"I was very likely half awake. I have no recollection of this apprentice saying these things at all."

Sir Rufus returned to the questioning. "Why did you ask whether they were white rockets?"

"Because company's signals usually have some colours in them."

"So that if they were really white they would not be company's signals?"

Lord's answer to this question is his only one during the Inquiry that smacks of fencing. "No, some companies have white signals." "Do try to do yourself justice, Captain. If you will allow me to say so, you are not doing yourself justice. Was not the point of your asking about the rockets in order to ascertain whether they were not distress signals?"

"I really do not know what the object of my question was."

One can imagine this answer confirming Mersey and the Court in their scepticism. And yet it is an absolutely logical and straightforward answer if taken with the rest of his evidence on the point. He was asleep. He did not recall saying anything; how, then, could he know what had been the object of any question he might have asked?

Sir Rufus passed on to the next impossible proposition which Lord wished the Court to believe. "Do you remember Mr Stone reporting at 2.40 through the tube that the steamer had disappeared bearing SW by ½ W?"

"I do not remember it. He has told me since."

"Is he a reliable man?"

"As far as I know he is."

"He says, 'the Captain again asked me if I was sure there were no colours in the lights that had been seen.' Do you remember that?"

"I do not."

"And that he [Mr. Stone] assured you that they were white lights?"

"He has told me about it since, but I have not the slightest recollection."

"You know he says, 'I assured him that they were white lights', and that you said, 'All right'?"

"I have no recollection of anything between 1.30 and 4.30."

That sentence was the pith of the Captain's story, and he stuck to it throughout—never deviating a fraction despite the most determined efforts to shake him by Sir Rufus Isaacs and Mersey.

Impossible to believe as this may be for the landsman or the man who, safely tucked up in his bed each night, has never wanted for sleep, it is not only possible, but highly probable to any sailor. A man who has never stood watch and watch or has never been in the habit of calling his relieving watch in the middle of the night, or calling the Captain after that poor man has already spent hours or even days on the bridge in heavy weather, fog, or proximity to ice, cannot be expected to appreciate Lord's story. But the sailor sleeps deeply because he always has plenty of leeway to make up; he often has to be called twice, three times before he is fully awake, often has to be literally shaken, often never wakes fully until he has dressed and gone outside into the cold night air. This is the background against which Lord's story has to be tested. Remember, he was asleep, fully clothed in a steam-heated room and he had been up and about the decks all the preceding day since seven in the morning, that he had not only been up, but constantly on the alert after the hours of darkness for ice. Remember too, that his ship was stopped and that his subconscious was not therefore alert to danger. The apprentice, Gibson, had, according to Lord who had questioned him closely, only come to the door; he had not come across and shaken him, or spoken close to. There is a vast gulf in station between the Captain of a ship and an apprentice. A liner Captain is a man on a pinnacle, clothed with awe before the sight of the junior officers—let alone the apprentice, who is the "lowest and greenest form of marine life". Unless there is urgency it is extremely unlikely that an apprentice will seize the Captain and shake him and make absolutely certain he is awake before delivering a message—and often this is the only way to rouse a deep sleeper. If Captain Lord's story of not remembering

Gibson's visit was true, it is a very significant pointer to the lack of urgency which the officer and the boy on the bridge read into the rockets which they saw.

As to both Gibson's and Stone's story that Lord questioned them about the rockets, this too is a well-known phenomena at sea. Men can be quite lucid, or they can ramble on unintelligibly when called without remembering anything of it afterwards—without even being awake, so that they have to be called again. Others, instead of talking, make movements with their limbs or even sit up and switch on the light while still asleep. There is nothing odd or in the least extraordinary about Lord's questions while asleep.

The next point touched upon in examination was Lord's conversation with the Chief Officer when the latter woke him at daybreak—just before 5 a.m.

"Well, I was conversing with him about the probability of pushing through the ice to commence with. I was undecided whether to go through it or turn round and go back, and we decided to go on, so I told him to put the engines on 'stand by'. He did so. Then he said, 'Will you go down to look at this steamer to the southward?' I asked him 'What is the matter with it?' He said, 'He might have lost his rudder,' but I said, 'Why? He has not got any signals up.' 'No, but,' he said, 'the Second Officer in his watch said she had fired several rockets.' I said, 'Go and call the wireless operator.' "

The steamer was of course the one showing two masthead lights when the Chief Officer relieved the Second Officer at four o'clock, and which later turned out to be a yellow funnel ship.

"The Chief Officer came back some time after . . . I suppose fifteen to twenty minutes."

"And what did he say?"

"He said, 'There is a ship sunk.' "

"Did he tell you what ship?"

"No. He went back to the wireless room straight away. . . . Some time after that he said, 'The *Titanic* has hit a berg and sunk.' I left the bridge and went to the wireless room myself."

"Were you quite comfortable in your mind when you heard the *Titanic* had sunk in reference to your own actions?"

"Well, I thought we ought to have seen her signals at 19 miles, that was the only thing that was worrying me."

"Does it not strike you now that that steamer that you saw sending up rockets must have been the *Titanic*?"

"No."

"Not now?"

"No, I am positive it was not the *Titanic*."

"Why are you positive it was not?"

"Because a ship like the *Titanic* at sea is an utter impossibility for anyone to mistake."

"That must depend upon the distance you are from her?"

' "Well, my distance—according to my estimate is 4 to 5 miles." "But might she not have been a good deal further off?"

"I do not think so. I do not think we would have seen her sidelights." Isaacs made the fatuous comment, especially from a man who had, however shortly, been to sea, "If she was 4 or 5 miles away her light must have been at a high elevation from you must it not, for you to see it?"

"A steamer something like ourselves, as I said before."

"I mean her sidelight must have been pretty high from the water if you could see it 4 to 5 miles distant?"

"The *Californian* is 40 feet above the water, and I said she was a steamer something like the *Californian*."

Having received the official message from the *Virginian* with the *Titanic*'s position given as 41° 46'N, 50° 14'W—PASSENGERS IN BOATS, SHIP SINKING—he at once started for that position. From 6 a.m. to 6.30 he had made anything between south and south-west, endeavouring to make S 16°W as near as possible through the field ice.

"Was that direction the one from which you had seen the rocket?"

"I did not see the rocket."

"Or from which you had heard the rocket had been seen?"

"I did not hear as to the bearing of the rocket then."

He thought he reached the position given by the *Titanic* at 7.30. He passed the *Mount Temple* there, stopped, and received a verbal message from his wireless operator (Evans) that the *Carpathia* was standing by the *Titanic*'s position, and to have boats ready and lifebelts. He did not see any wreckage where the *Mount Temple* was. Later he saw the *Carpathia*, steamed up to her, and saw several boats, deck-chairs, cushions and planks, two collapsible boats, no bodies and no lifebelts in the water. He searched around and left the wreckage in position 41° 33'N, 50° 1'W.

Thomas Scanlan, M.P., appearing for the National Sailors' and Firemen's Union of Great Britain and Northern Ireland, questioned Lord on his practice in ice. Lord replied that he had not much experience in ice, that on this occasion he had doubled the lookout, that in fact he himself had seen the ice first, and that it was not customary to reduce speed in the vicinity of ice in clear weather. While he was stopped he was displaying two mast lights and his coloured sidelights. He described the lifeboat and fire drills which he practised regularly once a passage.

He was asked by Sir Robert Finlay, K.C., M.P., for the White Star Line, to describe his course after seeing the *Mount Temple.*

"I steered as far as I recollect about South or south by east true from there along the edge of the ice—the western edge of the ice." He had arrived at the wreckage at 8.30. The Chief Engineer estimated the speed at 13½ knots, he himself estimated it at 13.

"Had you observations to enable you to fix the spot where the wreckage was found?"

"I had very good observations at noon and that afternoon."[6] Lord's noon position had been 41° 33'N, 50° 9'W.

After various counsel had questioned him, Sir Rufus Isaacs returned to the question of the apprentice Gibson, saying that he had woken the Captain.

Lord replied, "I have no reason to suppose that he is telling anything but the truth. He is still an apprentice in my ship." Again he explained the apparent inconsistency by saying that he was half asleep at the time.

He was subjected to repeated questions about the Second Officer calling him up on the voice pipe at about 2.40 and saying that that ship was disappearing or had disappeared bearing SW ½ W. And Lord again denied that he had had any conversation at all with the Second Officer after he had told him about the first rocket at 1.15.

---

6 Taken and agreed by his officers—not by himself.

Mersey cut in, "You knew next morning that the *Titanic* had gone down. Did you make any record in the log of the rockets you had seen?"

"Well, we did not think they were distress rockets."

"Do you think that nobody on board your ship supposed they might be distress signals?"

"The Second Officer—the man in charge of the watch—said most emphatically they were not distress signals."

"Is there anybody on board your boat who thinks they were?"

"Not to my knowledge."

The examination continued. Lord had been called by the Chief Officer at 4.30 and told that the Second Officer had seen rockets in his watch.

"And did you reply, 'Yes, I know'?"

"I said, 'Yes, they certainly had told me something about a rocket.'"

"Do you observe the difference in the question I put to you and your answer?"

"You mentioned rockets. I mentioned rocket."

Finally Sir Rufus said, "I have the report from America and I think it is right to put this to the witness." He read from his notes of Lord's testimony to the Senate Committee. "When I came off the bridge at half-past ten I pointed out to the officer that I thought I saw a light coming along, and it was a most peculiar light. We had been making mistakes all along with the stars, thinking they were signals."

Lord interrupted. "Most peculiar night, I think that should be."

"It may be." Sir Rufus continued reading. "We could not distinguish where the sky ended and where the water commenced. That is right, is it not?"

"Yes, that is what I have said."

Presently Robertson Dunlop, still holding a watching brief only for the Leyland Line and the *Californian* officers, rose and established that Lord had been on duty—on deck—practically the whole of the day of the 14th from seven o'clock on the watch for ice in consequence of the reports. He referred to Lord's first hearing that the *Titanic* had sunk. "You were surprised about it. Did you question your Second Officer as to why you had not been called?"

"I did . . . He said that he had sent down and called me—he had sent Gibson down, and Gibson had told him I was awake, and I had said, 'All right, let me know if anything is wanted'. . . I was surprised at him not getting me out, considering rockets had been fired. He said if they had been distress rockets he would most certainly have come down himself, but he was not a little bit worried about it at all."

Lord went on to describe to Dunlop how the ice had run in a "T" North and South, with the "T" dividing the *Californian's* position from the place where the *Titanic* was supposed to have sunk. "I suppose for 2 or 3 miles all the way down to where she was it was studded with bergs and loose ice." He produced a sketch of the icefield and the *Californian's* course through it which he had made after Gill's rumours in the Boston papers that the *Californian* had disregarded distress signals.

Dunlop: "Assuming that she sank somewhere between two and three a.m. could you, in fact, if you had known at 1.15 in the morning that the *Titanic* was in distress to the southward and westward of you, have reached her before, say, three a.m.?"

"No, most certainly not."

"Could you have navigated with any degree of safety to your vessel at night through the ice that you in fact encountered?"

"It would have been most dangerous."

Lord Mersey: "Am I to understand that this is what you mean to say, that if he had known that the vessel was the *Titanic* he would have made no attempt whatever to reach it?"

Dunlop: "No, my Lord, I do not suggest that." He turned to Lord. "What would you have done? No doubt you would have made an attempt?"

"Most certainly I would have made every attempt to go down to her . . . I do not think we would have got there before the *Carpathia* did, if we would have got there as soon."

CHAPTER TWELVE

Following Lord came the rest of the *Californian*'s deck officers. The evidence they gave was confusing, to say the least. It is significant that none of the engine-room staff were called—except for Gill at a later date—and none of the seamen or quartermasters who would have been on lookout or at the wheel on that night. As statements were taken from these men when the *Californian* had docked on May 11th, it is safe to say that the engine-room staff had not refuted Captain Lord's statement that he was stopped from 10.21 p.m. to about 5.15 a.m., and the lookouts had nothing to add to the story told by the officer and apprentice of the watch—or perhaps they hadn't seen anything—or perhaps their story conflicted with the picture the Board of Trade had decided upon. Whatever they said, it is doubtful if we will ever know at this length of time because the statements have been lost. They are not in the files on the *Titanic* Inquiry in the archives of the Ministry of Transport, which has taken over merchant shipping administration from the Board of Trade.

The first witness after Captain Lord was the apprentice, Gibson. His story was that he had gone on watch at 12 midnight, had seen the vessel referred to at about 12.20 for the first time as a white light. On looking through the glasses he had seen her red sidelight and a glare of lights on her after deck. He was not sure whether he saw a second masthead light. She was right on the starboard beam, from 4 to 7 miles away.

"Do you know at all which way your ship was heading?"

"I was told afterwards she was heading ENE."

"So she was really pointing in the opposite direction to that which she had been steaming?"

"I could not say."

It comes out in this exchange and in many later ones that Gibson was not good at expressing himself, and that he was either remarkably unobservant, not very bright, or so overawed by the presence of his inquisitor, and the row of venerable gentlemen watching his every action that he did not acquit himself well. The *Californian* was quite obviously heading westerly before she stopped; she was heading easterly in the early part of his watch, and it is difficult to see how the answer to that question could have been anything but a brisk and positive 'Yes'.

"She was going from Europe to America?"

"Yes."

"And she was pointing how?"

"ENE."

Gibson had thought the stranger was calling up by morse lamp, he had thought the mast light was flickering a signal.

"That would be using her masthead light to send morse?"

"I did not know it was the masthead light then."

He had tried morsing her, but had then realised it was in fact her masthead light that he had seen flickering. At 12.35 he had gone below, and had returned to the bridge at 12.55. The light had still been there although it had been two and a half points forward of the starboard beam then instead of abeam. Questioned on whether his own ship was swinging, he had replied that she was swinging to northward. In fact, of course, as testified by everyone else, the *Californian* was swinging her head to the southward.

The Second Officer had told him that the strange ship had fired five rockets after he had gone below, and that he (the Second) had reported them to the Captain. Gibson had then seen three more rockets, first with the glasses, then two more with the naked eye. They had all been white. *He was not asked to describe them.*

"When you got the glasses on the vessel and saw the first rocket going up through them, could you make out the vessel at all?"

"No, sir, just her lights."

Lord Mersey: "Still this glare of light?"

"Yes."

"Did that indicate—that glare of light—that this was a passenger steamer?"

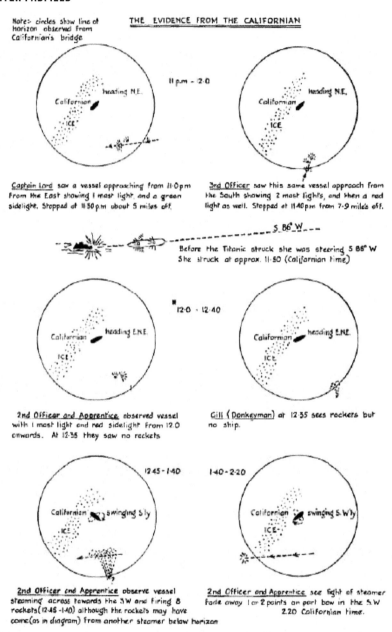

Note:- circles show line of horizon observed from Californian's bridge

THE EVIDENCE FROM THE CALIFORNIAN

11 p.m - 12.0

heading N.E.

Californian

ICE

heading N.E.

Californian

ICE

Captain Lord saw a vessel approaching from 11.0 pm from the East showing 1 mast light, and a green sidelight. Stopped at 11.30 pm about 5 miles off.

3rd Officer saw this same vessel approach from the South showing 2 mast lights, and then a red light as well. Stopped at 11.40 pm from 7.9 miles off.

S 86° W - - -

Before the Titanic struck she was steering S 86° W She struck at approx. 11.50 (Californian time)

12.0 - 12.40

heading E.N.E.

Californian

ICE

heading E.N.E.

Californian

ICE

2nd Officer and Apprentice observed vessel with 1 mast light and red sidelight from 12.0 onwards. At 12.35 they saw no rockets

Gill (Donkeyman) at 12.35 sees rockets but no ship.

12.45 - 1.40

Californian   swinging S.ly

ICE

1.40 - 2.20

Californian   swinging S.W.ly

ICE

2nd Officer and Apprentice observe vessel steaming across towards the SW and firing 8 rockets (12.45 - 1.40) although the rockets may have come (as in diagram) from another steamer below horizon

2nd Officer and Apprentice see light of steamer fade away 1 or 2 points on port bow in the S.W
2.20 Californian time.

* About midnight the vessel was described thus: *Lord:* "Medium-sized tramp." *3rd Officer:* "Large passenger vessel *with lights out.*" *Gill:* Large passenger vessel with rows and rows of lights *ablaze.*" *2nd Officer:* "Medium-sized cargo ship." *Apprentice:* "Medium-sized cargo ship."

No, sir.

After this the Second Officer had remarked to him that she seemed to be steaming away towards the SW, and had later said, "Look at her now—she looks very queer out of the water—her lights look queer." Gibson went on, "I looked at her through the glasses after that and her lights did not seem to be natural."

Lord Mersey jumped in, "What do you mean by that?"

"When a vessel rolls at sea her lights do not look the same. . . ."

"You were not rolling?"

"No. . . . She had a big side out of the water. . . . She seemed as if she had a heavy list to starboard."

The Solicitor-General, Sir John Simon, who was examining, said, "What was there to show you that?"

"Her lights did not seem to look like as they did do before when I first saw them."

Mersey: "What was the difference?"

Solicitor-General: "Could you describe them at all, Gibson?"

Gibson: "No, sir."

The Second Officer had been saying to him, "A ship does not fire up rockets for nothing," to which he had agreed. They had talked about her until she disappeared at about 2.5. Asked what he thought the ship had been, Gibson replied, "A tramp steamer."

When the ship had disappeared the Second Officer had told him to go down and call the Captain and tell him that she had gone and that she had fired eight rockets altogether. He had gone into the chartroom, where the Captain was, opened the door and reported. The Captain had asked if they were all white and asked him the time, after which he had left.

Gibson's story on this vital point agrees with Lord's evidence that Gibson had merely opened the door and reported.

The Solicitor-General asked, "Was he awake?"

"Yes, sir."

At 3.40 the Second Officer had again whistled down to the Captain and said he had seen a further three rockets.

So it appeared from one of Gibson's answers, but he and his various questioners then became really confused about whether the Captain had been called after he (Gibson) went down to him or not. After some bewildering exchanges, Mersey asked, "Now am I to understand you to say that at twenty minutes to four the same morning you saw three more rockets?"

"Yes, sir. I reported them to the Second Officer."

"Did he report them to the Captain?"

"No."

"Why not?"

"I really do not know if they were really there."

"Why were they not reported to the Captain?"

"I do not know, sir."

This passage in the transcript of the Inquiry is contradictory and impossible to understand. As can be seen, though Gibson's final words were that he had seen three rockets after the ship had disappeared towards the SW, that he had reported them to the Second Officer, and the Second Officer had *not* reported them to the Captain. Before that he had volunteered that the Second Officer *had* whistled down the tube at 3.40 and reported the further three rockets.

Further questioning about the ship's heading elicited the information that the *Californian* had swung around from ENE to WSW and the ship had disappeared a point or so on the port bow. Asked if the lights he had seen on the after deck had been in a row, he said, "No."

Asked again to explain how it was that she looked "queer", he at last said that her red sidelight seemed to get higher out of the water and that was why he thought she had a list to starboard. Of course, if Gibson really did see anything like this it would rule the *Titanic* right out, as she had a list to port and from the moment she struck, her red light would have actually been getting lower in the water as she went down by the head. Gibson had no command of English though, was probably awed by the proceedings, and did not explain himself coherently at all.

Mersey asked, "What was it made you think it was a tramp steamer? You saw nothing but the lights?" From which it sounded as though Mersey had never seen a great passenger ship at sea all ablaze with rows and rows of lights.

Gibson replied, "Well, I have seen nearly all the large passenger boats out at sea, and there was nothing at all about it to resemble a passenger boat."

Robertson Dunlop, for the *Californian*, rose and established that Gibson had seen only one masthead light, and that he had not seen her turn after starting to steam away to the SW.

Dunlop asked, "Do you think you could have missed the second masthead light if it had been there?"

"No."

Despite this, when Gibson stood down most of the people in the court-room must have felt sure that the *Californian* was indeed the "mystery ship". The *Daily Mirror* expressed it the next day. "The luncheon interval brought a welcome relief to the strain of examination to which the youth had been subjected, and the laymen in the audience went out convinced that they had heard the story of one who had seen from a distance the last hours of the *Titanic*."

After him came a short, thick-set man, Herbert Stone, the *Californian's* Second Officer, who, with Gibson, had been on watch from midnight until 4 a.m. He had gone on watch shortly after midnight, met the Captain on charthouse deck level and had the ship pointed out to him. She was then showing one masthead light and a red light and two or three small indistinct lights. He thought she was approximately 5 miles away. (It is doubtful if he saw the sidelights with glasses from the lower bridge, although he may have done.) The Captain had asked him to notify him if the bearing of the ship altered or if she came any closer. He had gone *up* to the bridge and relieved the Third Officer, who had told him the ship had stopped at about one bell (11.40) and that he had called her up by morse and received no reply. The Third Officer had gone below. The ship had been bearing then SSE by standard compass (SE true).

About 1.10 he had called the Captain by speaking tube down to the chartroom and said he had seen white lights in the sky in the direction of the other vessel *which he took to be white rockets*. "First of all I was walking up and down the bridge and I saw one white flash in the sky immediately above this steamer. I did not know what it was. I thought it might be a shooting star . . . it was just a white flash in the sky. It might have been anything." He had taken his glasses and looked, and seen four more at intervals of three or four minutes. They were white rockets. He thought she might have been signalling to another steamer at a greater distance, or telling him that there were big icebergs around.

He was questioned at great length about why he had not thought they were distress signals, and what they could be if they were not distress signals. Poor Stone got tied up. He could not adequately explain that had they been distress rockets they would have gone high in the sky and made an exceedingly loud noise—he kept on saying they might have been company's signals or signals to or from another vessel over the horizon. *At no time did he admit that they could have been distress signals.*

Lord Mersey: "You know, you do not make a good impression on me at present."

The Captain had asked Stone if they were company's signals when he had told him about them.

"I said, 'I do not know—but they appear to be white rockets.' "

Afterwards he had remarked to the Chief Officer that the rockets did not appear to go very high—they were very low lying—*they were only about half the height of the steamers masthead light* ". . . and I thought rockets would go higher than that." One light, however, had been brighter than the rest and he was sure that this had come from the deck of the steamer, although the other lights might have come from further away. When the navigation lights of the ship altered their bearing the lights (rockets) had altered in the same way, which had made him almost certain that they were from the visible ship.

He had seen the last of the rockets about 1.40 and sent Gibson down at about two o'clock. During the interval he had been watching the steamer through binoculars and saw her change her bearing from SSE towards the S towards W.

"Under way apparently?"

"Yes."

"On one occasion I noticed the lights looked rather unnatural, as if some were being shut in and others being opened out—the lights appeared to be changing their bearing—the deck lights. . . and I lost sight of her red light."

He had thought that she was, maybe, changing course for an iceberg. He did not remember Gibson saying anything about her red sidelight, although he himself had said something about the lights looking peculiar.

"Did you suggest to Gibson that she was probably in distress and needed assistance?"

"I said nothing about distress, because I did not think so at the time."

Mersey could not believe this. "What did you think they were sent up for?"

"I just thought they were white rockets, that was all. The first thought that crossed my mind was that she was in trouble; but as she steamed away I did not think any more of it. I was not sure that they came from the ship. I thought it possible that they might have come from another ship at a greater distance."

"Did you tell that to the Captain?"

"Yes—the next day."

Continuing his story, Stone said, "I told Gibson to go down to the Master and be sure to wake him and tell him that altogether we had seen eight of the white lights like rockets in the direction of this other steamer—that this steamer was disappearing in the south-west, that we had called her up repeatedly on the morse lamp and received no information whatsoever. . . . When Gibson returned he told me he had woken the Captain up and given him my report. The Captain asked him the time and asked him if he was sure there were no colours in them, red or green. Gibson assured him they were all white rockets. . . . Then he told me that as he shut the door he heard the Captain say something—what, he was not quite certain about."

Again this agrees with Lord's evidence that he heard someone open and close the door and had called out to whoever it was, but had received no reply.

Stone went on to describe how the steamer's lights had gradually faded out as if she was steaming away. Pressed to describe, by Lord Mersey, how fast she was steaming and how he knew she was steaming at all, he replied that she was altering her bearing and two stationary ships could not possibly alter their compass bearing from each other.

He had told Gibson, when he had ordered him to call the Captain, to say that she was disappearing in the SW—he could not have said disappeared because he continued to see her stern light for some time—about twenty minutes—afterwards.

Here is another of the pseudo-coincidences which Mersey was to pick on in his report. This ship which Stone was keenly observing disappeared about 2.20, and so did the *Titanic*—at least the *Titanic* went down at 2.20 *Titanic* time, and Stone's ship disappeared at 2.20 *Californian* time—but that was near enough. It was a strange coincidence. Here is Stone being questioned on the manner in which the lights disappeared.

". . . Did they have the appearance of lights of a ship that had foundered?"

"Not by any means."

"Did you think that anything had happened to her?"

"No."

About twenty minutes after he had seen the light disappear (about forty minutes then after he had sent Gibson down) he had called the Captain again by the speaking tube and the Captain came and answered, and he had told him that the ship, from the direction of which he had seen the rockets coming, had disappeared bearing SW by half W, the last he had seen of the lights.

The very good question was then raised by Mersey why he had thought it necessary at just that particular time to tell the Captain about a steamer that had disappeared twenty minutes earlier. "But why? Why wake up the poor man? It was of no consequence if the vessel was steaming safely away."

"Simply because I had had the steamer under observation all watch and that I had made reports to the Captain concerning her, and I thought it my duty when the ship went away from us altogether to tell him."

This answer may have meant that Stone waited for some time to be sure the ship had finally disappeared before he called the Captain for what he thought would be the last time.

Just before 3.30 Gibson had reported to him that he had seen a white light in the sky to the southward just about on the port beam, and he had crossed over to the port wing and watched in that direction through his binoculars. The *Californian* was then heading about west.[1] "Shortly after I saw a white light in the sky right dead on the beam at a very great distance. . . . It was so far away it was difficult to judge whether it was a rocket or not." He had not thought that it came from the other ship as it was not on the same bearing.

The most likely explanation of these later rockets is that they were the *Carpathia*'s rockets as she approached the scene. At that time about 3.30 (*Californian*) she was practically upon the first lifeboat, which was Boxhall's. Her clocks were some twenty minutes ahead of the *Californian*'s and she reached this first boat about ten minutes after Stone saw the rockets—at 4 a.m. Although we do not know how far Boxhall's boat had rowed by then, she cannot have gone far with her strange assortment of oarsmen and women, and her position can be assumed to be within a very few miles of where the liner foundered. The *Carpathia* was therefore within a very few miles of the disaster position when first Gibson and then Stone saw the rockets, which in the absence of any other reported rockets that night must be assumed to be hers. Here again is Stone's description of this later rocket he saw: ". . . a white light in the sky at a very great distance. . . . It was so far away it was difficult to judge whether it was a rocket or not." And, bearing out that description, here is one of Gibson's answers to the questions about the three later rockets, "I really do not know if they were really there."[2]

Shortly after four o'clock Stone had been relieved by the Chief Officer. "I gave him a full report of everything I had seen and everything I had reported to the master. . . the whole information regarding the watch. He looked over on the port beam and he remarked to me, 'There she is—there is that steamer. She is all right.' I looked at the steamer through the glasses and I remarked to him, 'That is not the same steamer—she has two masthead lights. I saw a steamer then just abaft the port beam showing two masthead lights apparently heading in much the same direction as ourselves."

---

1 Whether compass or true west is not clear.
2 *See also* Stone's original statement—Appendix B.

Questioned why, in view of his evidence about the steamer showing rockets having steamed away, the Chief Officer should remark, "She's all right", he said he did not know why he should say that.

Cross-examined on the earlier period of his watch again, he said that he Had never noticed the other steamer having a list. Asked repeatedly about how he had seen her red light although she had been steaming roughly westerly or southwesterly and could only therefore have shown him a green light, he kept on saying that he had seen no green light and had only seen the red light. He would not agree that he ought to have seen her green light. (This must have been Inquiry hypnosis; there is no other explanation.) Finally he said, "I did not see her red light after she started steaming away—only her stern light."

Then he was subjected to another gruelling examination on what he imagined the rockets could have been if they had not been distress rockets; his best reply was merely, "A ship in distress does not steam away from you, my Lord."

The nearest Stone ever came to admitting that they might have been distress rockets was in this exchange:

"Did you think they were distress signals?"

"No."

"Did not that occur to you?"

"It did not occur to me at the time."

"When did it occur to you?"

"After I had heard about the *Titanic* going down."

Pressed as to whether, when he had heard about the *Titanic*, he had then thought they were distress signals which he had seen, he said he thought they *might* have been. Further pressed to name the ship he saw as the *Titanic*, he said, "They may have been from some other steamer. I did not think *that* vessel was the *Titanic*."

It was plain throughout these exchanges that neither Mersey nor counsel for the Board of Trade could conceive that an officer who had sat for and obtained a certificate of competency could possibly have seen white rockets throwing stars being fired in the night and not have wondered whether they were distress signals; this was precisely what he had been taught to recognise as a distress signal.

In reply to questions from Dunlop he said that he judged the stranger to have been a smallish steamer, and she could not by any means have been the *Titanic*. He was positive that he had seen only one masthead light.

He stood down.

Despite Stone's vigorous denials of having seen distress signals, and his repeated descriptions of the vessel near the *Californian* as a smallish steamer with only one masthead light, his evidence merely served to convince most people that that vessel had in fact been the *Titanic* sinking. The *Daily Express*, picking out the salient features of the day's sensational evidence in a manner which Sir Rufus or Lord Mersey would have been proud to own to, headed their report THE MYSTERY SHIP.

"A question of absorbing interest was raised at yesterday's sitting of the court of Inquiry . . . when remarkable evidence was given by witnesses from the Leyland liner *Californian* which must have been within the vicinity of the ill-fated liner when she sank.

"It was shown that:

"The rockets fired singly in the manner of distress rockets were seen by the *Californian* from a steamer thought to be about 5 miles away.

"That the steamer's lights were watched for some time through binoculars and that she seemed to have a 'heavy list' to starboard.

"That no effort was made to get into touch with her by wireless, although her lights looked 'funny' and she took no notice of morse signalling.

"That a glare of light was seen on her after part and that her lights eventually disappeared."

Later in the article the *Express* quoted Mersey in heavy black type, "It is in my brain that the vessel the *Californian* saw was the Titanic. . . . Clear it up if you can."

***

The following day, May 15th, as Gill had torpedoed Captain Lord in the American Inquiry, Groves, his Third Officer, stepped up to the witness stand to torpedo him in the British Inquiry.

Charles Victor Groves was a Second Officer serving as Third of the *Californian*, a well-groomed, clean-shaven young man who had served his apprenticeship in the P & O company. He started off prosaically enough, describing the atmospheric conditions during his watch that night—the 8 to 12. "You could not see where the horizon and the sky finished but you could see the stars right down as far as the sea. ... There was nothing in the shape of a haze." The Captain had been on the bridge from the beginning of the watch until about 10.35 and when he left had told him to let him know if he saw any ship approaching.

"As I said before the stars were showing right down to the horizon. It was very difficult at first to distinguish between the stars and a light—they were so low down. About 11.10 ship's time I made out a steamer coming up a Little abaft our starboard beam." Groves was then keeping his watch on the upper bridge where there was no clock, but he had set his watch at six o'clock.

He had not paid much attention to the ship at first, thinking it may have been a star rising, but at 11.25 he made out two lights. At the time the *Californian* was heading NE and the ship was three points abaft the beam—making her bearing S by E. At which the counsel leading him through his story, Mr S. A. T. Rowlatt for the Board of Trade, made a slight mistake in his mental calculation, and gave the bearing of the ship then as S½W. No one corrected him. Groves thought she was 10 to 12 miles off.

"Was she changing her bearing?"

"Slowly."

"Coming round more to the south and west?"

"More on our beam, yes—more to the south and west, but very little."

This statement means nothing. If she was coming more round on the beam she was coming more to the south and *east*, not as he said in the second half more to the south and *west*.

About 11.30 he had gone down to the lower bridge and reported this ship to the Captain, had told him there was a ship approaching, coming up on the starboard quarter.

"Captain Lord said to me, 'Can you make anything out of her lights?' I said, 'Yes, she is evidently a passenger steamer coming up on us.'"

"How many deck lights had she? Had she much light?"

"Yes, a lot of light. There was absolutely no doubt about her being a passenger steamer—at least in my mind."

"Could you see much of her length?"

"No, not a great deal—because as I could judge she was coming up obliquely to us."

The Captain had told him to call her up on the morse lamp, which he did, but received no reply. The Captain came up on the bridge and thought he saw a flickering light, but she was not answering. "When he came up on the bridge he said to me, 'That does not look like a passenger steamer.' I said, 'It is, sir. When she stopped her lights seemed to go out, and I suppose they have been put out for the night.'"

This was the first time Groves had mentioned her stopping and he was asked at what time. He replied "11.40". He was not, however, taken in greater detail through her movements, or her distance when she stopped, or her bearing at that time.

"And you told the Captain this, did you?" (About the lights going out.)

"Yes."

"What did he say to that?"

"When I remarked about the passenger steamer, he said, 'The only passenger steamer near us is the *Titanic*.'"

Mersey raised his brows. "He said that did he?"

"Yes, my Lord."

This evidence is not at all clear. Groves had previously said he had told the Captain about her being a passenger steamer on the lower bridge when he first called him. Now he has said that the *Titanic* remark occurred on the upper bridge (at least by inference) when he had told Lord about the lights going out and after he had tried signalling her.

Anyway, the point was not pressed.

Groves had remembered that the lights of the stranger went out at 11.40 because that was the time one bell was struck.

Counsel for the Board of Trade, Mr Rowlatt, went on with the questioning, "Did the steamer continue on her course after that?"

"Not so far as I could see."

"She stopped?"

"She stopped."

"Was that at the time her lights appeared to go out?"

"That was at the time her lights appeared to go out."

"Were the lights you saw on her port side or her starboard side?"

"Port side."

"I want to ask you a question. Supposing the steamer whose lights you saw turned two points to port at 11.40, would that account to you for her lights ceasing to be visible to you?"

"I quite think it would."

The gloves are off. The cards are down in full view. The Board of Trade and the Court have their witness, and they are going to play him to their fullest advantage. At which stage it is worth looking at Groves' evidence up to this point because if it is believed it proves conclusively, absolutely, and without the slightest shadow of a doubt that this steamer, whatever she was, tramp as everyone else has said, or passenger liner as Groves has said, could not have been the *Titanic*. The *Titanic* was steering S 86°W. The ship Groves saw was approaching from somewhere about south—between south and south by east probably—and showing her port side. In which case she must have been heading between the reciprocal bearing of north by west and somewhere about north-east. Surely—surely this was apparent to at least the nautical men who were sitting as Lord Mersey's assessors. If that ship was the *Titanic* and she had, as Groves said, been sighted on the starboard quarter of the *Californian* which was heading north-east, she must have quite shortly disappeared further aft on the starboard side—she could by no stretch of imagination approach the *Californian* from a southerly bearing unless she was steering northerly. Remember he had first seen the light about 11.10, and whatever time the *Titanic* was keeping this was before she struck. Suppose, as seems very probable, that *Titanic* time was twelve minutes ahead of *Californian* time—then this ship was first seen at 11.22 *Titanic* time, and was reported to the Captain (*when she was much closer from a southerly direction*) at 11.42 *Titanic* time, and her lights went out at 11.52 *Titanic* time. However we needn't go too much into times because the Board of Trade were obviously assuming that both ships were keeping the same time, as was Lord Mersey, who jumped straight in.

"Mr Rowlatt, at 11.40 the engines were stopped on the *Titanic*?"

"Yes, my Lord. I do not know whether that would cause a large number of lights to go out. They had a supplemental dynamo. I think the only evidence about lights going out was that at some time after this the lights in a particular stokehold went out for a short time." (It appears from the transcript that Mr Rowlatt was quite correct here.)

"Oh yes, I know that," Mersey replied, "but is it not the fact that at some time the lights in the ship, except the lights in the alleyways and the working parts of the ship did go out?"

"I do not remember that there is any evidence of that. I do not know how it would be. I do not know whether those who sit with you could indicate whether it would necessarily follow the engines stopping. I should imagine the engines stopping would not put the lights out."

Whereupon the proceedings became farcical. It is some indication of the state of confusion and conviction which held sway over Mersey's mind that he argued for some minutes with various counsel to the effect that the lights, except for emergency lights, must go out directly the engines stopped.

Mr Rowlatt kept his head. "It can hardly be that when they stopped the ship going forward the ship is plunged in darkness automatically. It only means they stop the engines which actuate the propellers."

Lord Mersey was adamant. "At some time the light which was produced by the main engines did go out."

After a great deal more argument he was finally convinced that the" generators for the electric light were located somewhere abaft the main engines and would not be affected in any way by an order from the bridge to stop the engines.

All was not lost however. Mr Rowlatt went on, "I have got an answer from the witness which might throw some light on it. He said that in his opinion the turning of the ship——"

Lord Mersey interjected. "I heard him. That would be when the order was given to change direction."

Rowlatt was as quick as he. "Hard a-starboard, and your lordship remembers we had evidence that the ship did answer her helm to the extent of two points at once."

"Yes, she did answer her helm. Very well, two points you were saying?"

"Two points, my Lord. The man at the compass said she altered her course two points."

"A change of two points to port would conceal the lights in the ship?"

Rowlatt turned to Groves. "Did you say would or might? I do not want to put it too high."

"In my own private opinion it would."

Here Groves might well be right. If the ship was coming up on him from the southward slightly inclined to the east and she turned two points to port to head straight for him it could well have shut out all her broadside lights. But if she was steering a course to the east of north how in heaven's name could she have been the *Titanic*? If the Admiral and the two Commanders R.N.R. did not see this, heaven help them. If they did see it why did they not prevent Mersey from making a fool of himself?

Rowlatt went on. "Did you continue to see the masthead lights?"

"Yes."

"Did you see any navigation lights—sidelights?"

"I saw the red port light."

Lord Mersey: "When did you see that?"

"As soon as her deck lights disappeared from my view."

Further questioning established that in his view the glare of the deck lights had prevented him from seeing the red light before, that the Captain had not been on the bridge with him when the lights went out, and that he did not think the Captain was on the bridge with him for more than three minutes at the outside.

The *Californian* had continued swinging slowly to starboard, the lights of the strange ship coming round ahead as she did so. Groves was relieved by Stone at about 12.15 and remarked to him that the ship was a passenger steamer, that she had stopped and put her lights out. He used the word "put", which has a different connotation from "shut" out, although under examination he said it was his impression that she had *shut* them out as she turned.[3]

After several exchanges about it Lord Mersey summed up his *personal* interpretation of this puzzling section of the evidence. "It comes to this, Mr Rowlatt, at first he thought the lights had been put out, but when he reflected about it, and observed she changed her position, he thought she had shut her lights out, which is a very different thing."

Rowlatt was still struggling to keep the record straight. "I do not know that he said he observed her change her position." He turned to Groves, "She was stopped at the time was she not?"

"Yes."

Rowlatt went on, "He accepted my suggestion, my Lord, that if the vessel did change her course it might shut her lights out—it would shut her lights out."

Groves then said, in reply to questioning, that he did not think he would detect a swing of two points to port by the masthead lights and had not done so at the time in question. Now, if Groves had seen the broadside lights *shut out* the only way they could have been *shut out* would have been for the ship to point directly or very nearly directly at him, in which case the two masthead lights would come in a line one above the other, or very nearly in a line. This would have been very noticeable.

After handing over the watch to the Second Officer Groves had gone below to the wireless operator's cabin, found him asleep, woken him up, and said, "What ships have you got, Sparks?" The man had said, "Only the *Titanic*." Groves had put the earphones over his head for a brief moment but had not heard anything, and had retired to bed. The following morning he had been woken some time after six by the Chief Officer who told him that the *Titanic* had sunk and the passengers were in lifeboats ahead of them. He had jumped into the Second's cabin and said, "Is that

---

3 Shutting out means turning in such a fashion that the lights become hidden.

right, Mr. Stone, about the *Titanic*?" and the Second had said, "Yes, that is right—hurry up and get dressed, we shall be wanted in the boats. I saw rockets in my watch."

Mersey interjected, "That conveys to me the notion that when he said he saw the rockets in his watch he was referring to the rockets which he believed had come from the *Titanic*. Did he give you that impression?"

"Well, it is rather difficult for me to say what impression I got then because I was rather excited, but I have told you what he said to me and what I said to him."

Groves dressed and went up to the bridge, by which time the ship was under way with ice all around and icebergs. While dressing he could feel her bumping the ice and knew by that that she had a good speed on. The lifeboats were being swung out when he came up. Getting on for seven o'clock when he came to the bridge he saw the *Mount Temple* stopped about a mile and a half on the starboard bow,[4] and to port, abeam, a four-masted ship with a red funnel and black top with house flag at half mast (*Carpathia*)—further away than the *Mount Temple*. His impression was that the *Californian* almost immediately turned to port straight for her. She was then some 5 miles away. There was another vessel in the vicinity with a black funnel.

They reached the *Carpathia* about 7.45[5] and exchanged signals with her. The Captain suggested searching down to leeward, which they did and saw some wreckage and boats. At nine o'clock exactly as he heard the bells the *Carpathia* steamed off. The *Californian* continued the search until 10.40.[6]

Thomas Scanlan, for the Sailors' and Firemen's Union, rose to examine him, and established that the ship he had seen approaching from 11.10 the night of the 14th had come to a stop between 7 and 9 miles away.

---

4 This timing does not agree with Captain Moore's evidence from the *Mount Temple*.
5 Captain Rostron of the *Carpathia* didn't see the *Californian* until eight o'clock, and then she was still over to the westward of him.
6 The other officers' evidence was all for *11.40*.

"In the position to which you had swung round . . . if any person from that ship or from a boat lower down saw you, would they have seen the light you were showing then, your red starboard light?"

"It is a green light."

"I beg your pardon—your green light?"

"Yes."

"And the white masthead light?"

"They would have been able to see it from the ship undoubtedly but as to a boat I am rather doubtful."

Mr A. Clement Edwards, M.P., for the Dockers' Union, rose and established that the *Californian* had been under way when Groves was awakened in the morning.

Afterwards Robertson Dunlop took Groves through the position of the *Californian* when stopped, and went on, "If the *Titanic* was in latitude 41° 33', which is the position she has given, and the position in which the wreckage was found, and your vessel was, as stated in the log, in latitude 42° 05', the *Titanic* would be some 33 miles to the southward of the position where you were lying stopped?"

Here Dunlop had the wrong figures: the *Titanic's* wirelessed latitude was 41° 46'—thus 19 miles, not 33, to the South of the *Californian*. Nevertheless 41° 33' N was approximately where the wreckage was found. No one quarrelled with him, and Groves answered, "Yes, about 30 miles."

"And if the *Titanic* was 30 miles to the southward of the position where you were stopped I do not suppose you could see any navigation lights at that distance?"

"No—none whatsoever."

"If this vessel which you did see was only some 4 or 5 miles away to the southward of you, do you think she can have been the *Titanic*?"

Before Groves could answer Lord Mersey interjected, "That is a question I want this witness to answer." He looked at Groves. "Speaking as an experienced seaman and knowing what you do know now, d'you think that steamer that you know was throwing up rockets, and that you say was a passenger steamer, was the *Titanic*?"

"Do I think it?"

"Yes?"

"From what I have heard subsequently?"

"Yes?"

"Most decidedly I do, but I do not put myself as being an experienced man."

Dunlop came back again. "That would indicate that the *Titanic* was only 4 or 5 miles to the southward of the position in which you were stopped."

Mersey seemed determined to stop this question being put. "If his judgement on the matter is true it shows that these figures—latitudes and longitudes that you are referring to are not accurate; that is all it shows."

"The accuracy we will deal with, my Lord."

"I mean to say," Mersey continued, "if what he says is right it follows that the figures must be wrong."

There followed some questions about how he thought she was a passenger steamer, to which he replied, "By the brilliance of her lights."

"Before she stopped at 11.40 you had her under observation for some time, noticing her movements?"

"Yes, but I took no notice of the course she was making except that she was coming up obliquely to us."

Dunlop probed on.

"Was she making to the westward or the eastward?"

"She would be bound to be going to the westward."

"Was she?"

"She was bound to."

"Did you see her going to the westward?"

"Well, I saw her red light."

"If she was going to the westward and was to the southward of you you ought to have seen her green light?"

"Not necessarily."

"Just follow me for a moment. She is coming up on your starboard quarter you told us?"

"On our starboard quarter."

"Heading to the westward?"

"Yes."

ARCS OF VISIBILITY OF SHIPS LIGHTS

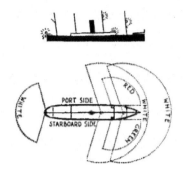

DIRECTIONS FROM OWN SHIP

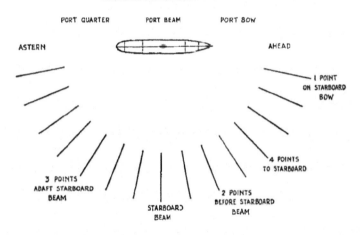

"And she is to the southward of you?"

"She is to the southward of us."

"Then the side nearest to you must have been her starboard side, must it not?"

"Not necessarily. If she is going anything from north to west you would see her port side. At the time I left the bridge we were heading ENE by compass."

Of course Groves is talking nonsense. The heading of his own ship had nothing whatever to do with the lights of the ship to the southward of him. On the bearing of that ship as testified by Groves she could only have been showing a green light if there was any appreciable West in her course. If, like the *Titanic,* she had been heading almost due West she must have shown a very broad green light. Perhaps Groves, like Stone before him, was afflicted with some sort of hypnosis in the atmosphere in which he found himself, although his previous answers did not suggest it. There is no doubt that on his showing in the courtroom on a perfectly simple problem of bearings and courses he would not have passed the oral examination for the Second Mate's Certificate which he held.[7]

However, Dunlop could not get Groves to admit his simple proposition, and no one else tried. Why should they? Once this obvious fact was stated the whole of Grove's evidence about this ship having been the *Titanic* stood revealed as lunacy.

Dunlop tried and tried over and over again but failed to get Groves to see reason. Eventually he changed his tack. "Did you see her green light at all?"

"Never."

This one simple question and answer finally, absolutely and irrevocaby expunges Groves' entire testimony about the ship he saw having been the *Titanic.* If Lord Mersey or the Board of Trade had then wanted to reincarnate the idea they should have sought to prove that on this particular night the *Titanic* was actually, and by mistake, burning her green light on the port side and her red light on the starboard side. No one suggested this, and so the matter ought to have rested. In fact it didn't rest. There was a way out. *Captain Lord* had seen a green light on this same steamer. He had only seen one masthead light, but no matter, the green light was good enough—Groves had seen the two masthead lights, and all the saloon lights. Groves had been mistaken about the red light. It couldn't have been a red light because the *Titanic* would have shown her green—and obviously this ship *was* the *Titanic.*

But this is anticipating the Report. After eliciting the response that Groves had never seen a green light on this vessel to the South of him

---

7 Groves later went on to obtain an Extra Master's Certificate, and himself sat as an assessor at marine inquiries, becoming noted for his humane attitude towards those in error before him.

Dunlop rested his case, and the next witness was called. He was the *Californians* Chief Officer, George Frederick Stewart.

Stewart confirmed that he had relieved Stone some time after 4 a.m. and had been told about the steamer which had fired rockets and gone away. He did not think he had been told the number of rockets. When asked what he thought the rockets might have been he admitted he thought they may have been distress signals, or they might have been answering the *Californian*'s morse light—although he had never seen this done before. He confirmed that he had then scanned the horizon to port and had seen the two masthead lights of a ship but Stone had not thought it was the same steamer that he (Stone) had seen.

At about 4.30 he had called the Captain and told him about the rockets Stone had seen. The Captain had replied, "Oh yes, I know—he has been telling me." The Captain had then come on the bridge and they had discussed the possibility of continuing through the ice on their voyage. Stewart had asked Lord if he intended going to the southward to see what that ship was.

"When you asked him that, was the ship you referred to a ship that you thought had been in distress?"

"Yes."

"When you asked him that, what did he say?"

"He said, "No, I do not think so—she is not making any signals now.""

The Solicitor-General, Sir John Simon, questioned him about the *Californian*'s position at 10.21, and discovered it was the Captain's dead reckoning position. Simon seemed to think it odd that the noon latitude for April 13th had been 43° 43'N and for April 14th 42° 05'N—or 99 miles of southerly latitude—and yet the *Californian* had then stopped making southing the next day, and altered to due West. It's difficult to know why he should have thought this if he had been in Court while the *Titanic*'s course had been described in exactly similar terms; perhaps he was just testing the witness.

Stewart went on to say that the 10.21 position was not only dead reckoning, but he himself had had a pole star at 7.30 which had fixed the latitude. He then said he *believed* that from noon they were going more westerly.

"Keeping on the same latitude since noon?"

"Yes."

Looking at the log-book Stewart found the course to have been about West. He was questioned about the odd fact that there had been no mention made of the distress rockets in the scrap log, which he had copied into the fair log. The system was that a scrap notebook was kept in which the officers of the watch made their observations, and afterwards he (Stewart) wrote it up each day in the fair copy, tore out the page of the scrap log and destroyed it. This was in fact a fairly general practice, although some ships still kept the scrap log on a slate, which was afterwards rubbed off. He could give no explanation of why the rockets had not been reported in the scrap book.

He was taken through to the time he had called the wireless operator. The Solicitor-General suggested that he had called Evans and asked him to find out what was amiss with that ship to the southward. Stewart thought he had called Evans and just said, "See what the ship is to the southward." He did not remember (as the Solicitor- General again suggested) that he had gone to the operator's room and said that rockets had been seen during the night.

He thought the ship had started moving at 5.15, crawling through the ice very slowly.

Examined further about the navigation of the vessel he said that the latitude of 42° 03' wirelessed to the *Antillian* with the message about the three icebergs had been a dead reckoning position before he had taken a pole star at 7.30 which had given him 42° 05'N.

It was then established that sights on the following day, after leaving the *Titanic*'s wreckage had been good, that they had been taken and agreed by all the officers. The position at noon on the 15th had been 41° 33'N and 50° 09'W. Previously they had stopped close to the *Carpathia* at 8.30 and had left the area of the wreckage at 11.20 and had travelled some 4 or 5 miles between the wreckage and the noon position.

"Were you encountering ice at the time?"

"Yes."

Dunlop, questioning him after he had been through his story, established that if his navigational figures were right the ship seen in the 8 to 12 and the 12 to 4 watches could not have been the *Titanic,* and the rockets from the *Titanic* would probably not have been seen. Whereupon Mersey came in, "All this does not impress my mind much. It all proceeds upon the assumption that these figures are right. The other evidence is to my mind of vastly more importance. However, I do not want to shut you out from it, you know."

Dunlop came back, "You have heard my Lord's observation. Have you any reason to doubt the accuracy of these latitudes?"

No, sir.

Mersey said to Dunlop, "The previous officer told me in answer to a question that I think you yourself suggested, that he was satisfied that it was the *Titanic,* and at present I do not mind telling you that is my attitude of mind. You may perhaps change it."

"I hope to succeed, my Lord." Dunlop turned back to Stewart. "Have you ever considered whether the vessel which was reported to have been sending up rockets was, or could have been, the *Titanic*?"

"I do not think it could have been, sir."

Mersey: "What?"

"I do not think it was, sir."

"You think it may have been?"

"I think if it had been the *Titanic* there would have been no doubt about it."

But Mersey was determined. "Do you think it may have been the *Titanic*?"

"No, sir."

Dunlop established that if the *Titanic* to New York and the *Californian* to Boston had both been on their proper courses they would have been some 30 or 40 miles apart. He further elicited that the rockets which the Second Officer had described to Stewart at four o'clock had not made any report or left a trail in the sky or been at a higher altitude than the ship's masthead lights, which was why he (Stone) had thought she may have been signalling to a ship to the southward, and why he had thought they were not distress rockets.

Stewart stood down.

The next, and last, *Californian* witness, with the exception of Gill some days later, was Cyril Evans, the Marconi man. It was established that he had been keeping New York time to which x hour 55 minutes had to be added to obtain ship's time on the 14th. He was taken through the story he had told in New York up to the time the Captain had come to his cabin and asked what ships he had got.[8] This had been at 9.05 New York time— ix p.m. ship's time. He had replied "The *Titanic*" and the Captain had told him he had better call her up and tell her they were stopped and surrounded by ice. When he called her the *Titanic* had said "Keep out". This was a normal thing to do ". . . one did not take it as an insult or anything."

Afterwards he had turned in. He remembered Groves coming in some time after twelve and asking him what ships he had. This was Groves' normal practice. He had replied, "Only the *Titanic*—the new ship on her maiden voyage." Then Groves had left.

He was not asked whether Groves had told him about the passenger ship which had stopped and put out her lights some 7 miles away. Neither did he state anything more that Groves had said. Now if Groves really had seen a large passenger liner haul up and stop close by, and then learned from the wireless operator that the only ship in the vicinity was the *Titanic,* wouldn't he have said something about it? Perhaps he did. But if he did, either Evans did not remember it, or the Board of Trade counsel did not think it worth while leading him to say anything about it—which is singularly out of character with the rest of the proceedings.

When woken in the morning Evans had heard from the *Mount Temple* that the *Titanic* was sinking and the position, and then the *Frankfurt* jumped in and told him the same thing. He wrote the position down on a piece of paper and handed it to Mr Stewart and afterwards got the official message from the *Virginian.* He was also in touch with the Russian *Birma.* The ship had not been moving when the Chief Officer came to his cabin, but started moving ten minutes to quarter of an hour afterwards.

After Evans had left the witness stand the Solicitor-General asked if the *Californian* witnesses could go.

Mersey replied "As far as I am concerned they may go. I do not want them. I do not suppose anyone else does."

---

8 This differs from his statement in New York, when he said, "and I *went to the Captain* and I asked him if anything was the matter . .. and the Captain asked me, if I had any boats, and I said, the *Titanic*..." See also Lord's account of where Evans received the order to call up the *Titanic*—Appendix A.

So Lord, Stewart, Stone, Groves, Evans and Gibson were released. So far as Lord was concerned, it must have been a gruelling experience, especially when his Third Officer suddenly decided that it *had* been the *Titanic* that they all saw that night. But there were no questions for the Court to answer which specifically affected him or the *Californian* and certainly no charges against him. He had appeared as a witness, and that was the end of it; he had told what he knew.

It had not been the *Titanic* they had seen—that was so obvious it hardly needed saying, but he had said it because he had been asked. The rockets had not been distress rockets—that again was obvious because they had not made a sound and they had not even reached mast height and the ship had been steaming away. This part of the Inquiry had been thoroughly unpleasant and Mersey had been hostile from the start; so had the Attorney-General. He was glad it was over.

But by now practically everyone else in England who read the newspapers must have been convinced that the ship he and the others saw *was* the *Titanic*. And they must have been concerned about other headlined disclosures—the *Daily Mirror* for instance:

MYSTERY OF *CALIFORNIAN'S* LOG-BOOK
No mention of Rockets seen on Night of Titanic Wreck

LORD MERSEY'S VIEW
President of Opinion that Signals were those of Sinking Liner.

CHAPTER THIRTEEN

James Henry Moore, the master of the *Mount Temple,* was the next witness called, and he repeated what he had said in New York—only in rather less detail. He was not questioned thoroughly about the green lights of the small sailing vessel he had passed shortly after three o'clock. Why? This time he estimated his distance from the *Titanic's* wirelessed position as 15 miles when he saw the schooner. Three o'clock—15 miles—why was he not questioned on it? About the tramp steamer ahead of him which later turned out to have a black funnel he said he had first seen it ahead shortly *after* he turned—between about 1 a.m. and 1.30. He had sighted the *Carpathia* and the *Californian* shortly before 8 a.m.

It seems reasonable to suppose that the Court showed so little interest in Captain Moore's adventures and the various ships he had seen because they thought they already had their man.

After him came the *Mount Temple's* wireless operator, who read from his log that the *Californian* had called asking for information at 5.11 (5.20 *Californian* time).

* * *

Before the next landmark in this story, which was the publication of the Senators' Report, several more members of the *Titanic's* crew gave evidence about the mystery light or lights. To prevent tedious repetition it is summarised below.

John Hart—Third Class steward: two lights like masthead lights of a steamer while he was on board *Titanic* off starboard side of the ship—roughly to the North—said he was no judge of distances.

Charles Mackay—bathroom steward: a "supposed" light on the starboard side of the ship after he had got into boat—reddish tinge to it—only one light.

George Symons—A.B.: A steamer's light visible on port bow before he left the ship—one white light 1½ points on port bow, distant between 5 and 10 miles—no sidelights—took it to be a cod bankman. (Steamer and cod bankman?)

Lightoller—Second Officer: "A white light about two points on the port bow—whether it was one or two lights I could not say . . . I could not distinguish any coloured lights but merely it was a white light distinct and plain . . . I was perfectly sure it was a light attached to a vessel, whether a steamship or a sailing ship I could not say."

Mersey: "Can you form any estimate of the distance of that light from the *Titanic*?"

"Yes, my Lord, certainly not over 5 miles away."

"Was there any field ice or pack ice about the *Titanic* about this time?"

"No, my Lord."

"Then there was nothing to prevent a vessel, as far as you could see, from coming to the *Titanic*?"

"Not as far as I could see."

Conversely there was nothing to prevent the *Titanic* going to this vessel *unless it had not appeared until after the decision had been taken to get the women and children away in the boats, and some boats had been lowered.*

Herbert Pitman—Third Officer: a white light which he judged to be the stern light of a sailing vessel—about 5 miles away.

Boxhall—Fourth Officer: two white masthead lights, close together as if she was a four-master, approaching end on, later saw green and red sidelights, then red sidelight only with naked eye—came to 5 or 6 miles, slowly turned around—finally saw her white stern light.

Harold Lowe—Fifth Officer: two white masthead lights and red sidelight—no distance mentioned.

George Rowe—Quartermaster: one white light half a point on the port bow while he was firing rockets—thought *Titanic's* stern was swinging due South at the time—later the light was two points on port bow.

Before the next witness was called the Court was adjourned for several days, and during the adjournment, on May 28th, the U.S. Senate published its report.

"OH, WHAT AN ASS!" screamed the *Daily Express* in huge type, and followed it with "MAD SPEECH".

"Senator Smith, who presided over the American Commission which inquired into the loss of the *Titanic* yesterday delivered the most amazing speech ever heard in any parliament in the world."

It headed the report of the amazing speech "BOMBASTIC BOSH".

The *Daily Mail* was equally uncomplimentary.

"Flowers of turgid rhetoric are scattered so freely through his eccentric composition that its meaning is not always clear. Senator Smith's great maxim appears to be 'Look after the sound and let the sense take care of itself.' He has buried a grave and terrible event beneath a mountain of foolish fustian. . . . Where he descends to technical questions his now notorious want of knowledge of the sea renders his queries absolutely worthless."

Unfortunately by no means everyone agreed with these strictures, and despite them the general result of the Senators' judgement was a stiffening—if this was possible—of the censorious attitude towards Lord and the *Californian*.

The *Daily Mirror*, for instance—"the paper with the largest net circulation"—had no criticism of the Senator whatever; instead it printed in bold type a list of his own criticisms. One of them, naturally, was:

"*Captain Lord* of the *Californian*, whom he (Smith) holds responsible for the unnecessary sacrifice of all the lives lost."

And *The Times* reported in sober vein, "It is a comparatively brief document, and the somewhat florid speech with which Senator Smith accompanied its presentation only served to accentuate the sobriety of its tone and to lend substance to the theory that Senator Smith's colleagues played a more marked part in its preparation than they did in the investigation. . . ."

Notwithstanding the "comparative brevity" of the document *The Times* carried it over half a page of small type, and included the large sections of adverse comment on the *Californian*. Those who read the paper must have come away with the strong impression that Captain Lord had been guilty of inhumanity—for there had been only condensed reports of the evidence taken by the Senators from day to day and the final Report, as witnessed, was absolutely damning. There was no reason why anyone who had not studied the full transcripts from America—and few can have had the opportunity—should have questioned the verdict on Lord.

Other sections of the Press certainly didn't. *John Bull*, to take the most scurrilous example, had actually anticipated the Senators' verdict by three days. On May 25th they printed an open letter addressed to Lord.

To Captain Stanley Lord, s.s. "Californian"

Sir—Perhaps by this time you are heartily ashamed of yourself. Although you were called by the officer of the watch, by your apprentice, Gibson, and through the speaking tube, and informed that a vessel was firing rockets of distress, you took no heed of the signal.

No doubt it was a cold night, and it was not pleasant to turn out of a warm bed, to go on the bridge, and drive through the ice. But surely you might have taken the trouble to instruct somebody to call up the Marconi operator, and get him to try and find out what was the matter. Yet on your own evidence you slept on, and largely through your inaction 1,500 fellow creatures have perished.

There is no doubt that your officers saw the *Titanic* (it is quite evident that your vessel was within a few miles of her), and had you acted like a man, turned out at the first call, and driven your ship with all possible speed, you would have been able to save every soul on board.

I fear you are a remnant of an old type of skipper, and it strikes me that your officers were somewhat too timid in expressing their views to you. They should have insisted on your going to the assistance of the distressed vessel. They should have chanced your displeasure, and pulled you out of bed.

Another matter I don't like is the utter absence of any reference to these distress signals in your log-book. Was the idea to say nothing about it, had the donkeyman not split?

Your whole action is, to say the least of it, reprehensible and un-British, and if the Board of Trade were a real live business body, I rather think they would take stringent action without waiting for the findings of the Court. You have brought discredit on the fair name of the British Marine service. I rather fancy some of my American friends will give you a warm reception when next you reach New York.

JOHN BULL

The Commission of Inquiry, the Press and the public were already convinced of Lord's guilt. The Senators' Report put any other interpretation of the evidence from the *Californian* right out of the question; it also appeared to quicken the Court's desire to add their verdict to the already impressive weight of opinion.

When the Inquiry resumed it was a mere nineteen questions after the day started before counsel arrived at THE LIGHT.

"And before you left the ship's side did Captain Smith give you any directions with regard to a light?"

"Yes," replied Alfred Crawford, bedroom steward, First Class. "He pointed to a light on the port side, the two masthead lights of a vessel and told us to pull for there and land the people and return to the ship."

It is unnecessary to go through all the questions, but after three more Lord Mersey asked, "Is there anyone here representing the *Californian*?"

He was told that Mr Dunlop would be arriving in a few minutes, and then Sir Rufus Isaacs rose and said, "Someone will be here because we are calling someone from the *Californian* today, and we have given them notice of it."

Butler Aspinall for the Board of Trade continued the questioning. "I do not know whether you are a judge of distance of lights at sea, but what would you say?"

"I should say she was 5 to 7 miles away from us."

"The Captain gave the directions?"

"Yes, he pointed the ship out."

Mersey came in, "Does 5 to 7 miles agree with the information from the *Californian* as to the position she took up when she anchored?"[1]

Aspinall replied "It is widely different, my Lord."

"That is what I was thinking. The distance would be about 20 miles would it not?"

"Yes, 19 was in my mind—19 to 20."

"We have had the log of the *Californian*?"

"We have."

Sir Rufus entered the field. "The point, your Lordship, is one which wants a little clearing up. Our attention has been directed to the same point."

Lord Mersey: "Very well, I will not say anything about it now."

The questioning continued. Crawford's boat had pulled towards the light for the whole night. At one stage he could make out both sidelights—he didn't know when.

Of course he didn't. Listen to him at the U.S. Inquiry: "No, I could not say I saw any sidelights."

"Did you see any more of the light than you have described?"

"No. At daybreak it seemed to disappear. . . ."

The sidelights had grown in his imagination since he had left New York.

Thus, dramatically, was the stage set for the opportune arrival of Ernest Gill, donkeyman, formerly of the *Californian*.

His story as it unfolded was much as it had been in New York. He didn't mention the exact time here but it was before he went off watch that he was walking along the starboard rail and saw a large steamer.

". . . It could not have been anything but a passenger boat—she was too large. I could see two rows of lights which I took to be porthole lights and several groups of lights which I took to be saloon and deck lights. I knew it was a passenger boat. That is all I saw of the ship . . . she was a good distance off I should say not more than 10 miles and probably less." Gill also saw the edge of the ice floe 4 or 5 miles away. He went and called his mate, and later came on deck again, sometime after 12.30, by which time the ship had disappeared. He saw a flash near where the steamer

---

1 The water was 2 miles deep!

had been which might have been a falling star—it descended and then disappeared.

"I did not pay any attention to that. A few minutes after, probably five minutes, I threw my cigarette away and looked over and I could see from the water's edge—what appeared to be the water's edge—a great distance away—well, it was unmistakably a rocket—you could make no mistake about it."

"Now can you tell me whether that was in the same direction from you as the steamer had been that you had seen?"

"It was slightly astern of where I had seen the steamer. The steamer was more than ahead of us, just on our quarter as we say, and the light was more astern. It was more abeam of our ship."

This passage means nothing: the nautical terms used are all contradictory. But he was not asked to explain himself.

"Do you know whether you had swung at all?"

"I could not say."

"Was the rocket in the same direction as what you took to be the falling star?"

"Yes, in the same direction."

"Did you watch any more?"

"I stayed for about three or four minutes after that but it was extremely cold, and I was just dressed in a thin flannel suit and I did not care to stay any longer on deck. I went below."

Could it be that Gill was the only person on the *Californian* who did see the *Titanic*'s rockets? There is no doubt that these lights which he saw were not the ones seen by Stone and Gibson, the apprentice, over the ship which they were watching, because there was no ship in Gill's story—or rather a ship which had disappeared over the horizon. And yet from his garbled description of the direction he saw the rockets—on the beam to starboard—the ship should have been there if Stone and Gibson reported correctly.

The only positive things which emerge from Gill's evidence are that these were not the same rockets described by Stone and Gibson, and if his was the ship described by Groves she must have steamed over the horizon in about a quarter of an hour, because Groves had pointed her out to

Stone when he came on to the upper bridge at about 12.15, and Gill saw she had gone at 12.30 approximately. Did the *Titanic* steam at some speed between 12.15 and 12.30? The evidence is quite clear that she was stopped while her boats were lowered, but what time did the first boat get in the water? Wherever and for whatever distance she may have steamed—if she did much steaming at all—it is extremely unlikely that she would have steamed away from the *Californian*.

* * *

Leaving Gill, and passing back to the *Titanic*'s witnesses again, Frederick Fleet, the lookout who had said in New York that he had seen a single white light on the port bow which he had thought might have been a fisherman, was not asked about the light by counsel for the Board of Trade. In New York he had said positively that there were no lights visible while he was in the crow's-nest. In the British Inquiry he was at first not asked. Why? His mate Lee, who had given evidence before the *Californian* officers were called, had been asked whether any lights had been visible while he was on lookout and had said, "No."

When Fleet was being examined it was left to Mr Scanlan, appearing for the National Sailors' and Firemen's Union, to ask him the *only* question that was directed to him about ships visible during his watch.

"Did you see this light on the port bow before you left the crow's-nest?"

"No, it must have been about one o'clock."

He was examined at great length about whether his eyes were all right, and how long it had been since he had his last eyesight test and who had examined him, to his gradually increasing disgust, until, when Mr Harbinson for the Third Class passengers rose, he at first refused to answer, and then asked belligerently "Is there any more likes to have a go at me?"

Mersey turned to the Board of Trade benches. "Do you want to ask him anything more?"

Sir Rufus: "Oh no!"

Fleet: "A good job too."

Mersey: "I am much obliged to you. I think you have given your evidence very well, although you seem to distrust us all ."

"Thank you," said Fleet and withdrew.

When Bruce Ismay was called to give his account of the night's events he said he thought he saw a light on the starboard bow when his boat was in the water. They had pulled towards it but it seemed to disappear as daylight came.

"If you will excuse me saying so," he went on, "I do not think it was a steamer at all—I think it was a sailing ship we saw."

Mersey took notice immediately. "Am I to understand that you do not think it was the *Californian*?"

"I am sure it was not."

"I am rather sorry to hear that."

"This was on the starboard side of the ship. I understand the *Californian* was seen on the port side of the ship—or the ship that was supposed to be the *Californian*. This light I saw was on the starboard side."

"Never mind about what side it was at all. Have you come to the conclusion that the vessel whose lights were seen for so long a time was not the *Californian*?"

"No, sir."

"I thought you said you had come to that conclusion," said Mersey, perplexed.

"No, I said that the light we pulled for I do not think was the *Californian*'s light. . . the only light I saw was the one we rowed for."

Later Sir Rufus pointed out to him, "The *Californian* is of course a vessel under the control of your company—the company of which you are president?"

"Financially, yes. So far as the management of the company is concerned I have nothing to do with it."

The following day Ismay was still giving evidence to the great variety of counsel who were examining him in minute detail. Lord Mersey returned to the subject of the *Californian*.

"I want you to tell me about this light you rowed for. Your impression is that that was not the light of the *Californian*?"

"That is my impression," Ismay replied, "because it was a dull white light. . . . When we left the ship it would be on the starboard side. . . . We rowed on and we thought the light became more distinct and then it seemed to draw away from us again."

"Have you any doubt, having heard the evidence, that the *Californian* did see the rockets from the *Titanic*?"

"Judging from the evidence I should say not."

"Judging from the evidence you would say——?"

"That our rockets were seen by the *Californian*."

"I thought yesterday I misunderstood you. Your opinion is that the rockets sent up from the *Titanic* were seen by the people on board the *Californian*?"

"*Yes, from what I have read.*"

Ismay was not examined by Robertson Dunlop.

∗ ∗ ∗

On the twenty-fourth day of the Inquiry, in the middle of hearing evidence from the man who had succeeded Sir Alfred Chalmers as chief nautical adviser to the Board of Trade, Sir Rufus Isaacs gave the first official intimation that the *Californian* incident would be brought before the Court in the questions which the Board of Trade wished the Court to consider.

"It does occur to me and to my friend the Solicitor-General associated with me in it that it is important that the question should be specifically put and that your Lordship should take it into account, and that it ought not to be passed over merely as a matter throwing some general light upon the Inquiry. It has already been examined into, and my friend Mr Dunlop has been representing the *Californian*, and therefore we put the question and ask your Lordship to answer it."

Mersey nodded. "Quite so. I do not suppose that I have any jurisdiction to direct that the Captain's certificate should be interfered with?"

"No, I think that only arises in a collision between two vessels. Then there is jurisdiction."

Captain Lord and the other officers of the *Californian* had been called only as witnesses, the Court had disallowed their being made parties to the proceedings, they had returned to their homes or their ship without any further notice of investigation being served upon them, and now, towards the end of the Inquiry the first question in any way relating to the *Californian* or the conduct of her Captain was being placed before the Court.

On June 19th, the twenty-seventh day of the Inquiry the specific additions to the questions were given. To question 24: "What was the cause of the loss of the *Titanic* and of the loss of life which thereby ensued or occurred?" Sir Rufus proposed to add, "What vessel had the opportunity of rendering assistance to the *Titanic,* and if any, how was it that assistance did not reach the *Titanic* before the *Carpathia* arrived?"

Mersey asked, "Will that involve my dealing with the *Frankfurt?*"

"Well, only a reference. It is quite simple I think. The only one that gives any difficulty with regard to this—any examination—is the *Californian.* As to the *Mount Temple* you have the evidence about that. The question will cover the *Californian.*"

Now, what did Sir Rufus mean when he said that the Court had the evidence about the *Mount Temple?* The only *Mount Temple* men called were the Captain and the wireless operator. The operator was in his Marconi room. The only navigational evidence, the only evidence of anyone who was about the decks at the time, was that of the Captain. Why was Captain Moore's evidence as to his position more sacrosanct than Captain Lord's?

The next day Captain Rostron gave his evidence. About the weather conditions he said, "I never saw a clearer night. It was a beautiful night." And of Captain Smith, "He was a very experienced officer."

"Of very high standing?"

"Very high indeed."

Dunlop was not in Court, but he had briefed Mr Bucknill (later Lord Justice Bucknill) to read out on his behalf an affidavit which had been made by Captain Rostron in New York.

"I approached the position of the *Titanic,*" read Bucknill, "42° 46'N, 50° 14 W, on a course substantially N 52°W true. . . . At five o'clock it was light enough to see all round the horizon. We then saw two steamships to the northwards, perhaps 7 or 8 miles distant. Neither of them was the *Californian*. One of them was a four-masted steamer with one funnel, and the other a two-masted steamer with one funnel. I never saw the *Mount Temple* to identify her. The first time I saw the *Californian* was about eight o'clock on the morning of 15th April. She was then about 5 to 6 miles distant bearing WSW true and steaming towards the *Carpathia*. The *Carpathia* was then in substantially the position of the *Titanic* at the time of the disaster as given to us by wireless. I consider the position of the *Titanic* as given to us by her officers to be correct.

"During the night previous to getting to the *Titanic's* position we saw masthead lights quite distinctly of another steamer between us and the *Titanic*. That was about quarter past three . . . and one of the officers swore he also saw one of the sidelights . . . the port sidelight. This was about a quarter past three. . . bearing about two points on the starboard bow— about N 30°W true."

Rostron agreed that he had said all this.

CHAPTER FOURTEEN

On the thirty-third day of the Inquiry Robertson Dunlop rose to make his final speech in defence of the *Californian.*

"Now, Mr Dunlop," was Mersey's caustic greeting, "how long do you think you will take to convince us that the *Californian* did not see the *Titanic's* lights?"

"I think, my Lord," Dunlop replied slowly, "I will take about two hours.

"Now I wish to say a word on behalf of myself because although I have been present very rarely during the course of this Inquiry some of my friends who have been present have told me that my position as an advocate for the *Californian* is not altogether an enviable one."

What better statement could there be of the attitude of mind with which the Court viewed "the *Californian* incident"? And it was not long before it was given form and words from the bench.

Dunlop started by detailing the navigational evidence from the *Californian* as recorded in her log-book[1]—times, positions and courses from noon to the Chief Officer's pole star sight and up to the time she stopped 20 miles North of the *Titanic's* CQD position. Whereupon Mersey, who had been following this on a chart which Dunlop had marked for him, exclaimed "But then, you know, the Admiral who sits on my right tells me that the information to be obtained from the log does not enable anyone to lay down the track."

Dunlop replied, "The reason for that is that the course which was mentioned in the log is the course by compass, and until your Lordship has the deviation book you cannot obtain the magnetic course."

---

1 See Appendix G.

"I am told that there ought not to be a log of this kind without the error of deviation being put down."

"There is no column in it that I can see, for entering the deviation I think."

"Is it not as a rule put in the remarks column?"

"Sometimes it is, my Lord. I do not know whether it is done on board the *Californian*. The log-book will show that."

Lord Mersey looked through the log. "Apparently it is not done aboard the *Californian*."

"Apparently not."

Had the Admiral or Lord Mersey looked at the regulations issued by the White Star Line, the big brother of the Leyland Line, they would have seen that the deviation was not required to be written in the log books of their ships. Had they wanted to check up on the deviation they might well have been able to do so from the log-book they had in their possession by looking back until they found a course similar to the one in question.

Dunlop continued. But he had not proceeded very much further before he was interrupted again by Mersey.

". . . Are you going to say they were not distress signals. . ." (seen from the *Californian*).

He replied that they were taken to be company's signals.

"It does not concern me whether they were distress signals or whether they were not for the moment. What concerns me is were they signals from the *Titanic*? If they were not signals from the *Titanic* we do not know what signals they were, or why they were fired until we have the vessel that fired them." After which he returned to the subject of the deviation book.

Dunlop replied to repeated questions that Lord had not come prepared—not even with the log-book, which had to be sent for.

Mersey: "Telegraph to Liverpool for the deviation book."

Dunlop went on, "My Lord, I submit that the Master, if he is to be judged at all, must get the benefit of his log. It is the log-book kept by the Chief Officer, a person whose conduct is not in any way the object of this Inquiry and who is not concerned in the result of what your Lordships views may be."

Mersey then wanted to know what course Lord had been steering the following morning to get to the position of the *Titanic*'s wreckage. In the log it was simply "Various courses—proceeding slow, pushing through thick field ice, cleared the thickest ice, proceeding full speed, pushing ice." The Commissioner for Wrecks thought that all the various courses should have been stated in the log.

Suffice it to say that this is impracticable with a large number of sudden alterations, and the invariable practice on these occasions is that which Lord followed.

When Dunlop was allowed to continue with his address he made the point that as the steamer approached the *Californian* on the night of the 14th, Captain Lord had said she was not the *Titanic*, and both the Second Officer and Gibson had said that she had no appearance at all of being a passenger boat. ". . . And even Gill, the donkeyman, with his imagination stimulated by what had taken place in New York could not and did not say that she was the *Titanic*—Gill thought she was a passenger steamer."

Gill had thought this after twelve o'clock. "According to Groves, whose evidence was the more dramatic of the two, he said he saw the deck lights go out at 11.40. Gill nevertheless sees them all ablaze a few minutes after twelve. If Groves is right Gill must be wrong and if Gill is right Groves must be wrong. So much for Gill. . . .

"Groves, the Third Officer, when he was pressed at the end of his evidence—I will not say by whom—to say he thought it was the *Titanic*, my Lord, he answered this——"

Mersey interrupted, "Did I press him?"

"Your Lordship asked the question."

"I thought so."

Dunlop continued. "Up to that moment, my Lord, he had not the courage to say that she was the *Titanic*, but thus stimulated, he said this: 'From what I have heard subsequently I do, but I do not put myself forward as an experienced man.' My Lord it is perfectly clear, I submit, that Groves did not think so at the time, because at the end of his watch he went to have his usual chat with the Marconi operator who was a kind of 'Evening News' to him. He went there to find what ships there were and what news there was, and according to the operator's version of the conversation that took place at the end of Groves' watch, not a word was said about the steamer which Groves described in the witness-box. . . .

"Groves attached no importance at the time to the vessel which he had seen, and he attached no importance at all to any of the incidents which he described when here in the witness-box; and I submit that his evidence was largely the result of imagination stimulated by vanity. So much with regard to the class of vessels seen."

He then drew attention to the fact that all the witnesses on the *Californian*, with the exception of Groves, had seen only one masthead light, and went on to describe the due West course which the *Titanic* was steering before 11.40 which must have presented her green sidelight to any ship to the North of her. "The sidelight the witnesses in the *Californian* saw was the red light—that is the Third Officer, the Second Officer and Gibson."

When Dunlop described the effect of the *Titanic*'s starboarding as certainly not such as to open the red light Lord Mersey drew his attention to Lord's evidence that he saw a green light. Dunlop agreed, but reiterated that neither the Third Officer, the Second Officer nor Gibson saw it. He referred to Boxhall's evidence that the *Titanic* had not swung at all after the engines had been stopped.

Mersey came back again to Lord's statement about the green light.

Dunlop replied, "But the Third Officer—and it was the Third Officer on whose evidence your Lordship seemed to be placing most reliance at the time——"

"What was his name?"

"Groves." Dunlop went on to list the questions he had asked Groves about the sidelights. ". . . He said the steamer when he first saw her was bearing South . . . half an hour later he sees her about 6 miles distant bearing SSE. That indicates a vessel steering somewhere about NE—not a vessel during that time going to westward as the *Titanic* was." Dunlop then dealt with Gill's evidence very shortly as unreliable, ". . . the evidence of a donkeyman going forward to call his mate." Mersey: "Do you suggest he came here with a desire—I will not say with an intention to deceive—but with a desire to make out that it was the *Titanic* they did see?"

"Yes, my Lord, I think he did, and he did for this reason. This donkeyman, hearing of the loss of the *Titanic* the next morning, a few days later arrived in New York, interviewed by New York reporters, giving evidence at the American Inquiry, his imagination got fired by all this excitement and he began to imagine the steamer of which he had had a momentary glimpse was in fact the *Titanic*.

"I submit that from whatever point of view you test the evidence of the *Californian*, either as regards class of vessels seen, the lights seen, the movements which they describe as having seen, they all point to the same conclusion, that the vessel which they saw was not and could not have been the *Titanic*.

"This is further corroborated by the evidence of the Master of the *Carpathia* whose evidence your Lordship will probably be inclined to accept."

Dunlop went on to list the evidence of the lookouts of the *Titanic*, none of whom saw the *Californian*, either before or after twelve. And he listed the *Titanic*'s Second Officer, Third Officer, two quarter-masters, three lookout men, and also Mr Ismay who saw the light or lights of what they thought was a fishing boat.

"Only Boxhall, the Fourth Officer, Lucas, an A.B., and Hart, a steward, saw sometime between one and two a steamer which approached and to which they signalled by morse signals, and later on saw her steam away. They are the only witnesses who mentioned seeing a steamer at all, and that was not until something between one and two—obviously not the *Californian*, because the *Californian* at that time was lying stopped in the ice. . . . The steamer which Boxhall said he saw was never heard of or seen again."

Dunlop did not have his names complete or his times quite accurately, but this is not surprising considering the conflicting evidence, and the fact that the Court never did find out what time the *Titanic* was keeping. His statement is nevertheless generally correct if "between twelve and two" is substituted for "between one and two".

"I do not know whether this steamer which Boxhall is referring to," he went on, "is or is not the steamer which the Chief Officer of the *Californian* saw at four o'clock, a vessel which had been steaming to the SW and afterwards was seen steaming in a northerly and easterly direction. That is the only evidence which seems to connect the vessel which Boxhall saw with any vessel which the *Californian* saw."

Dunlop, having, so far as he was concerned, proved that the *Titanic* and *Californian* could not have been in sight of one another was asked by Mersey if he had made any attempt to find out what steamers were in the vicinity. He replied that it did not concern him or the Leyland Line to endeavour to ascertain the name of a steamer which may have seen the *Titanic*'s rockets and did not go to her assistance. Nevertheless he had from *Lloyd's Weekly Shipping Index* compiled a list of steamers which he had put upon the chart for Lord Mersey.

"It is no part of my purpose and certainly no part of theirs [his clients, the Leyland Line] to attempt to throw blame upon any other vessel."

Mersey: "This is a very high sense of duty. I do not appreciate it at all."

Dunlop referred to the deposition of Captain Rostron of the *Carpathia* about the two vessels which he had seen at or about five o'clock. "We do not know to whom they belonged, where they were bound, or where they came from; but clearly these two vessels were at this time near the neighbourhood of the *Titanic*'s loss."

He went on to describe the vessels which Captain Lord and Groves had seen near the *Mount Temple* and the one the Chief and Second Officers of the *Californian* had seen at four o'clock in the morning. After which he detailed the movements of one of the ships he had obtained from Lloyd's. This was the *Trautenfels*—a two-masted, single funnel (black with red stripes) steamer of 2,932 tons belonging to the Hansa Line of Bremen, bound Hamburg-New York, which was not fitted with wireless apparatus. She had left Hamburg on March 31st—was spoken on April 7th—and on April 14th, in 42° 1′N, 49° 53′W, sighted two icebergs fully 200 feet high. "Soon afterwards heavy field ice was encountered which extended for a distance of 30 miles and made it necessary for the steamer to run in a SW direction for 25 miles to clear it. In the field ice thirty bergs were counted, some very large. In the northward no clear water was seen so that the Captain estimated that the ice in that direction must have extended fully 30 miles. . . ." Dunlop at this point was reading from *Lloyd's Weekly Shipping Index* for May 2nd, 1912. He agreed that the limitations of this description were that no times were given, but submitted that the *Trautenfels* did do what the witnesses from the *Californian* said their steamer did.

Apart from the weakness in lack of any evidence of time there is the point that it is doubtful if the Captain of the *Trautenfels* could have seen 30 miles to the northward or even judged what conditions were, at the time of night that the *Californian* witnesses saw their ship. Nevertheless Dunlop had proved that she was in the vicinity on the day in question, and undoubtedly met the same icefield. It is interesting that Captain Knapp of the U.S. Hydrographic department also listed the steamer *Trautenfels* as one of those in the vicinity, in his evidence to the Senate Committee.

Mersey asked what sidelight this vessel would be showing to the *Californian* and so started what, in the light of his subsequent report, is the most interesting exchange in this part of the Inquiry.

"She would be showing her green light," Dunlop replied.

Mersey kept on, "Yes, but what is your (*Californian*) evidence of the light you saw?"

"One of the witnesses saw the green light."

"Two of the witnesses saw a red light."

"Three," Dunlop corrected him. "The others all saw a red light."

"Then you know this cannot be the ship if the red light is the thing—this cannot be the one you saw."

"I am quite content if it is not. If your Lordship takes it as the red light we saw of a steamer, then it is clearly not the *Titanic*. That throws the *Titanic* out."

(Game, set and match.)

Mersey: "I quite appreciate that."

After Sir Rufus Isaacs had read out a letter he had received from Boston detailing the arrival dates of the *Trautenfels* and a sister ship, the *Lindenfels*, as the 18th and 20th of April respectively, Dunlop continued to describe another steamer he had extracted from *Lloyd's*—the petroleum steamer *Paula*. She was a three-master of 2,748 tons gross with a black funnel and a red "R" on a yellow backing, belonging to the Deutsche Americana Petroleum Co. of Hamburg. She also gave her position on the 14th, and Dunlop had marked it on Lord Mersey's chart. This was not given aloud in the British Court, but, turning back to Knapp's evidence at the Senate Committee we find that on April 14th, 5.30 p.m., the master reported heavy pack ice and thirty large icebergs in one field from 41°

55'N, 50° 13'W, to 41° 40'N, 50° 30'W. In other words the *Paula* reached the *Titanic*'s icefield during daylight on the 14th, and we do not know what she did subsequently. Dunlop went on to read out other ships which he had been able to discover in the area, the *Memphian, Campanillo* and the *President Lincoln*, and followed up by submitting that the evidence as to which steamer it may have been was incomplete. "And as to the question of why this steamer exhibited rockets the answer is that we do not know because nobody has been called as a witness from that steamer."

Mersey interjected, "You may be wrong about that. A number of people were called from the *Titanic*."

"Yes, but if it was not the *Titanic*."

"I agree that if it was not the *Titanic* nobody has been called from this steamer."

Dunlop mentioned the evidence from the *Carpathia* that she had sent up rockets; this suggested that rockets were in fact used as signals. He submitted that the conduct of the Second Officer of the *Californian* was inconsistent with that of a man who thought he had seen distress signals; that he would certainly have roused the Master had he done so.

Mersey questioned him on the number of rockets that had been seen, and Dunlop replied "eight" and questioned by Lord Mersey on the number sent from the *Titanic* replied that one witness thought about eight—they were going up for an hour, and he didn't suppose that anyone counted them. Mersey, however, thought this a coincidence.

Dunlop went on to deal with Lord's actions directly he knew of the disaster, how he had passed a steamer blocked in the ice at full speed, and not content when he reached the *Carpathia* to accept their word that they had picked up everyone, he had steamed around for another two hours. "The conduct of Captain Lord that morning was not the conduct of a man who was callous or indifferent to the duties which he owes to humanity. I submit that his inaction was purely the result of ignorance of the conditions that were existing some 20 or 30 miles away from him on this particular night. . . . Had he known he would have rushed to the *Titanic*'s assistance, and no one regrets more than he does that he did not do so, but the remorse for his apparent inactivity during these fatal hours of midnight is relieved by the knowledge that if he had gone to this vessel's assistance when called by Gibson at five minutes past two he could not by any possibility have got to her before the *Carpathia* had herself arrived on the scene.

"As I have already explained to your Lordship the *Californian* was distant two hours steaming from the position of the *Titanic,* and if she had gone to her assistance at five past two it is perfectly obvious that he could not have reached her until after about 4.30, which was half an hour after the *Carpathia* got there. That is assuming that he could have made at night the progress which he was able to make in the daytime. . .

"In the interests of justice the Court ought not to pass any censure on Captain Lord. In the first place the Commission was not appointed to inquire into his conduct at all. His conduct had absolutely nothing to do with the object of the Inquiry as stated by the Attorney-General in his opening speech. There was no jurisdiction to hold an Inquiry into Captain Lord's conduct. . . . Under the rules which regulate these proceedings at these Inquiries if a charge is to be made against a Master he must be told what that charge is. That is required by the Merchant Shipping Act. . .

"No such notice was given to the Master of the *Californian.* On the 26th April Captain Lord and Gill gave their evidence at the American Inquiry and a transcript of that evidence was in due course transmitted to the Board of Trade. On the 11th May, on the arrival of the *Californian* in Liverpool, statements were taken by the officers of the Board of Trade from Captain Lord, the three officers, two apprentices, an A.B., and some of the engine-room staff. On the 14th May Captain Lord attended here and gave his evidence, and his testimony was relevant to some of the questions which have been submitted to your Lordship. I asked on that occasion to be allowed to appear on behalf of the *Californian* and the Master, and my application was very properly resisted, or certainly not assented to by the Attorney-General, who properly explained that although the evidence showed that the *Titanic* was not very far from the *Californian,* it was very difficult to say that the evidence had any bearing on the questions submitted to your Lordship, and therefore, as the *Californian* was sailing, he proposed to put a few questions to the witnesses. . . .

"No charge was made at that time against Captain Lord, no intimation was made that any charge would be made, and he was not made a party to the Inquiry. He appeared here in no other capacity than as a witness to give the Court such assistance as he could . . . and the capacity in which I appeared is properly stated on the front pages of the various records of the days' proceedings as having watched the proceedings on behalf of the owners and officers of the *Californian,* as distinct from appearing on behalf of the *Californian,* which are the words I see opposite more distinguished names.

"It is not until the 14th June, a month after Captain Lord has left the witness-box, that an intimation is given that the Board of Trade propose to formulate a question relating to the *Californian,* which would give the Court an opportunity of censuring Captain Lord. . . . It is manifest from the statements of fact as I have stated them that Captain Lord has been treated here in a way which is absolutely contrary to the principles on which justice is usually administered, or on which these Inquiries are usually conducted."

This part of Dunlop's address is absolutely unassailable on legal grounds, and remarkably little time was taken up by Sir Rufus Isaacs in his closing address to refute it. The answer is that it is irrefutable.

Dunlop went on with the same theme and considered whether the question should have been put at all. "The object of it is explained by the Attorney-General on page 649. There it is stated that the law officers of the Crown should get from your Lordship a finding of the facts relating to the *Californian* incident in order to enable them to make up their minds whether in the public interest they ought to institute criminal proceedings under section 6 of the Maritime Convention Act. If that is the object of the question, I submit it is a wholly unfair object. If this man may be prosecuted hereafter he ought to have had notice of this question before he entered the witness-box; he ought to have known precisely what the charge against him was, and he ought to have had the opportunity of hearing the evidence given by other witnesses before he himself had to give his own evidence.

"If you deal with this question, my Lord, and find the facts against Captain Lord, what chance would he have of a fair and impartial trial before a jury which had read your Lordship's report?"

Again Dunlop seemed convinced, although he had presented a watertight legal and evidential case against either the right to censure Captain

Lord or the likelihood of the *Californian* having been less than 20 miles from the *Titanic*—he still seemed convinced that there was a strong likelihood of the Court's censure.

He continued, "The ordeal of public criticism and public censure through which he has already passed will, without further censure, be a sufficient warning to him and to other Masters of the strict duty that lies upon those who go down to the sea in ships of rendering assistance to other vessels in distress. . . . That counsel have to appear here to vindicate his reputation and defend his honour is not the least humiliation that this man has had to undergo."

Dunlop was weakening. He had made his case and shown how insubstantial was the evidence against the *Californian,* shown how unjust the question which had been added, as it were behind Lord's back, but now he was changing tack and making a plea for mercy.

"For all the reasons I have urged I do ask your Lordship not to pass any censure upon this man, and I venture to think that if your Lordship does not censure him then truth and justice and mercy will meet together in your Lordship's report."

Why this extraordinary *volte face* after his excellent address? Could it be that he felt the hostility, or perhaps the apathy[2] of the Bench he was trying to get through to? Could it be that he knew the issue was already judged? There seem no other explanations for his climb-down.

---

2 Dunlop's submission occupies fourteen pages of the official Report. The first eleven pages record almost constant interruptions; the last three have *no interruptions at all.*

CHAPTER FIFTEEN

The legal, if not the nautical and factual part of Dunlop's speech obviously exercised Lord Mersey's mind. Here he is discussing his reservations with Sir Rufus Isaacs in the latter's closing address.

"I said a long time ago that I doubted whether I ought to find a dead man, or a man who is not represented, guilty of negligence."

Isaacs replied, "Your Lordship will decide upon that when you come to your judgement."

"Taking the *Californian,*" Mersey went on. "That man is not represented. He came here merely as a witness."

"Who?"

"Captain Lord."

"Oh yes, my Lord, he was represented."

"Yes, he is here, in the sense that somebody sent by his owners did speak for him."

"Then, my Lord, I would sooner deal with that separate if I may—I know what your Lordship has in your mind."

"What I mean is that he has not been cited here to defend himself against the charge made against him of negligence."

"Your Lordship is speaking now of the Captain of the *Californian*?" Isaacs was not usually so obtuse; the inference that he was gaining time to think is inescapable.

"Yes, Captain Lord."

"But that is quite a different thing."

"I am not sure. You are talking about Captain Smith. What I am pointing out is this, that Captain Smith could not be here—he is dead—he could not have been cited. But the Captain of the *Californian* is here really merely as a witness. He has not been cited to answer a charge of negligence, and I have great reluctance to find people guilty of negligence when they are not cited and not charged with it, and have not had a proper opportunity of answering that charge."

"I will deal with Captain Lord's case, my Lord."

Sir Rufus slid off the subject. Mersey's conscience as a Law Lord had activated this exchange, and he had presented the case against censuring Captain Lord as well as it could have been presented from the legal angle. But little more was said about it. Sir Rufus continued his wide-ranging speech which covered all aspects of the *Titanic's* approach to the icefield, foundering, and the escape of those who survived, until he reached the last question, the *Californian* incident.

"I have been most anxious, and I have been throughout, to find some possible excuse for the inaction on the part of the *Californian*. It is not a case of desiring to bring home to them that they did not do their duty—our anxiety and your Lordship's anxiety would be, if possible, to find some reason to explain the failure by them to take any steps when they had seen the distress signals. I can only say that to me it is a matter of extreme regret that I have come to the conclusion that the submission I must make to you is that there is no excuse. . . ."

At which point it is worth noting that Sir Rufus has plunged in straight away with the fact of distress signals, although no one on the *Californian*—with the possible exception of Gill who was a donkey-man—admitted seeing distress signals. And lest this sounds too academic it cannot be repeated too often that no one mistakes distress signals on clear, dark nights from ships 5 to 6 miles away—especially when there is evidence to prove that human voices (cries from drowning) carried some miles over the water, and that the distress rockets from the *Carpathia* were *heard before her lights were seen.* Sir Rufus was not a sailor—if we discount his one voyage as ship's boy—and could be excused, perhaps, for not knowing this; but *he was instructed by the Board of Trade.* Mersey may not have known, but he had already had the International Signals of Distress pointed out to him. These were:

"At night:

1) A gun or other explosive signal fired at intervals of about a minute. (Rowe, remember, had been asked to bring up the *detonators* from the after bridge.)

2) Flames from the vessel as from a burning tar barrel.

3) Rockets or shells, throwing stars of *any colour or description* fired one at a time at short intervals. (Author's italics.)

4) A continuous sounding with any fog signalling apparatus. (Although the *Titanic* did not use her whistle, the officers, remember, could not make themselves heard above the noise of steam from the funnels when the crew first came on deck.)"

And Mersey, in his Report, listed all the *Titanic's* life-saving appliances, among which were "36 rocket signals *in lieu of guns*". Lightoller had already described the effect of these: "It's really a timed shell." Distress rockets were not just bright lights; they were timed shells carried *in lieu of guns,* and their object was to make a loud explosion such as all those on board the *Californian* must have heard if they had been even 10 miles from the liner.

It was common knowledge, and common practice, that the transatlantic liners also carried their own distinguishing flares—and used them. It was not until *after* the *Titanic* went down that this practice was held to be bad. It was not until 1952 that the colour of distress rockets was stipulated, and then they became *red.*

Perhaps Mersey didn't know much about distress signals, but he had three sailors on the Bench with him who should have known.

Sir Rufus went on to point out that when the case opened all that he had known about the *Californian* were Gill's reported statements in the American Press, and the statement of the master to the American Inquiry. Mr Dunlop for the owners and crew had in fact examined Captain Lord in the box. Sir Rufus quoted some questions that Dunlop had put to Lord. "That makes it quite plain my friend appeared, and appeared from the first moment, for the Master.

"May I just call your Lordship's attention to the Rules. My submission with regard to it is that by appearing he becomes a party."

It is difficult to understand how Sir Rufus came to this conclusion because Robertson Dunlop had specifically asked for his clients to be made a party and had been refused. It might seem that this is being unnecessarily pedantic—after all, as Sir Rufus said, Dunlop *had* appeared for Captain Lord from the first. But this is only half the story. He had not been present in Court to challenge the evidence of many of the witnesses whose evidence appeared to incriminate Lord; he had, for the most part confined himself to being present only while the *Californian* witnesses had been on the stand. Apart from the opportunities he thus missed for showing up flaws in the evidence apparently against Lord, particularly from the lookouts and the men who had remembered differently in America, and emphasising the evidence for him, it is well known that no judge likes an advocate who is absent from Court for long periods. It could well be that Dunlop, despite an excellent argument in his final address, actually lost the case for Lord by his lax attendance.

Sir Rufus continued, "I am not asking your Lordship in any way to deal with this matter, except to state the conclusion to which you arrive."

"Have I any jurisdiction to do more?" Mersey asked.

"I think not. . . I submit to you that all we are asking your Lordship to deal with is the conflict of fact that arises upon the evidence, and nothing more. . . . There is a conflict between the various witnesses called from the *Californian*. The facts alleged on the one hand are these, that the *Californian* saw distress signals. As to that there is no conflict." What is he saying? He must have known from the evidence that no one on the *Californian* admitted to seeing distress signals, although they were interrogated for a very considerable time.

"To be quite accurate I think one might say that the Captain does not admit that they were distress signals, but he admits they might have been. . . . Further that those distress signals came in from a vessel in the direction in which the *Titanic* was. That there is no dispute about." This again is not clear, because to make this statement with regard to the ship seen from the *Californian*, he must dispute the position given by the *Californian*, in which case there could have been no certainty in which direction the rockets should have been seen. Further, there *was* a conflict of evidence about the position of the *Titanic*, which could be roughly summed up as

Captain Moore (*Mount Temple*) and Captain Lord versus Captain Rostron and Boxhall. So again, this statement is completely untrue.

"The further point is that, having seen these distress signals the *Californian* took no steps except to attempt to do morse with a light. . . ." It would be tedious to repeat that these were not proved to be distress signals. But it should be mentioned that it is perfectly reasonable to call up a ship 5 miles away with the morse lamp if you have reason to suppose she has no wireless—indeed this is the *only* way it is possible to call up a ship whose name is not known. Lord thought she had no wireless because he had been told by his operator that the only ship in the vicinity was the *Titanic,* and this ship close to him had no appearance of being a passenger vessel at all, let alone the largest passenger vessel in the world—ergo, she must be a ship without wireless. This was 1912—very early days for radio and by no means all ships were fitted.

"The comment I make upon it is that for the Master of a British vessel to see distress signals—whether they come from a large passenger steamer or not—is a very serious matter. . . . Supposing your Lordship came to the conclusion that we were right in saying that she did see distress signals and that they were the signals of the passenger steamer *Titanic,* and took no steps, that is a finding of fact which I should ask your Lordship to give in the Report which you may make. I do not ask you to do anything more."

Mersey: "Let me put it quite plainly. If Captain Lord saw these distress signals and neglected a reasonable opportunity which he had of going to the relief of a vessel in distress, it may well be that he is guilty of a misdemeanour. That is so is it not?"

"Yes, under the Merchant Shipping Act, 1906."

"Am I to try that question?"

"Certainly not."

"I think not."

"Certainly not, my Lord. I never asked and could not ask your Lordship to try that question, but nevertheless the facts, which you are asked to find, whether they reflect upon him or not, are material to the Inquiry."

This then, was the way the Attorney-General proposed to get around the legal objections. The Court was only to be asked to find the facts, not to censure Captain Lord in any way, although the facts themselves, if found as submitted, would be a sufficient censure.

Mersey: "The facts I can find, but I do not want, unless I am obliged to do it, to find a man guilty of crime."

This was nonsense. Mersey was not obliged to do anything. He was the President of the Court. His intention from the first day he had seen the *Californian* witnesses had been to find Lord guilty; he had made no attempt to disguise it.

Sir Rufus continued his address about the rockets seen, and then reiterated what he wanted the Court to find. "What I am asking you to find is the fact that they did see on the *Californian* distress signals from the *Titanic,* and that the distance of the *Titanic* from the *Californian* was only a few miles."

Mersey asked, "How many?"

"I should put it at something like 7 or 8. It is very difficult to say. I do not profess to be able to say with precision."

He could not say with precision because all the reliable evidence—in fact the entire evidence with the exception of a steward and a donkey-man—pointed to *a ship* having been seen 5 miles from the *Titanic,* and *a ship* having been seen about 5 miles from the *Californian.* But this was much too close to be credible. A greater distance had to be invented. And further than 8 would be to all intents and purposes over the horizon.

Sir Rufus went on to speak of the evidence. "Now the evidence, which is voluminous, is undoubtedly to some extent very conflicting on some points. I am not sure that it is at all possible to reconcile some of these statements that are made, from whatever aspect you look at them. But upon the material points I submit there is not any real difficulty. The material points are first of all whether the *Californian* saw the distress signals. One answer of Captain Lord it seems to me quite disposes of that——"

Mersey interjected, "I do not know if it will relieve you at all in the trouble you are taking, but I think we are all of the opinion that the distress rockets that were seen from the *Californian* were the distress signals of the *Titanic.*"

So Sir Rufus passed on from his pertinent quotation to describe the Captain hearing about the rockets by voice pipe and Gibson's conversation with him later. He attempted "to be quite fair to the Captain", and recalled how he admitted hearing the door close. "On the other hand the boy's statement is very definite and very specific as to what happened." He went on to submit that although the boy said 1.15 he really meant 12.45,[1] and then recalled Captain Lord's words in the witness-box about the rocket reported to him by Stone. "I asked the Second Officer, I said is that a company's signal? and he said he didn't know. Question: Then that did not satisfy you? Answer: No, it did not. Question: I mean, whatever it was it did not satisfy you. Answer: It did not. But I had no reason to think it was anything else."

Mersey: "That is a curious condition of mind."

"Very. And if your Lordship looks at the question just opposite to that we get eventually to question 6943: Very well, that did not satisfy you? Answer: It did not satisfy me. Question: Then if it was not that it might have been a distress signal? Answer: It might have been. Question: And you remained in the chartroom? Answer: I remained in the chartroom.

"Now, my Lord, that establishes quite clearly this, that he thought it might have been, and the moment a man thinks it might have been a distress signal and does not know what else it could be, I should have thought it really means he knew—I will not say he was quite certain—but he knew at any rate this, that there was a serious possibility of some vessel being in urgent need of assistance close by. . . I find it very difficult to understand why it was in those circumstances he remained in the chartroom and made no step . . .

"The shifting of time, according to the evidence that is given has some bearing upon it. It is said, for example, that this white rocket, the first distress signal, was not seen until a quarter past one. It is very difficult to explain this in view of the evidence of the *Titanic,* which is that they were sending up rockets from 12.45. I should have thought upon this evidence and the evidence that follows it, that the estimate of time must be quite wrong."

Sir Rufus was on treacherous ground here. To start with no one has found out the exact difference between the clocks of the two vessels. The *Titanic's* time was undoubtedly ahead of the *Californian's* because she had

---

1 Although Gibson at this time was below attending to the log line!

been considerably further East at noon on the 14th, but how much further had not been probed. It is probable that the difference was between five and twelve minutes, which would make 1.15 *Californian* time between 1.20 and 1.27 *Titanic* time. Secondly, on what was the theory based that the first *Titanic* rocket went up at 12.45? Presumably on the quartermaster Rowe's evidence at the British Inquiry that he had left the after bridge at 12.45. But at the American Inquiry he had been equally positive about leaving the after bridge with the detonators at 12.25. The evidence at the British Inquiry from Boxhall and Pitman is that there was at least one starboard side boat in the water just before the first rocket was fired. The conclusion the British Court came to was that the first boat went away at 12.45 and the first rocket was fired at 12.45—but again Rowe's evidence at the American Inquiry casts some doubt on this. And Rowe is the only man who was noting times at that stage.

Continuing his address, Sir Rufus thought it very striking that no mention of the distress signals was found in the *Californian*'s log. He went on to describe a great deal of Gibson's story, and then came to the apprentice seeing three more rockets at 3.40.

Mersey: "I do not understand this boy's evidence—that he saw three rockets at twenty to four."

"It might be one of two things. It might be that they were some of the signals which were sent up from the boats, but if they were rockets it may be they were the *Carpathia*'s."

"She sent up rockets?" Mersey asked. Where had he been during the Inquiry?

"Yes."

"That is quite possible. . . . However you can pass it by. It does not affect my mind."

Sir Rufus passed it by, and went on to dismiss Lord's claim to being asleep when Gibson called him. He quoted Lord as saying that, "he does not doubt the boy is telling the truth. Question: Just think. You say you do not doubt it for a moment. Do you see what that means? That means that the boy did go into the chartroom to you. He did tell you about the rockets from the ship, and you asked him whether they were white rockets and told him that he was to report if anything further occurred? Answer: So he said. That is what he said. Question: Have you any reason to doubt that is true? Answer: No, I was asleep.

"Yes, well, my Lord, I must say that with the greatest desire to accept that evidence, if possible, I find it impossible. He cannot have been asleep in view of what he was expecting. He had had the report—he was waiting to know whether they had managed to call up this other vessel or not. . . .

"I do submit that the true view of the evidence is that what this boy Gibson is stating is correct, and if you take that view it means this——"

Mersey interrupted, "He struck me as a perfectly honest witness, and the Captain himself, when he is asked if he thinks the boy is speaking the truth, says he does."

This piece of reasoning is breath-taking.

"Yes, and may I add one further factor to your Lordship's consideration. That boy, when he was called was certainly very reluctant to say anything which he thought would tell against the Captain."

"Certainly."

"I mean he was not anxious to make a case against him—quite the reverse, and I think the same observation would apply to Mr Groves, the Third Officer, who also gives very pertinent evidence. But when you have got as far as this, I submit it is really as far as one needs to go in this case. . . . It means this, that that establishes that signals were sent, that they were seen by the *Californian,* that they came from the *Titanic,* that the Captain knew that these signals had been sent up and that the Captain remained in the chartroom and did nothing. Those are the facts which are relevant for the purpose of the Inquiry."[2]

---

2 The whole of Sir Rufus's closing address on the subject of the *Californian* and particularly this paragraph is a perfect illustration of his methods as outlined by his biographer in the *Dictionary cf National Biography:* "He was not a profound lawyer, but hard work and good sense made him the master of all the law that mattered for winning success. . . . His speeches in Court, expressed in commonplace language and directed strictly to the matter in hand, had a verdict-getting quality which showed how well he understood what the tribunal was thinking. Indeed Isaacs's greatest asset at the Bar was not eloquence *but a penetrating power of judgment which enabled him to see the point on which the case would ultimately turn,* the main difficulty of fact to be surmounted, and sometimes the moment when compromise could wisely be effected."

Of course this was as far as the Attorney-General was prepared to go. On every side of him stretched the icy slopes of the evidence that those signals were either *not* from the *Titanic* as he had stated categorically without proving, or that they were from the *Titanic* which lay at a great distance behind this other ship some 5 miles away from the *Californian*. He was not prepared to discuss all the conflicting evidence of Groves and Gill and Gibson, the three men *unaffected* by censure, because he knew that once in amongst it all his case would slide in ruins. He had to stick to the two concrete facts which he had and plug away at them—rockets *were* seen, the Captain *was* called. He dared not even describe the rockets, because once he mentioned that they did not even reach up to the mast lights of the near-by ship, and neither did they make a bang, he would have had an impossible job to reconcile them with the *Titanic's* rockets at that distance.

To put the record straight he was, however, prepared to make the few woolly and entirely misleading statements which follow—which are frankly nonsense.

"There are two factors to bear in mind in that connection (the discrepancies in the various lights) which I think are essential to bear in mind in order to understand this evidence. The one is that the *Californian* was swinging during the whole of this time. It explains what otherwise might be inexplicable—that is why, at first the green light is seen and subsequently the red light. It explains it. I was going to say, for this reason——"

"Seen by the *Californian*?" Mersey interjected.

"Yes. The *Californian* first of all sees the green light; the *Californian* is then heading ENE; it is after she stopped. The *Titanic* is proceeding to the westwards, and at that time the *Titanic* would expose her green light to a vessel which is heading ENE."

The really inexplicable thing about that passage is how it came to be made at all in a serious Inquiry by an advocate briefed by the Board of Trade. It wouldn't have made any difference to the *Titanic's* sidelights if the *Californian* had been heading for the centre of the earth; the *Californian's* heading had no bearing whatsoever on what light a vessel to the south of her and heading westwards would show. "The *Titanic* would be exposing a green light quite clearly."

When questioned by Mersey, Sir Rufus cited Captain Lord's evidence of having seen a green light.

"Then after that the *Titanic,* when she comes into collision with the iceberg, also swings. The evidence about that is the evidence of Rowe."

Rowe's evidence was that the stem was swinging to the South when he was on the fore bridge at either 12.25 in the American Inquiry or 12.45 in the British Inquiry. To show a red light the *Titanic*'s stern would have had to swing past South to SSW, assuming the *Californian* was to the NNE as the Attorney-General obviously did assume from the direction of the rockets seen from the *Californian.* This means, taking Rowe's evidence, as he is, that the *Titanic* did not show a red light until after 12.45—this time of Rowe's having been accepted for the rockets. Groves, who saw the red light from the *Californian,* had then been off watch for well over half an hour. Even if the earlier time of 12.25 is taken, Groves would still have been off watch.

Sir Rufus, determined to make his case, went on to cite the evidence from the *Californian* that she was swinging from north-easterly, through South to WSW, and thus explained Boxhall's evidence of the ship he saw showing a green and then a red light. In fact Boxhall's evidence was that the ship was coming almost directly for them at first, that he saw both the green and the red, *and then the stern light.* To have shown a stern light the *Californian* would have had to turn considerably further than WSW if, as claimed, the disappearing ship bearing SW½W was the *Titanic.* The chief factor in Boxhall's evidence, though, had been that his "mystery ship" had been *moving towards him,* and he had known this because although only her mast lights had been visible to start with, he had eventually seen her sidelights as well.

Sir Rufus's explanations of the lights were all woolly and inaccurate, and came from a man who had either not done his homework, or was not prepared to state the exact truth for fear it would injure his case. As indeed it would. And here is another example from his next submission that the ship seen from the *Californian* was without doubt a large passenger steamer. Gibson's evidence, he said, spoke of a blaze of light, ". . . and you would not associate this with a cargo vessel." But he must have known that Gibson was asked repeatedly whether this ship had any appearance of being a passenger ship, and had always replied that it had not, that it was a cargo ship. Yet he took this one, isolated phrase from Gibson's evidence and *used it against the actual meaning of the evidence* as witnessed by the boy.

"Once we have got as far as having established that these distress signals came from the *Titanic*," he repeated, "that the Captain knew of them, and that he did not proceed either to the rescue of the vessel in distress... or [take] the step to call up the wireless operator and let him get into communication with the vessel one gets really a state of things which is quite inexplicable."

Mersey, of course, was in full agreement. "It is a most extraordinary thing that no attempt was made to communicate with the *Titanic*."

Does this mean that the vessel they tried morsing was *not* the *Titanic*, does it presuppose that Captain Lord knew the *Titanic* was foundering, or is it just another nonsensical jumble of words of a piece with the rest of this lamentable episode in the Inquiry?

"Quite," Sir Rufus replied, "the more extraordinary inasmuch as I have certainly understood as the rule which everybody who goes to sea would never fail to observe, that if you see a vessel in distress you must do your utmost to get to it...."

Of course it would have been extraordinary not to try and get to a vessel firing distress rockets. Apart from the humanitarian motives which would have been uppermost in any sailor's mind there might well have been the possibility of salvage. The simplest, and thus completely overlooked theory of why the *Californian* did not go is that no one thought they were distress rockets. They did not look or sound like them—*and the ship firing them was steaming away.*

"In this particular case," continued Sir Rufus, "I am unable to find any possible explanation of what happened, except it may be the Captain of the vessel was in ice for the first time. ... One can only conjecture, and I do not know that it is perhaps quite safe to speculate upon the reasons that made Captain Lord neither come out of his chartroom to see what was happening, nor to take any step to communicate with the vessel in distress...."

This nasty, oblique reference to insobriety on the part of Captain Lord was entirely unsupported by any evidence, was immaterial and quite indefensible. It was, moreover, entirely untrue in so much as Lord *had* taken steps to communicate with the vessel. The *Californian* had been morsing her for an hour.

"That this vessel, the *Californian,* could have got to the *Titanic* and might have got to the *Titanic* in time to save the passengers is, I am afraid, the irresistible conclusion from this evidence. If she was at this distance of 5 to 7 miles, and she could steam 11 knots an hour—she did steam 11—even allowing for her having to deviate so as to avoid an icefield there still would have been a very considerable opportunity for her to have got there in time.

"Of course the Captain says he was 19 miles away. That evidence I submit is quite unsatisfactory." (No reasons given.) "One understands of course why he should be anxious to put himself as far away as he can from the *Titanic*. . . . But if you bear in mind what I submit are the salient features of the evidence, that is that the sidelights were seen of the *Titanic,* you get rid altogether of this distance of 19½ miles. No human being would suggest that the *Californian* could have seen the sidelights of the *Titanic,* either her red light or her green light at a distance of 19½ miles. She must have been within easy distance in order that her masthead lights and her sidelights were seen, as they were by the *Californian*."

Imagination shudders at the juries who may have been swayed by similar facile sophistry during the course of this man's brilliant career. And I do not know whether it is perhaps quite safe to speculate upon whether the same fallacious evasions would have been so earnestly put forward had Captain Lord been up on a charge of capital murder with the same evidence against him.

CHAPTER SIXTEEN

That portion of the Mersey Report which deals with "the *Californian* incident" is a clear statement of Lord Mersey's attitude from the earliest days of the Inquiry, and by implication a clear indictment of his method of sweeping confusing or complicated evidence to one side in order to penetrate into the heart of the matter. It is given below in full.

"It is here necessary to consider the circumstances relating to the S/S *Californian:*

"On the 14th April the S/S *Californian* of the Leyland Line, Mr Stanley Lord, Master, was on her passage from London, which port she left on April 5th, to Boston, U.S., where she subsequently arrived on April 19th. She was a vessel of 6,223 tons gross and 4,038 net. Her full speed was 12½ to 13 knots. She had a passenger certificate, but was not carrying passengers at the time. She belonged to the International Mercantile Marine Company, the owners of the *Titanic.*

"At 7.30 p.m. ship's time on 14th April, a wireless message was sent from this ship to the *Antillian,* 'To Captain, *Antillian* 6.30 p.m. apparent ship's time, lat 42° 3'N, long 49° 9'W. Three large bergs 5 miles to southward of us, Regards—Lord.'

"The message was intercepted by the *Titanic* and when the Marconi operator (Evans) of the *Californian* offered this ice report to the Marconi operator of the *Titanic* shortly after 7.30 p.m. the latter replied: 'It is all right. I heard you sending it to the *Antillian* and I have got it.'

"The *Californian* proceeded on her course S 89°W true until 10.20 p.m. ship's time, when she was obliged to stop and reverse her engines because she was running into field ice which stretched as far as could then be seen to the northward and southward.

"The Master told the Court that he made her position at that time to be 42° 5'N, 50° 7'W. This position is recorded in the log-book which was written up from the scrap log-book by the Chief Officer. The scrap log is destroyed. It is a position about 19 miles N by E of the position of the *Titanic* when she foundered and is said to have been fixed by dead reckoning and verified by observations. I am satisfied that this position is not accurate. The Master 'twisted her head' to ENE by the compass and she remained approximately stationary until 5.15 a.m. on the following morning. The ship was slowly swinging round to starboard during the night.

"At about 11 p.m. a steamer's light was seen approaching from the eastward. The Master went to Evans' room and asked, 'What ships he had.' The latter replied, 'I think the *Titanic* is near us. I have got her.' The Master said, 'You had better advise the *Titanic* we are stopped and surrounded by ice.' The *Titanic* replied: 'Keep out.' The *Titanic* was in communication with Cape Race, which station was then sending messages to her. The reason why the *Titanic* answered 'Keep out' was that her Marconi operator could not hear what Cape Race was saying as from her proximity the message from the *Californian* was much stronger than any message being taken in by the *Titanic* from Cape Race which was much further off. Evans heard the *Titanic* continuing to communicate with Cape Race up to the time he turned in at 11.30 p.m.

"The Master of the *Californian* states that when observing the approaching steamer as she got nearer he saw more lights, a few deck lights and her green sidelight. He considered that at eleven o'clock she was approximately 6 or 7 miles away, and at some time between 11 and 11.30 he first saw her green light, she was then about 5 miles off. He noticed that about 11.30 she stopped. In his opinion this steamer was of about the same size as the *Californian*, a medium-sized steamer 'something like ourselves'.

"From the evidence of Mr Groves, Third Officer of the *Californian*, who was the officer of the first watch, it would appear that the Master was not actually on the bridge when the steamer was sighted.

"Mr Groves made out two masthead lights; the steamer was changing her bearing slowly as she got closer, and as she approached he went to the chartroom and reported this to the Master; he added: 'She is evidently a passenger steamer.' In fact, Mr Groves never appears to have had any doubt on this subject; in answer to a question during his examination, 'Had she much light?' he said, 'Yes, a lot of light. There was absolutely no doubt of her being a passenger steamer, at least in my mind.'

"Gill, the assistant donkeyman of the *Californian,* who was on deck at midnight said, referring to this steamer, 'It could not have been anything but a passenger boat, she was too large.'

"By the evidence of Mr Groves, the Master, in reply to his report said, 'Call her up on the morse lamp and see if you can get any answer.' This he proceeded to do. The Master came up and joined him on the bridge and remarked: 'That does not look like a passenger steamer.' Mr Groves replied: 'It is, sir; when she stopped her lights seemed to go out, and I suppose they have been shut out for the night.' Mr Groves states that these lights went out at 11.40[1] and remembers that time because 'one bell was struck to call the middle watch'. The Master did not join him on the bridge till shortly afterwards, and consequently after the steamer had stopped.

"In his examination Mr Groves admitted that if this steamer's head was turning to port after she stopped, it might account for the diminution of lights by many of them being shut out. Her steaming lights were still visible and also her port sidelight.

"The Captain only remained on the bridge for a few minutes. In his evidence he stated that Mr Groves' morse signalling appears to have been ineffectual (although at one moment he thought he was being answered) and he gave it up. He remained on the bridge until relieved by Mr Stone, the Second Officer, just after midnight. In turning the *Californian* over to him, he pointed out the steamer and said: 'She has been stopped since 11.40, she is a passenger steamer. At about the moment she stopped she put her lights out.' When Mr Groves was in the witness-box the following questions were put to him by me. 'Speaking as an experienced seaman and knowing what you do know now, do you think that steamer that you know was throwing up rockets, and that you say was a passenger steamer, was the *Titanic*? Do I think it? Yes. From what I have heard subsequently?—Yes, most decidedly I do, but I do not put myself as being an

---

1 Compare this with preceding paragraph.

experienced man. But that is your opinion so far as your experience goes? Yes, it is, my Lord.'

"Mr Stone states that the Master who was also up (but apparently not on the bridge), pointed out the steamer to him with instructions to tell him if her bearings altered or if she got any closer, he also stated that Mr Groves had called her up on the morse lamp and had received no reply.

"Mr Stone had with him during the middle watch an apprentice named Gibson, whose attention was first drawn to the steamer's lights at about 12.20 a.m. He could see a masthead light (with glasses) and 'a glare of white lights on her after deck'. He first thought her masthead light was flickering and next thought it was a morse light 'calling us up'. He replied, but could not get into communication and finally came to the conclusion that it was as he had first supposed, the masthead light flickering. Some time after 12.30 a.m. Gill, the donkeyman, states that he saw two rockets fired from the ship which he had been observing, and about 1.10 a.m. Mr Stone reported to the Captain by voice pipe that he had seen five white rockets from the direction of the steamer. He states that the Master answered: 'Are they company's signals?' and that he replied: 'I do not know, but they appear to me to be white rockets.' The Master told him to go on morsing and when he received any information to send the apprentice down to him with it. Gibson states that Mr Stone informed him that he had reported to the Master, and that the Master had said the steamer was to be called up by morse light. This witness thinks the time was 12.55; he at ᵒⁿᶜᵉ proceeded again to call the steamer up by morse. He got no reply, but the vessel fired three more white rockets; these rockets were also seen by Mr Stone.

"Both Mr Stone and the apprentice kept the steamer under observation, looking at her from time to time with their glasses. Between one o'clock and 1.40 some conversation passed between them. Mr Stone remarked to Gibson: 'Look at her now, she looks very queer out of the water, her lights look queer.' He is also said by Gibson to have remarked: 'A ship is not going to fire rockets at sea for nothing,' and admits himself he may possibly have used that expression.

"Mr Stone states that he saw the last of the rockets fired at about 1.40, and after watching the steamer for some twenty minutes more he sent

Gibson down to the Master. 'I told Gibson to go down to the Master, and be sure and wake him and tell him that altogether we had seen eight of these white lights like white rockets in the direction of the other steamer; that this steamer was disappearing in the south-west, that we had called her up repeatedly on the morse lamp and received no information whatsoever.'

"Gibson states that he went down to the chartroom and told the Master; that the Master asked him if all the rockets were white, and also asked him the time. Gibson stated that at this time the Master was awake. It was five minutes past two and Gibson returned to the bridge to Mr Stone and reported. They both continued to keep the ship under observation until she disappeared. Mr Stone describes this as 'a gradual disappearing of all her lights which would be perfectly natural with a ship steaming away from us'.

"At about 2.40 a.m. Mr Stone again called up the Master by voice pipe and told him that the ship from which he had seen the rockets come had disappeared bearing SW½W, the last he had seen of the light; and the Master again asked him if he was certain there was no colour in the lights. 'I again assured him they were all white, just white rockets.' There is considerable discrepancy between the evidence of Mr Stone and that of the Master. The latter states that he went to the voice pipe at about 1.15 but was told then of a white rocket (not five white rockets). Moreover between 1.30 and 4.30 when he was called by the Chief Officer (Mr Stewart), he had no recollection of anything being reported to him at all, although he remembered Gibson opening and closing the chartroom door.

"Mr Stewart relieved Mr Stone at 4 a.m. The latter told him he had seen a ship 4 or 5 miles off when he went on deck at 12 o'clock and at 1 o'clock he had seen some white rockets and that the moment the ship started firing them she started to steam away. Just at this time (about 4 a.m.) a steamer came in sight with two white masthead lights and a few lights amidships. He asked Mr Stone whether he thought this was the steamer which had fired rockets and Mr Stone said he did not think it was. At 4.30 he called the Master and informed him that Mr. Stone had told him he had seen rockets in the middle watch. The Master said, 'Yes, I know, he has been telling me.' The Master came at once to the bridge and apparently took the fresh steamer for the one which had fired the rockets and said, 'She looks all right. She is not making any signals now.' This mistake was not corrected. He, however, had the wireless operator called.

"At about 6 a.m. Captain Lord heard from the *Virginian* that the *Titanic* had struck a berg, passengers in boats, ship sinking, and he at once started through the field ice at full speed for the position given.

"Captain Lord stated that about 7.30 he passed the *Mount Temple* stopped and that she was in the vicinity of the position given him as where the *Titanic* had collided (lat 41° 46'N; long 50° 14'W). He saw no wreckage there but he did later on near the *Carpathia* which ship he closed soon afterwards, and he stated that the position where he subsequently left this wreckage was 41° 33 'N, 50° 1'W. It is said in the evidence of Mr Stewart that the position of the *Californian* was verified by stellar observations at 7.30 p.m. on the Sunday evening and that he verified the Captain's position given when the ship stopped (42° 5'N, 50° 7'W) as accurate on the next day. The position in which the wreckage was said to have been seen on the Monday morning was verified by sights taken on that morning.

"All the officers are stated to have taken sights and Mr Stewart in his evidence remarks that they all agreed. If it is admitted that these positions were correct, then it follows that the *Titanic's* position as given by that ship when making the CQD signal was approximately S 16°W (true) 19 miles from the *Californian,* and further that the position in which the *Californian* was stopped during the night was 30 miles away from where the wreckage was seen by her in the morning, or that the wreckage had drifted u miles in a Little more than five hours."

After this clever dance through the evidence, picking gems from here and there, and trying to skirt, so far as possible, anything which might give the lie to the original hypothesis that the popular view of the *Californian* as a monster ship was the correct view—after this delicate minuet the Mersey X-ray was turned upon it.

"There are contradictions and inconsistencies in the story as told by the different witnesses. But the truth of the matter is plain. The *Titanic* colided with the berg at 11.40. The vessel seen by the *Californian* stopped at this time. The rockets sent up from the *Titanic* were distress signals. The *Californian* saw distress signals. The number sent up by the *Titanic* was about eight. The *Californian* saw eight. The time over which the rockets from the *Titanic* were sent up was from about 12.45 to 1.45 o'clock. It was about this time that the *Californian* saw the rockets. At 2.40 Mr Stone called to the Master that the ship from which he had seen the rockets had disappeared. At 2.20 a.m. the *Titanic* had foundered. It was suggested that the rockets were seen from some other ship not the *Titanic*. But no other ship to fit this theory has ever been heard of."

It was all as simple as that.

The Report continued, "These circumstances convince me that the ship seen by the *Californian* was the *Titanic* and if so, according to Captain Lord, the two vessels were about 5 miles apart at the time of the disaster. The evidence from the *Titanic* corroborates this estimate but I am advised that the distance was probably greater though not more than 8 to 10 miles. The ice by which the *Californian* was surrounded was loose ice extending for a distance of not more than 2 or 3 miles in the direction of the *Titanic*. The night was clear and the sea was smooth. When she first saw the rockets the *Californian* could have pushed through the ice to the open water without any serious risk and so have come to the assistance of the *Titanic*. Had she done so she might have saved many if not all of the lives that were lost."

Mersey had spoken. His advisers had concurred. Most of the Press paid them the compliment of believing that they had sifted through the evidence and arrived at the right answer. They had sifted through the evidence, there is little doubt of that, or they would not have been able to eliminate so successfully most of the arguments which proved as conclusively as it was possible to prove anything on the evidence available that the two ships were never in sight of one another.

The popular Press had already convicted their man. Now it was the turn of some of the 'serious' papers to weigh in.

The Daily Telegraph, July 31st, 1912

After patiently sifting through all the evidence the Commission has reported that "the lights seen by the steamer *Californian* were those of the *Titanic*; that the *Californian* could have pushed through the ice" . . . etc., etc.

This is the indictment which is held to have been proved against a British shipmaster. It stands on record for all time; it calls for no comment for the condemnation is as unmitigated in its simple severity as it is unmerciful in its stem recital of the probable consequences of this fatal lapse from the high standards of conduct on the sea. . . . This part of the Report stands out as a thing apart—a horror which in the days to come will wound the human instinct of the race whenever the story of the *Titanic* is recounted. . . .

The last sentence was prophetic indeed!

***

Without going into technicalities, without trying to determine where the *Titanic* actually foundered, or what was done with the wheel after she struck the berg, or how she pointed then, or thereafter, or what time she was keeping, or any of these facts which the Inquiry failed completely to probe, it can be stated that the overwhelming majority of the evidence is against Mersey's judgement.

To start with the *Californian* was stopped and no attempt was made to suggest anything else. All witnesses on the *Californian* appear to have seen a ship of some description, *but only one,* which stopped some 5 miles off. Yet all the lookouts from the *Titanic* saw nothing before they left the crow's-nest—either before she struck, or before the change of watch or after the change of watch. How is it possible to reconcile this ?

The majority of evidence from the *Titanic,* including that of the Second Officer, Lightoller, was that the light they saw was from a fisherman of some sort. One does not mistake a fisherman for a 6,000- ton steamer on a clear dark night at 5 miles. Were it not for Boxhall's evidence it is safe to say there would have been no *"Californian incident"*. Yet what is his evidence: that the steamer whose mast lights he saw approached head on *until he could see her sidelights*. This is how he knew she was moving, because after a while her sidelights became visible—she had not changed direction; he could see that from the mast lights. She afterwards turned around and showed her stern light, and she was so far away when he left in number 2 emergency boat that *he did not even bother to pull towards her.* He pulled in a north-easterly direction, and was the first boat to be picked up by the *Carpathia* from the south-east. The boats that had pulled for the light were the last to be picked up by the *Carpathia.* Ergo the light was to the westward. The point though is that Boxhall was absolutely clear that this steamer he saw was *moving.*

So much for the *Titanic's* witnesses.

As to the ship which approached the *Californian* as seen by the various officers and others who testified, it was first seen by the Captain and the Third Officer. Captain Lord saw it on the starboard bow showing eventually one masthead light and one green light—heading west. Groves saw it on the starboard quarter showing eventually two masthead lights and one red light—heading west according to Groves, but quite obviously it could only have been heading somewhere about NE. They both saw it stop in about the same position 5 miles off (Lord)—7 miles (Groves). Mersey has cannibalised their evidence; he has taken Lord's green light and westerly heading and Groves' two masthead lights. He has also taken Groves' description of a large passenger ship, added them together and made the *Titanic.*

Not content with that he has also produced Gill, the donkeyman, and although Groves has said that this passenger steamer's lights were put out at 11.40, Gill sees her ablaze with light at about midnight. Possibly icebergs are passing to and fro between the ships and shutting out the lights at intervals!

While still on Groves' evidence Mersey sees fit to perpetuate a bit of nonsense about the *Titanic's* lights being diminished if she turned to port after striking the berg, although her steaming lights were still visible and also her port sidelight. It would be interesting to see this statement described graphically.

But Gill is the star witness. It is he who has made the newspaper headlines. Mersey has to get him in again when he is *actually seeing the rockets.* What excitement! This is how he does it: "Gill, the donkeyman, states that he saw two rockets fired from the ship *which he had been observing*." But this is quite untrue. Gill never made this statement. Here is a portion of his evidence at the British Inquiry where he is being questioned about the rockets he saw which came from a point on the horizon.

"No, I could not see anything of the steamer at all. She had disappeared. She had either steamed away or I do not know what she had done. She was not there."

Mersey: "What time was this?"

"After one bell."

Rowlatt: "Between half-past twelve and one."

Mersey: "I do not understand that."

Perhaps he didn't understand it, and Like Senator Smith in America he misstated the evidence and produced a ship from which Gill saw the rockets fired in order that Gill's evidence would not conflict with Gibson's or Stone's, or with his own conviction that the *Californian* was in sight of the *Titanic*.

But the most conclusive evidence that these two vessels were nowhere near each other comes not from what anyone saw or thought they saw or remembered seeing—it comes simply from what they *didn't hear. No one in the* Californian *heard the rockets.* Now, those who have on a still night at sea listened to the cicadas, say, from a shoreline many miles away will appreciate that this would have been impossible on the kind of night that the *Titanic* foundered if the two ships had been in sight of one another. For those without this experience, the evidence is before them: first, it was the stillest, calmest night on the North Atlantic that many of the sailor witnesses had ever seen; second, the rockets from the *Carpathia* were *heard* by the *Titanic* survivors like cannon from over the horizon long before the ship or her mast lights even were seen;[2] third, the *Titanic* was carrying rockets *in lieu of guns*; fourth, Rowe, the quartermaster, was ordered to bring up the *detonators* from the afterbridge; and fifth, when Lightoller described a rocket he said, "It's really a timed shell." Yet *not one* of the *Californian* witnesses heard *anything*.

Finally, there is the navigational evidence. The first thing to remember here is that Lord broadcast his position to the world at 7.30 that night in his message to the *Antillian* long before anyone could have known that the

---

2 In which connection it is worth quoting from Lawrence Beesley's book, *The Loss of the Titanic:* "The cries which were loud and numerous at first, died away gradually one by one, but the night was clear, frosty and still, the water smooth, and the sounds must have carried on its level surface free from any obstruction for miles...."

Titanic was going to strike a berg. He also broadcast his course as practically due West, by inference, if his noon position by the log-book was not deliberately falsified. And why should Stewart, the Chief Officer, make incorrect entries in the log and perjure himself in the witness-box? No blame could possibly be attached to him as he was not on deck when the rockets were fired and was not told of them until the following morning.

Taking, as Dunlop did, the nearest parallel in law to the *Californian's* predicament with the log-book, here is what the standard textbook on the law of collisions at sea has to say about logs as evidence:

"Under the Evidence Act, 1938, it would seem since the decision of Wilmer J. in the *Springtide* that ship's logs are admissible for the vessel provided that the maker is called as a witness, subject to the exceptions in section 1 (1) and section 1 (2), and provided that the entries were written, made, or produced by a person with his own hand or signed or initialled by him or otherwise recognised by him in writing as one for the accuracy of which he is responsible, *not being a person interested*".[3] (The italics are mine.)

Neither Sir Rufus Isaacs nor Mersey ever gave any reason for summarily dismissing the *Californian's* log-book positions as hopelessly inaccurate.

These, then, are some of the most obvious facts which rule out any theory that the two ships were ever in sight of one another. There are so many more evasions and half truths in this section of the Mersey Report that it would be tedious to list them all

Reading through it and the relevant parts of the transcript with a critical eye it is difficult not to come to the conclusion that the Inquiry was "rigged". Why otherwise was the evidence of the *Titanic* lookout completely disregarded? Why was the last lookout man who was on watch after 12 midnight in the crow's-nest never called, and why did Mersey try and brush aside as unimportant the evidence of his companion in the crow's-nest, Alfred Hogg? Hogg was called after all the *Californian* witnesses including Gill, and therefore long after Mersey had made up his mind about the identity of the ship seen from the *Titanic*. Here is the tail end of Hogg's examination by Sir Rufus Isaacs, before which there had been no mention whatsoever of 'THE LIGHT'.

---

3 Marsden's *Collisions*.

17599 Q. "When you went to relieve them (Lee and Fleet) at 12 o'clock was anything said to you then?" A. "Nothing was passed on to me at all then."

Mersey: "I do not see what the importance of this is."

Sir Rufus: "Not of that, but I thought he might say something else. I quite agree it is of no importance at all."

17560 Q. "Eventually you were saved in boat number 7"? A. "Yes."

Sir Rufus: "We have had evidence about that boat so I am not going into any particular about it. I will tell your Lordship why we have called him. We wanted to exhaust the lookout men. You have had five out of six before you now. The only one who has not been called is Evans, and I do not think it is necessary to call him because he goes on with this witness to relieve at 12 o'clock."

Mersey: "It is of very little importance."

"Very little. It was only so that your Lordship should see him as the relieving watch."

And that concluded his examination by the Board of Trade counsel. Is it likely that nothing would have been passed on if there had been a ship 5 miles distant?

In case there is any doubt, here is Lee, the man who handed over to him. He was asked, "Before half-past eleven on that watch—that is seven bells—had you reported anything, do you remember?"

"There was nothing to be reported."

What were the lookout men doing if all those people on the *Californian* saw the *Titanic* approach to within 5 miles, and they saw—*nothing*? What were they doing?

But the real point at issue here is that this question is so obvious, so fundamental to any theory about the two ships that it could not have been simply overlooked by Mersey and his assessors or by Isaacs and the Board of Trade counsel. And yet they made no attempt to probe it; quite the reverse. Mersey brushed aside Hogg's evidence and the sixth lookout was never heard—this although at the American Inquiry Frederick Fleet, the collision lookout, had said, "The other lookout reported it (the light)". If this "other lookout" hadn't been Hogg, as appeared from Sir Rufus's single question, it must have been his mate. The proposition that the *Californian* and, by this time, the *Titanic* were both stopped, and so could not have suddenly appeared to each other was so obvious that, after the question relating to the *Californian* was added to those before the Court, it was their duty to examine the lookouts especially in an effort to find out *when* the "mystery light" was first visible. That they didn't do so could scarcely have been oversight; it must have been either boredom or design. Although the Court had the American transcript available, Frederick Fleet, remember, was not asked one single question about the "mystery light" by the Board of Trade counsel at the British Inquiry.

And while on this point, why was the overwhelming evidence for the lights in question (from both ships) having been seen *at five* miles disregarded, and a fictitious figure which had only appeared in Groves' evidence substituted? Probably because not even Mersey's tame nautical assessors could stomach it. Five miles was a complete impossibility; the ships would not have been much outside hailing distance.

Then again, in the summary of evidence, why was that from the *Californian* carefully cannibalised so that it became feasible that the ship they saw approaching could have been the *Titanic*? Groves' evidence finally and absolutely rules out the ship which he thought he saw as having been anything but a North-bound steamer. His evidence is too explicit on the direction of approach—obliquely from the starboard quarter while the *Californian* was heading NE—and the heading of the mast lights—the lower one to the left as he viewed them—and the colour of the sidelight when it came into view—*red*—to have been a slip of the tongue or lapse of memory.

And most important of all, why was Gill's evidence mis-stated in the Report? Mersey himself had questioned Gill on this very point.

The evidence points to a "rigged" Inquiry. Mersey was a Law Lord who must have known the British legal system intimately, but he disregarded Dunlop's plea for Lord's elementary legal rights. In the face of grave doubts as to whether he had any right to do more than mention the name of the steamship *Californian* in his Report, he censured Lord for inaction. It was not even a question of "beyond reasonable doubt"; the doubt was the other way—there was no doubt on the evidence that the *Californian* was *not* the ship in question.

But could it have been rigged? Could the Board of Trade, Sir Rufus Isaacs, Sir John Simon, and the other Board of Trade counsel, besides the assessors and Lord Mersey all have agreed to mis-read the evidence so that the loss of 1,500 lives could be placed fairly and squarely on the broad shoulders of Captain Stanley Lord? It is almost impossible to believe that there was any explicit agreement. But there was considerable subconscious pressure so to do. The Board of Trade came badly out of the whole affair, a decade or so out of date with their regulations and thinking; Sir Rufus Isaacs and Sir John Simon were barristers trained to sway juries and get their man; while Mersey, as we have seen, was for some reason or other pre-conditioned to accept the *Californian*'s inaction in the face of rockets as something which was so self-evident that no proof was necessary.

The really puzzling thing is the silence of the nautical assessors.

And if the verdict was emotional and hysterical as it may well have been in the American Inquiry, there was less excuse because the *Titanic* had been sunk over three months before the British Report appeared.

One of the most significant and sinister aspects of the Board of Trade's part in the affair was that Lord was never afterwards taken to court by the Board, although, if Mersey's judgement was right, he had committed a very grave misdemeanour. Here is a section again from Dunlop's closing address: "The object of it (adding the question about the *Californian* to the list of questions already before the Court) is explained by the Attorney-General on page 649. There it is stated that the law officers of the Crown should get from your Lordship a finding of the facts relating to the *Californian* incident in order to enable them to make up their minds whether in the public interest they ought to institute criminal proceedings under section 6 of the Maritime Convention Act. . . ."

That was the object of adding the question. Mersey's answer could not have been more positive or more damning—Sir Rufus's plea could not have been more unequivocal—yet the law officers of the Crown took no action whatever. Why? Had they softened? Did they think that Lord had been through enough—that his public censure was in itself sufficient punishment? Or did they fear what might come out of another, and perhaps more competent approach to the question?

Whatever the reasons, or whatever the lack of reason, Lord Mersey had spoken; the burden of responsibility for all the tragic deaths had been placed, and Captain Stanley Lord was then and thereafter officially, popularly and publicly "Lord of the *Californian*"

CHAPTER SEVENTEEN

I t is now too far distant in time to make any categorical assertions about the meaning or nature of these rockets which were seen by Stone, Gibson and Gill from the decks of the *Californian*. They were low- lying, and it is possible that they were, as Stone first thought, fired by the ship which he was observing. If the *Titanic's* actual position of foundering was considerably to the South and East of her wirelessed position (as there is good reason to believe) it might account for no one on the *Titanic* having seen either this ship or her rockets.

But again we are too far distant in time to try and fix the *Titanic's* last position at all precisely. It can be stated that the accuracy of her wirelessed CQD position was accepted by the Court mainly on the evidence of Captain Rostron of the *Carpathia*. This was that he was at forced full speed from some time after 12.35—when he was called by his wireless operator—until he stopped at 4 a.m. He further considered that he was making 17 knots, although whether this was an estimate or checked by the log was not divulged. He was steering N 52°W and he had a distance of 58 miles to go. Supposing that he had turned and worked up to his extra speed by 12.40, which is allowing a minimum of time, he would indeed have covered 57.3 miles up to four o'clock, and would thus have been up to the position. But he was never specifically asked whether he had *slackened* speed at all during this time, while he was dodging the bergs.

In 1959 his then Second Officer, now Sir James Bisset, K.B., C.B.E., R.D.,R.N.R.,LL.D.(Cantab.), published his memories of that occasion in the second book of an excellent autobiographical trilogy. Many years had passed by then, and human memory is a funny thing—certainly Sir James' stated facts about the *Californian* are very wide of the mark—but it is of interest to see what his recollections are where his own ship, the *Carpathia* is concerned.[1]

He remembers the green light from Boxhall's lifeboat at 2.40, and agrees with Captain Rostron there. The point about this is that if they then continued at 17 knots to reach the boat at four o'clock the light must have been visible from 23 miles away—or well down over the horizon. But we know that it was only a green "White Star" roman candle, or little more than a hand flare. So this is plainly impossible.

At 2.45 Bisset sighted the iceberg ahead on the port bow, and he records that the Captain acted in a seamanlike manner, altering course to starboard and *putting the telegraphs to half speed.* When he had seen that they had cleared the berg he put them over to "Full" again. Here is one momentary slackening of speed and a small diversion. At 3.15 Bisset thinks that the *Carpathia* is 12 miles from the *Titanic's* wirelessed position—if correct she has either travelled 11 miles in half an hour (7 knots over her speed with Lloyds Register) or was nearer to start with than 58 miles. At 3.30 he records Captain Rostron reducing speed to "Half" and then to "Slow". At 4 a.m., like Captain Rostron, he arrives at the first boat.

This at least throws some doubt on the distance that the *Carpathia* actually travelled—especially as Bisset records the forced full speed as being 16—not 17—knots.

Probably, at this stage, it is best to say simply that the positions of *all* the ships in the vicinity that early morning (*some six hours after star sights*) were *approximate.*

And yet there is a remarkable and completely independent confirmation of Lord's and Moore's evidence on record in a report from the Russian steamer *Birma* (ex *Arundel Castle*) which was given practically a full page spread in the *Daily Telegraph* on April 25th, 1912, thus before either the *Californian* or the *Mount Temple* witnesses had given their evidence at the Senate Inquiry. The chart of the ice flow and the position where the *Carpathia* was seen rescuing survivors should be compared with Lord's and Moore's estimates to appreciate the striking similarities. Lord estimated the *Carpathia's* latitude when rescuing survivors as 41° 36'—so did the *Birma;* Lord estimated the longitude as about 50°W—the

---

1 These were based on *contemporary* notebooks.

Birma estimated it much further to the *East*, about 49° 45'W; Moore of the *Mount Temple* didn't mention a specific longitude, but the inference is that the wreckage was about 50°W, corresponding to Lord's estimate.

Here are brief passages taken from the *Birma*'s long report to the *Telegraph*:

"We ascertained from the *Frankfurt* that the ship's position as given by the *Titanic* had been confirmed by them. Nevertheless the position was given wrongly. . . .

"We herewith enclose a rude chart, drawn for the purpose of illustrating the course of the steamship *Birma* on the memorable morning of the 15th instant, and the approximate location of the disaster. The ice floe was approached by us from the south-west until we reached the point marked 'X', when it was obvious that the location given must be wrong. We then saw the *Carpathia* on the north-easterly side of the floe, and being asked merely to stand by, and seeing the vessel engaged in picking up the boats with the survivors, we circled around the floe, first to the south in order to avoid being crushed by the ice; then after turning the lower corner, we turned north-eastward, up to the point marked "XX", which is the spot on which the *Carpathia* stood while picking up the boats."

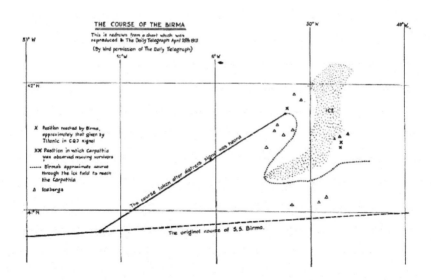

At the end of the report came this letter:

"To the Editor of the *Daily Telegraph*

"Dear Sir—We, the undersigned, commander, first officer, wireless operator, and wireless operator's associate, of the ss. *Birma,* herewith beg to state that the facts in the foregoing report, handed to you by Mr Charles Edward Walters, journalist, of San Francisco, California, are correct, to our knowledge and belief.

"The chart attached thereto has been prepared by Captain Stulping, of the ss. *Birma* . . .

Signed Ludwig Stulping, Captain
Alfr. Nielson, First Officer
C. Hesselberg, Purser
Joseph L. Cannon, Wireless Operator.
Thomas George Ward, Wireless Operator."

It was not of primary importance to Mersey's Court to probe the exact position of the disaster as the questions stood at the beginning of the Inquiry, for the precise geographical locality had no relevance to her loss unless it could be proved she was well outside the ice region. And she wasn't. But directly the question relating to the *Californian* and her inactivity was added, it became essential, if justice was to be done, to find out exactly where the various ships were that night, and especially the *Titanic* and the *Californian.* We have seen above that there was a serious conflict with the official (CQD) position for the *Titanic's* loss from four of the steamers in the immediate vicinity, the *Californian,* the *Mount Temple,* the *Birma* and the *Carpathia.* So far as the *Carpathia* is concerned there was the inference from Captain Rostron's evidence that White Star roman candles could be seen at 23 miles—plainly impossible—which was not probed, and there is now (although there was not then) the record of the Second Officer, Bisset, which conflicts with Captain Rostron's evidence. The Court sat for thirty-six days, examined ninety-eight witnesses with over 25,600 questions about various aspects of the disaster. Surely they could have spent another day and examined some of the serving officers from other ships in the vicinity had they wanted to arrive at the true navigational positions. It is possible that this was the last thing they wanted.

***

The most likely theory about the rockets is that they *were* the *Titanic's* rockets seen by a strange coincidence over the deck lights, but below the masthead lights, of the other ship which lay to the South of the *Californian*. It is tempting to believe that Stone may have been mistaken when he saw the rockets change bearing with the ship—that maybe all the rockets had been fired before the ship started to move, and thus appeared all to be over her. Stone's evidence is very positive, though, that the rockets were moving across from southerly to southwesterly *with the ship,* which made him believe that they were from the ship.

But again, maybe Gill was the only man actually to see the *Titanic's* rockets, and by making a mistake in the direction in which he said he was looking, failed to see the other, closer steamer.

Whatever the rockets or flares were or were not, no blame attaches to Captain Lord for inaction. He had a competent officer on watch, he was receiving reports from him and knew he was watching the other steamer closely and trying to contact her by morse, and was receiving no reply. A Captain is bound to rely on his senior officers; his life would otherwise be intolerable. And what had the Second reported to him? That the strange vessel was steaming off towards the South-West and had fired a rocket. There was no intimation that it had been a distress rocket, and in those days it was a perfectly normal and usual occurrence for ships to show each other company's flares for recognition by night. Secondly it was quite obvious that a vessel in distress and requiring assistance would not steam away. Finally the vessel had not answered his morse lamp. Lord had no reason whatever to suppose that she might be in distress.

But the two factors in his evidence which contributed greatly to the Court's adverse findings were the two times he had been called without being aware of it. The first time, by Gibson, could be a quite natural case of sleep-talking; the second call by Stone is harder to understand because to answer the voice pipe he would have had to rise from the chartroom settee and walk through to his own room. It is far more difficult to imagine him doing this without waking than in the first instance.

Now the evidence about this second call comes only from Stone. Gibson said in affidavit "At about 2.45 he (Stone) whistled down to the Captain again but I did not hear what was said." There may have been nothing said on this statement; the Captain may not have come to the voice pipe. In his evidence before the Court Gibson was confused and confusing in his answers about this second call of Stone's.

Stone's original statement goes thus: "At 2 a.m. the vessel was steaming away fast and only just her stern light was visible and bearing SW½W. I sent Gibson down to you and told him to wake you and tell you we had seen altogether eight white rockets and that the steamer had gone out of sight to the SW. Also that we were heading WSW. When he came back he reported he had told you we had called him up repeatedly and got no answer, and you replied, 'All right, are you sure there were no colours in them?' and Gibson replied, 'No, they were all white.' At 2.45 I again whistled down again and told you we had seen no more lights and that the steamer had steamed away to the SW and was now out of sight, also that the rockets were all white and had no colours whatever."

On the face of it this was an odd thing to do. The ship had disappeared twenty or so minutes before, there had been no more rockets, and the apprentice had already told the Captain everything. Why raise the subject again with a sleeping captain when there was nothing further to report?

Stone's answer at the Inquiry was that when he had sent Gibson down the steamer had not yet disappeared, but was *disappearing* in the SW. "I told him to say she was disappearing. I could not have said disappeared because I continued to see her stern light for about twenty minutes afterwards."

Gibson's evidence was quite categorical, though, that the vessel *had* disappeared at about 2.5 and that he had been sent down *after* she disappeared, and that Stone had told him to say that *she had gone,* and she had fired eight rockets altogether. This tallies with Stone's statement above and with his (Gibson's) own statement which goes thus: "Just after two o'clock she was then about two points on the port bow, *she disappeared from sight and nothing more was seen of her again.*"

So there is a conflict of evidence between each and every one of the vital witnesses from the *Californian* on practically every point under consideration: in the first place between Lord and Groves on the direction of approach and lights of the strange steamer, and upon its size and character; between Gill and Stone/Gibson about whether there was a vessel in sight when the rockets went up; between Groves/ Gill and Lord/Stone/ Gibson about the character of the steamer; between Stone and Gibson about whether the vessel disappeared at about two o'clock *before* Gibson called the Captain, or at 2.20 *after* he had called him and finally between Lord and Stone about whether he was called by whistle after Gibson came down. There is no conflict about Gibson's arrival because Lord remembered the door opening and banging shut again, and he had asked what time it was.

It is no part of my purpose to cast doubt on the integrity of any of the *Californian* witnesses. Captain Lord never did so, and there is no reason to start now, over fifty years later. It *is* my intention to show that the evidence was even more contradictory than Sir Rufus or Mersey admitted in their summing up and findings, and to point out the simplest explanation— that at the time these things were happening no one on the *Californian* thought anything of them at all—that it was only with hindsight after hearing the news of the tragedy that their minds started working, and in the closed, perhaps claustrophobic, atmosphere of a ship's accommodation the rumours mushroomed and became impossible to separate from the facts indistinctly remembered.

So again the conflict of evidence makes it impossible to resolve just what it was that Gill, Gibson and Stone saw that night. The most experienced man, Stone, admitted he was puzzled by the lights. He did not think they were distress signals because there was no explosion, no flash from the decks of the steamer—except in one instance—the steamer herself was going away from him, and the rockets only rose to about half the height of the masthead light. Had he thought for a moment that they might be distress rockets it is just impossible to believe that he would not have taken steps to *go down himself and* make sure the Captain was awake and fully alive to the situation. There was no necessity to stay on the upper bridge— no necessity whatever—the *Californian* was not even moving.

But there is one more difficult part of his evidence: the steamer disappeared bearing SW½W, and moving away quite fast. A glance at any of the charts of the ice shows that this puts her right in amongst the field. Three hours later Lord himself steamed through in about the same place, but then it was daylight, and he was able to pick out and dodge the growlers and bergs. While it is by no means impossible that an experienced North Atlantic man could have picked his way through such a field at night it argues a certain rashness on his part after he had originally stopped in much the same longitude as the *Californian*. Of course, if he had no wireless, as Lord believed from the fact that Evans knew nothing about him, he would not have guessed at the extent of the ice which lay in his path.

Lest this tends to cast another slur on Stone's recollection or his integrity, here is Gibson giving evidence—a youth who was in no way responsible for action or inaction, merely an apprentice without responsibility one way or the other—when he was asked, "Could you see whether she was steaming away?"

"No, the Second Officer was taking bearings of her all the time."

So whatever was happening to the other ship she was certainly under careful observation. They were not asleep on the *Californian*.

***

It is not my purpose here to give any description of the character of the man, Stanley Lord; he could have been anyone so far as this book is concerned—anyone who could have stood up to such rigorous examination by one of the leading advocates of the day and by a President so obviously prejudiced against him, and who could have given such straightforward, sailor-like answers to his tormentors, never contradicting himself, never wasting words, always perfectly certain of what he had seen and never doubting for a moment the truth or integrity of the other witnesses who had seen or reported something else.

At the conception of this book Lord was to have been a cardboard figure of "everyman" inextricably enmeshed in a web of viciousness and stupidity. That he would shine through his answers as rather bigger and more honest than "everyman" was none of my original intention.

POSTSCRIPT

After the publication of the Mersey Report Lord was forced to resign from the *Californian* and from the Leyland Line. He had at first been assured by the Liverpool management that he would remain in command of his ship, but later a director threatened to resign if Lord stayed in the company, so he had to go.

Meanwhile he was working hard to advance his side of the case and corresponding with anyone who might have been able to help him, including Lightoller from the *Titanic,* Rostron from the *Carpathia* and other officers from vessels which had been in the vicinity that night. And of course the Board of Trade. The Mercantile Marine Service Association was also working on his behalf trying to re-open that part of the Inquiry which concerned him. But they made a mistake by bringing the name of the *Mount Temple* into their appeals. Some sort of rockets or flares had been seen from this ship, and Lord had a letter from an officer who joined her after the voyage in question, saying that there was dissaffection among her officers over Captain Moore's failure to steam through the ice, and also that they had thought they were only some 10 to 14 miles from the sinking liner when they had seen not only her deck lights but also green flares. It is likely that what the *Mount Temple* officers actually saw was not the *Titanic* but the deck lights of the *Carpathia* and the green flares from Boxhall's lifeboat. Nevertheless the M.M.S.A. attempted to involve her in their efforts to clear Lord, and failed. The Board did not feel that the proximity or otherwise of the *Mount Temple* threw any real doubt on the findings of the Court so far as the *Californian* was concerned.

Lord himself was not interested in proving anyone else guilty; he only wanted to clear his own name. But when he wrote to the Board explaining his case and the anomalies of the judgement against him he came up against a stone wall of officialdom. Here is their reply—in its way a gem.

> Board of Trade,
>
> Whitehall Gardens, S.W.
>
> 29th August, 1912.
>
> Sir,
>
> I duly received your letter of the 10th August calling attention to certain remarks affecting yourself in the report of the recent Official Inquiry into the loss of the S.S. *Titanic,* and I regret that through an oversight this communication was not earlier acknowledged.
>
> In reply I fear all I can say is that as all the circumstances surrounding the casualty have formed the subject of a searching investigation by a Court of Inquiry, the Board of Trade would not feel justified in taking any steps with regard to your present statement.
>
> I am,
>
> Yours faithfully,
>
> (signed) Walter J. Howell.

Captain Stanley Lord.

There was no appeal. Lord could not force one because of an odd quirk of the law: no one had been censured for the disaster itself (the loss of the liner) and therefore no appeal was allowed to *anyone.*

In the January of the year following the disaster, 1913, Lord applied successfully for employment with Lawther Latta's Nitrate Producers' Steam Ship Co. Ltd., and was offered command of their *Anglo Saxon.* The following year the world was plunged into a war, whose horrors expunged the close memory of the *Titanic,* and afterwards Lord, finding that the *Californian* incident affected him neither personally nor professionally, let the matter drop. He continued to serve Lawther Latta's at sea until his premature retirement due to ill health.

Nitrate Producers' Steam Ship Company Limited,
Bilhter Buildings,
London, E.C.3.

It gives us very great pleasure to state that Captain Stanley Lord held command in this company from February 1913, until March 1927, during the whole of which period he had our entire confidence, and we regard him as one of the most capable commanders we have ever had. It was a matter of much regret to us that he felt compelled to retire owing to indisposition. He carries with him our grateful appreciation of his excellent services, and we earnestly hope that he will soon recover his wonted health.

(Signed) John Latta
Chairman.

Stanley Lord died in Wallasey in 1962, popularly and officially guilty of negligence and gross inhumanity.

And what of Mersey? His reputation was not impaired at all by the travesty he had played out; indeed it must have been enlarged by juxtaposition with the *Titanic*. He went on to even greater nautical fame: The International Conference on the Safety of Life at Sea—President, Baron Mersey; Court of Inquiry into the loss of the *Empress of Ireland*—President, Baron Mersey; Inquiry into the destruction of the *Falaba*—Baron Mersey; *Lusitania*—Baron Mersey; then 1916—Viscount Mersey.

Likewise Sir Rufus! Having, after the Inquiry, walked the tightrope of the Marconi scandal and preserved his public reputation by a hair's breadth, he subsequently became Lord Chief Justice of England, was created an Earl, became Ambassador to Washington, High Commissioner in the United States, Viceroy of India—it was an unbroken success story—First Marquess of Reading, G.C.S.I., G.C.I.E., G.C.V.O. Foreign Secretary—finally Lord Warden of the Cinque Ports.

Lastly the Board of Trade—ah, the Board of Trade—the grey eminence in the background of this tale; perhaps it is better that we leave them there—grey, impenetrable. Shortly after the outbreak of the last war their administration of the Merchant Marine was taken over by the newly created Ministry of Shipping whose duties subsequently came under the Ministry of Transport.

They have all gone, every one.

Only the Record remains—although of course some of the records have been mislaid by the Board and others are still on the secret list, unavailable to the public!

Appendix A

AFFIDAVIT OF CAPTAIN
STANLEY LORD

went to sea in 1891 as a cadet in the barque *Naiad* owned by Messrs. J. B. Walmsley. After obtaining my Second Mate's Certificate of competency I served as Second Officer in the barque *Lurlei*. In February, 1901, I passed for Master and three months later obtained my Extra Master's Certificate.

I had entered the service of the West India and Pacific Steam Navigation Company in 1897. This company was bought by the Leyland Line in 1900 and I continued in their service, being appointed to command in 1906 at the age of twenty-nine.

In April, 1912, I was in command of the liner *Californian,* having sailed from London for Boston, U.S.A. on April 5th. On April 13th, noon latitude by observation was 43° 43' North: on 14th April, the noon position by observation was 42° 05'N, 47° 25'W, and course was altered to North 6i° West (magnetic) to make due West (true). I steered this course to make longitude 51° West in latitude 42° North on account of ice reports which had been received.

At 5 p.m. on April 14th, two observations of the sun taken by the Second Officer, Mr H. Stone, to check the longitude were reported to me. These gave a run of 60 miles since noon, which was much ahead of dead reckoning. Another observation which I caused to be taken at 5.30 p.m. gave 64 miles since noon.

At 6.30 p.m. we passed three large icebergs 5 miles south of the ship. These I caused to be reported at 7.30 p.m. by wireless to the s.s. *Antillian,* the message being as follows: "*6.30 p.m. apparent ship's time, latitude 42°*

5'N, longitude 49° 9'W, three bergs five miles southwards of us regards Lord." A little later I was informed that a routine exchange of signals with the *Titanic* showed that she had also received the message sent to the *Antillian*. These would appear to have been the same icebergs sighted and reported by wireless during the day by the *Parisian* in position 41° 55'N, 49° 14'W.

At 7.30 p.m. the Chief Officer, Mr G. F. Stewart, reported to me a latitude by Pole Star of 42° 5½'N. This with the previous observation for longitude gave me proof that the current was setting to WNW at about 1 knot.

At 8 p.m. I doubled the lookouts, there being a man in the crow's- nest and another on the foc'sle head.

At 8.5 p.m. I took charge on the bridge myself, the Third Officer, Mr C. V. Groves, also being on duty. The weather was calm, clear and starry.

At 10.15 p-m. I observed a brightening along the western horizon. After watching this carefully for a few minutes I concluded that it was caused by ice. At 10.21 I personally rang the engine-room telegraph to full speed astern and ordered the helm hard aport. As these orders came into effect the lookout men reported ice ahead. Under the influence of the helm and propeller going astern the ship swung round to ENE by compass (NE true).

The ship was then stopped surrounded by loose ice and from one-quarter to half a mile from the edge of a low ice field. As I could not see any clear place to go through I decided to remain stopped until daylight. Allowing S 89°W (true) 120 miles from my noon position, and also taking into account the latitude by Pole Star at 7.30 p.m., I calculated my position as being 42° 5'N, 50° 7'W.

At 10.30 p.m. as I was leaving the bridge, I pointed out to the Third Officer what I thought was a light to the eastward which he said he thought was a star.

I went down to the saloon deck and sent for the Chief Engineer. I notified him that I intended to remain stopped until daylight but he was to keep main steam handy in case we commenced to bump against the ice.

I pointed out to him the steamer I had previously seen approaching from the eastward and southward of us and about 10.55 p.m. we went to the wireless room. We met the wireless operator coming out and pointing out the other vessel to him I asked him what ships he had. He replied: "Only the *Titanic*." I thereupon remarked, judging from what I could see of the approaching vessel, which appeared to be a vessel of no great size and comparable with our own: "That isn't the *Titanic*." I told him to notify the *Titanic* that we were stopped and surrounded by ice in the position I had calculated, and he left at once to do so.

Later I noticed the green (starboard) light of the approaching vessel, also a few deck lights in addition to the one masthead light previously seen.

At 11.30 p.m. I noticed that the other steamer was stopped about 5 miles off, also that the Third Officer was morsing him. I continued watching and noticed that she didn't reply.

At 11.45 p-m. I went on to the bridge, casually noticed the other vessel, and commented to the Third Officer that she had stopped and wouldn't reply to our morse signals. He answered in the affirmative.

At ten minutes after midnight, it now being April 15th, the Second Officer came on to the saloon deck. I drew his attention to the fact that we were stopped and surrounded by ice and that I intended to remain stopped until daylight. I pointed out the other steamer to him, told him that she was stopped and that he was to watch her and let me know if we drifted any closer to her. He then went on to the bridge to relieve the Third Officer, and I went into the chartroom.

I sat there reading and smoking until 0.40 a.m. when I whistled up to the bridge through the speaking tube and asked the Second Officer if the other ship was any nearer. He replied that she was just the same and I told him to let me know if he wanted anything as I was going to He down on the chartroom settee. I then did so, being fully dressed with boots on, etc., and with the electric light on. I left the watch on deck to the Second Officer with every confidence, as he was the holder of a British Board of Trade First Mate's Certificate of competency (foreign going) and my standing orders, which were well known to every officer, stated categorically that I was to be called at once in all cases of doubt.

At about 1.15 a.m. the Second Officer whistled down to say that the other steamer was altering her bearing to the south-west and had fired a white rocket. I asked him whether it was a company's signal and he replied that he didn't know. I thereupon instructed him to call her up, find out what ship she was, and send the apprentice, James Gibson, down to report to me.

I then lay down again in the chartroom, being somewhat relieved in my mind at the news that the other ship was under way and removing herself from her earlier relatively close proximity. For some time I heard the clicking of the morse key, and after concluding that the Second Officer had succeeded in communicating with the other ship, I fell asleep.

Between 1.30 a.m. and 4.30 a.m. I have a recollection of Gibson opening the chartroom door and closing it immediately. I said: "What is it?" but he did not reply.

At 4.30 a.m. the Chief Officer called me and reported that it was breaking day and that the steamer which had fired the rocket was still to the southward. I replied: "Yes, the Second Mate said something about a rocket."

I then went on to the bridge and was for some little time undecided as to the advisability of pushing through the ice or turning round to look for a clearer passage to the south-east. However, as daylight came in I could see clear water to the West of the icefield so put the engines on stand-by at about 5.15 a.m.

About this time the Chief Officer remarked that the steamer bearing SSE from us was a four-master with a yellow funnel and asked me whether I intended going to have a look at her. When I asked him why, he replied that she might have lost her rudder. I said: "She hasn't any signals up, has she?" He replied that she had not, but that the Second Officer had said that she had fired several rockets during his watch. I told him to call the wireless operator and see what ship it was. He did so but fifteen or twenty minutes later came back and reported that the *Titanic* had struck an iceberg and was sinking. Some delay was then experienced before we received an authoritative message giving the estimated position of the disaster but about 6 a.m. the following signal from the *Virginian* was handed to me: "Titanic *struck berg wants assistance urgent ship sinking passengers in boats his position lat 41° 46', long 50° 14', Gambell, Commander.*"

This position I calculated to be about S 16W, 19½ miles from our own estimated position. I immediately got under way and proceeded as quickly as possible on course between S and SW, pushing through about 2 to 3 miles of field ice. A lookout man was pulled in a basket to the main truck, given a pair of binoculars and instructed to look out for the *Titanic.*

At 6.30 a.m. I cleared the field ice and proceeded at full speed (70 revolutions). At 7.30 a.m. approximately, we passed the *Mount Temple* stopped in the reported position of the disaster. As there was no sign of any wreckage I proceeded further South, shortly afterwards passing a ship having a pink funnel and two masts, bound North, which turned out to be the *Almerian.*

A little later, I sighted a four-masted steamer to the SSE of us on the East side of the icefield, and received a verbal message from the wireless operator that the *Carpathia* was at the scene of the disaster. I steered to the South until the steamer was nearly abeam when I altered course and proceeded through the icefield at full speed, making for the other steamer. She proved to be *Carpathia* and I stopped alongside her at about 8.30 a.m. Messages were exchanged regarding the disaster and subsequent rescue operations.

At about 9.10 a.m. the *Carpathia* set course for New York and I continued the search for survivors, the ship steaming at full speed with the Second Officer and a lookout man in the crow's-nest. While carrying out this search, I saw the smoke of several steamers on the horizon in different directions. We passed about six wooden lifeboats afloat, one capsized in the wreckage; with the exception of two small trunks in a collapsible boat, the others appeared to be empty.

At about 11.20 a.m. I abandoned the search and proceeded due West (true) through the ice, clearing same about 11.50 a.m. The *Mount Temple* was then in sight a considerable distance to the South West of us and heading to the westward.

The noon position was 41° 33'N, 50° 09'W; the latitude was taken under the most favourable conditions by the three officers and reported to me. I did not personally take an observation this day. From this observation I placed the wreckage in position 41° 33'N, 50° 01'W, being about

SSE, 33 miles, from the position in which the *Californian* had stopped at 10.21 p.m. the previous evening.

I later called for written reports on the events of the night from the Second Officer and Apprentice (Appendices B and C). In amplifying his report, the Second Officer stated that the rockets he saw did not appear to be distress rockets, as they did not go any higher than the other steamer's masthead light nor were any detonations heard which would have been the case under the prevailing conditions had explosive distress signals been fired by a ship so close at hand. In addition, the ship altered her bearings from SSE at 0.50 a.m. to SW½W at 2.10 a.m.; assuming her to have been 5 miles from the *Californian* when she stopped at 11.30 p.m., the distance she must have steamed to alter her bearing by this amount I calculate to have been at least 8 miles.

While on passage to Boston, wireless messages about the disaster were received from Captain Rostron of the *Carpathia*; the American newspapers *New York American, Boston Globe, Boston American* and *Boston Post-*, a passenger in the *Olympic* called Wick; and the Leyland Line.

After our arrival at Boston at 4 a.m. on April 19th, I was summoned with the Radio Officer to appear before the United States Congressional Inquiry in Washington. I gave my evidence there in accordance with the above facts. Subsequently, I never had an opportunity to read a transcript of the proceedings or findings of this Inquiry, nor was the matter referred to by those I met on subsequent visits to American ports.

After the return of the *Californian* to Liverpool, I reported to the Wreck Commissioner and to the Marine Superintendent of the Leyland Line, Captain Fry. While in the latter's office, Mr Groves, the Third Officer, volunteered the opinion that the ship seen from the *Californian* on the night of April 14th was the *Titanic*. This was the first occasion I had heard him make such a statement and I duly commented to this effect to the Marine Superintendent.

I was summoned by telegram to appear before the British Court of Inquiry in London on May 14th and travelled down from Liverpool the previous evening. When I arrived in Court, Mr Roberts, manager of the Leyland Line, introduced, me to Mr Dunlop and told me he was watching the proceedings on behalf of the owners and officers of the *Californian.*

Apart from the questions asked by Mr Dunlop when I was in the witness-box, I had no further conversation with him nor at any time was I afforded an opportunity to discuss the proceedings with him or to suggest what navigational and other technical facts might be brought out which would verify the truth of the evidence which I had given.

Had I at any time been clearly warned—as I consider I should have been—that adverse findings in respect of the *Californian* were envisaged, I would have taken all possible steps during the Inquiry to call evidence to prove beyond doubt:

(a) *That the* Californian *was completely stopped,* with full electric navigation and deck lights burning, from 10.21 p.m. to 6 a.m. Additional evidence to prove this conclusively could have been provided by the production of the engine-room log-books covering that period and by the testimony of the Chief Engineer and those engineer officers who kept watch during the night.

If the Court could have been satisfied that the *Californian* was indeed stopped all night, then inevitably they would have had to conclude:

(i) that the *Californian* must have been beyond visual range of the actual position of the disaster, for in perfect visibility no other ship's lights were seen by the two lookout men and the two officers of the watch on the *Titanic* either before or immediately after she struck the iceberg, nor was the *Californian* in sight of the survivors as day broke. Additionally, none of the green flares burnt in the *Titanic's* boats which were seen at extreme range from the *Carpathia* were seen from the *Californian.*

(ii) that the *Californian* could not have been the ship later sighted from the *Titanic* which led to the firing of rockets, for this ship was clearly seen to be under way; to approach from a hull-down position to turn; and to recede.

(b) *That from the navigational evidence the* Californian *must have been at least 25 miles from the position of the disaster.* Additional proof could have been supplied from the engine-room log-books to show how far she steamed from the time of getting under way at 6 a.m. to reaching the wreckage at 8.30; in addition, further detailed consideration should have been given to the relative movements, positions and astronomical observations of the *Californian, Carpathia, Mount Temple* and *Almerian* from before noon on the 14th to the evening of the 15th April in an endeavour to fix as accurately as possible the *actual* as distinct from the *estimated* position in which the wreckage and survivors were found. A further point to which the Court gave no consideration was the fact that the area in which the *Californian* lay stopped all night was covered with field ice extending as far as the eye could see; the area in which the *Carpathia* found the *Titanic's* lifeboats contained very many large icebergs.

If the Court could have been satisfied that during the night the *Californian* was indeed at least 25 miles from the scene of the disaster, they would have had to conclude that even if the distant rocket signals beyond the near-by ship which were apparently seen from the *Californian* had been correctly identified as distress signals, and news of the disaster confirmed by wireless at the earliest possible moment, it would still have been quite impossible for us to have rendered any useful service, for bearing in mind the time taken to reach the wreckage in daylight, under the most favourable conditions, we could not have reached the survivors before the *Carpathia* did.

Finally, I would have submitted for the Court's consideration the following two important points:

(a) That had I or the Third Officer any reason to conclude that the ship seen approaching from 10.30 p.m. onwards was a passenger ship steaming towards an icefield at 21 knots, then instinctively as practical seamen either one of us would have taken immediate action to warn her that she was standing into danger.

(b) That it was perfectly reasonable for the Second Officer to decide that no emergency action was called for when a ship which had been so close to the *Californian* as to cause concern, and which had completely failed to respond to persistent attempts to call her up by morse light, got under way and passed out of sight after substantially altering her bearing. This positive action was more than sufficient to nullify any previous concern which might have been created by her apparently making use of confusing rocket signals of low power reaching only to mast height, and lacking any explosive content or detonation such as was customarily associated with a distress rocket and which should have been perfectly audible in the calm conditions then obtaining.

I was also in Court on May 15th. I clearly recall that when Lord Mersey, the President, pressed Mr Groves, the Third Officer, to express his opinion that the ship seen from the *Californian* was the *Titanic*, Lord Mersey commented that this was also his opinion—a comment which does not appear in the official record of proceedings.

I returned to Liverpool on the evening of May 15th, being due to sail in the *Californian* on 18th. However, after my return home I was verbally informed by the Marine Superintendent that I was to be relieved and I accordingly removed my gear from the ship.

I first read the findings of the Court of Inquiry in the Press and while naturally not at all pleased at the references to myself, I was not unduly concerned as I was confident that matters would soon be put right. I immediately approached the Mercantile Marine Service Association, of which I was a member, and a letter putting my side of the case was published in the September, 1912, issue of the Association's magazine, *The Reporter*.

At a later stage, Mr A. M. Foweraker, of Carbis Bay, a gentleman whom I never met, but who took a great interest in my case, supplied a series of detailed analyses of the evidence which were published in *The Reporter* and also in the Nautical Magazine under the title of *A Miscarriage of Justice* (April, May and June issues, 1913).

Letters were addressed to the Board of Trade both by the M.M.S.A. and by myself requesting a rehearing of that part of the Inquiry relating to the *Californian*. This request was consistently refused. The M.M.S.A. also sent a letter to the Attorney-General (Sir Rufus Isaacs) requesting an explanation of the comment in his closing address that *"perhaps it would not be wise to speculate on the reason which prevented the Captain of the* Californian *from coming out of the chartroom"* on receiving the Second Officer's message at 1.15. This obvious reflection on my sobriety I greatly resented, for it was my invariable practice to refrain from taking alcohol in any form while at sea, quite apart from the fact that no previous reference to such a possibility had been made during the course of the Inquiry. The only reply received was that Sir Rufus was on holiday and must not be troubled with correspondence.

I received a letter dated August 6th, 1912 from a Mr Baker, who had served in the *Mount Temple* on her return voyage from Quebec. This appeared to indicate that she was the ship seen to approach and recede from the *Titanic*. Although this letter was brought to the attention of the Board of Trade, no action was taken. . . . Through Mr Baker, I met Mr Notley, the officer referred to in Mr Baker's letters who had been taken out of the *Mount Temple*. He confirmed that he would give his evidence if called upon to do so, but could not volunteer information because of the adverse effect this might have upon his future employment—a conclusion with which I quite agreed.

I also corresponded with others whose evidence and opinion might prove of assistance to me and received letters from Captain Rostron of the *Carpathia*: Mr C. H. Lightoller (Second Officer of the *Titanic*); and Captain C. A. Bartlett, Marine Superintendent of the White Star Line.

Initially, I had been assured by the Liverpool Management of the Leyland Line that I would be reappointed to the *Californian*. However, I was later told privately by Mr Gordon, Private Secretary to Mr Roper (Head of the Liverpool office of the Leyland Line), that one of the London directors, a Mr Matheson, K.C., had threatened to resign if I were permitted to remain in the company, and on August 13th I was told by the Marine Superintendent that the company could not give me another ship. I then saw Mr Roper, who said that it was most unfortunate but the matter was out of his hands and public opinion was against me. I was therefore compelled to resign, up to which time I had been retained on full sea pay and bonus.

I continued my endeavours to obtain what I considered to be the justice due to me but without success, although I personally visited the House of Commons on October 23rd, 1912, and engaged in correspondence with the Board of Trade during 1913.

Toward the end of 1912, I was approached by Mr (later Sir) John Latta of Nitrate Producers Steam Ship Co. Ltd. (Lawther, Latta & Co.), who had apparently been approached on my behalf by a Mr Frank Strachan, United States agent for the Leyland Line, who had throughout done everything possible to assist me. After a visit to London to meet Mr Latta,

I was offered an immediate command with the company and entered their service in February, 1913. I served at sea throughout the First World War, and as the aftermath of the *Titanic* Inquiry in those days was not such as to affect me personally or professionally in any way, I decided to let the matter drop.

I continued to serve in Lawther Latta's until ill-health compelled me to retire in March, 1927. Sir John Latta's opinion of my service as a ship-master is given in the reference I received from the Company.

After my retirement, I was unaware of any adverse reference to the *Californian* in respect of the *Titanic* disaster, as I have never been a film-goer and was not attracted towards any books on the subject. Latterly, my eyesight also began to deteriorate and the amount of reading I could do was consequently considerably curtailed. However, I noted some extracts from a book called *A Night to Remember* in the Liverpool evening newspaper, the *Liverpool Echo,* although the brief extracts which I read—which did not contain any reference to the *Californian*—did not impress me.

In the early summer of 1958, however, I became aware that a film also called *A Night to Remember* apparently gave great prominence to the allegation that the *Californian* stood by in close proximity to the sinking *Titanic.* I therefore personally called on Mr W. L. S. Harrison, General Secretary of the Mercantile Marine Service Association, of which organisation I had remained a member without a break from 1897.

Acting on my behalf, Mr Harrison entered into correspondence with the producers of the film, the publishers of the book and later the author, asking for them to give consideration to my side of the story. However, those concerned maintained that the British Inquiry findings were authoritative and provided sufficient justification for the references to the *Californian* in their publications.

Being desirous of avoiding undue publicity, which owing to my present age and failing health would undoubtedly have serious effects, I am making this sworn statement as a final truthful and authoritative record of what occurred when I was in command of the *Californian* on the night of April 14th, 1912.

SWORN by the above-named deponent Stanley Lord at 13 Kirkway, Wallasey, in the County of Chester, on this twenty-fifth day of June, 1959, before me, Herbert M. Allen, Notary Public.

(Signed) STANLEY LORD.

Appendix B

ORIGINAL STATEMENT OF MR H. STONE, SECOND OFFICER

S.S. *Californian*,
At Sea.
(*18 April, 1912?*)

Captain Lord,

Dear Sir,

At your request I make the following report of the incidents witnessed by me during my watch on the bridge of this steamer from midnight April 14th—4 a.m. of the 15th.

On going up to the bridge I was stopped by yourself at the wheel-house door, and you gave me verbal orders for the Watch. You showed me a steamer a little abaft of our Star-beam and informed me she was stopped. You also showed me the loose field ice all around the ship and a dense icefield to the southward. You told me to watch the other steamer and report if she came any nearer and that you were going to lie down on the chartroom settee. I went on the bridge about 8 minutes past 12, and took over the Watch from the Third Officer, Mr Groves, who also pointed out ice and steamer and said our head was ENE and we were swinging. On looking at the compass I saw this was correct and observed the other steamer SSE dead abeam and showing one masthead light, her red side-light and one or two small indistinct lights around the deck which looked like portholes or open doors. I judged her to be a small tramp steamer and about 5 miles distant. The Third Officer informed me he had called him up on our morse lamp but had got no reply. The Third Officer then left the bridge and I at once called the steamer up but got no reply. Gibson, the apprentice, then came up with the coffee at about 12.15. I told him I had called the steamer up and the result. He then went to the tapper with the same result. Gibson thought at first he was answering, but it was only his masthead lamps flickering a little. I then sent Gibson by your orders to get the gear all ready for streaming a new log line when we got under weigh again. At 12.35 you whistled up the speaking tube and asked if the other steamer had moved. I replied "No" and that she was on the same bearing and also reported I had called him up and the result. At about 12.45 I observed a flash of light in the sky just above that steamer. I thought nothing of it as there were several shooting stars about, the night being fine and clear with light airs and calms. Shortly after I observed another distinctly over the steamer which I made out to be a white rocket though I observed no flash on the deck or any indication that it had come from that steamer, in fact, it appeared to come from a good distance beyond her. Between then and about 1.15 I observed three more the same as before, and all white in colour. I, at once, whistled down the speaking tube and you came from the chartroom into your own room and answered. I reported seeing these lights in the sky in the direction of the other steamer which appeared to me to be white rockets. You then gave me orders to call her up with the morse lamp and try and get some information from her. You also asked me if they were private signals and I replied "I do not know, but they were all white." You then said: "When you get an answer let me know by Gibson." Gibson and I observed three more at intervals and kept calling them up on our morse lamps but got no reply whatsoever. The other steamer meanwhile had shut in her red sidelight and showed us her stern light and her masthead's glow was just visible. I observed the steamer to be steaming away to the SW and altering her bearing fast. We were also swinging slowly all the time through S and at 1.50 were heading about WSW and the other steamer bearing SW x W. At 2 a.m. the vessel was steaming away fast and only just her stern light was visible and bearing SW½W. I sent Gibson down to you and told him to wake you and tell you we had seen altogether eight white rockets and that the steamer had gone out of sight to the SW. Also that we were heading WSW. When he came back he reported he had told you we had called him up repeatedly and got no answer, and you replied: "All right, are you sure there were no colours in them," and Gibson replied: "No, they were all white." At 2.45 I again whistled down again and told you we had seen no more lights and that the steamer had steamed away to the SW and was now out of sight, also that the rockets were all white and had no colours whatever.

We saw nothing further until about 3.20 when we thought we observed two faint lights in the sky about SSW and a little distance apart. At 3.40 I sent Gibson down to see all was ready for me to prepare the new log at eight bells. The Chief Officer, Mr Stewart, came on the bridge at 4 a.m. and I gave him a full report of what I had seen and my reports and replies from you, and pointed out where I thought I had observed these faint lights at 3.20. He picked up the binoculars and said after a few moments: "There she is then, she's all right, she is a four-master." I said "Then that isn't the steamer I saw first," took up the glasses and just made out a four-masted steamer with two masthead lights a little abaft our port beam, and bearing about S, we were heading about WNW. Mr Stewart then took over the watch and I went off the bridge.

Yours respectfully,

(Signed) *Herbert Stone,*

Second Officer.

Appendix C

ORIGINAL STATEMENT OF JAMES GIBSON, APPRENTICE

Thursday,
April 18th, 1912.

Captain Lord,

Dear Sir,

In compliance with your wishes, I hereby make the following statement as to what I saw on the morning of April 15th, 1911 [*sic*]:

It being my watch on deck from twelve o'clock until four o'clock, I went on the bridge at about 15 minutes after twelve and saw that the ship was stopped and that she was surrounded with light field ice and thick field ice to the southward. While the Second Officer and I were having coffee, a few minutes later, I asked him if there were any more ships around us. He said that there was one on the starboard beam, and looking over the weather-cloth, I saw a white light flickering, which I took to be a morse light calling us up. I then went over to the key-board and gave one long flash in answer, and still seeing this light flickering, I gave her the calling up sign. The light on the other ship, however, was still the same, so I looked at her through the binoculars and found that it was her masthead light flickering, I also observed her port sidelight and a faint glare of lights on her after deck. I then went over to the Second Officer and remarked that she looked like a tramp steamer. He said that most probably she was, and was burning oil lights. This ship was then right abeam. At about 25 minutes after twelve I went down off the bridge to get a new log out and not being able to find it, I went on the bridge again to see if the Second Officer knew anything about it. I then noticed that this other ship was about one point and a half before the beam. I then went down again and was down until about five minutes to one. Arriving on the bridge again at that time, the Second Officer told me that the other ship, which was then about 3½ points on the starboard bow, had fired five rockets and he also remarked that after seeing the second one to make sure that he was not mistaken, he had told the Captain, through the speaking tube and that the Captain had told him to watch her and keep calling her up on the morse light. I then watched her for some time and then went over to the key-board and called her up continuously for about three minutes. I then got the binoculars and had just got them focussed on the vessel when I observed a white flash apparently on her deck, followed by a faint streak towards the sky which then burst into white stars. Nothing then happened until the other ship was about two points on the starboard bow when she fired another rocket. Shortly after that I observed that her sidelight had disappeared but her masthead light was just visible, and the Second Officer remarked after taking another bearing of her, that she was slowly steering away towards the SW. Between one point on the starboard bow and one point on the port bow I called her up on the morse lamp but received no answer. When about one point on the port bow she fired another rocket which like the other burst into white stars. Just after two o'clock she was then about two points on the port bow, she disappeared from sight and nothing was seen of her again. The Second Officer then said, "Call the Captain and tell him that that ship has disappeared in the SW, that we are heading WSW and that altogether she has fired eight rockets." I then went down below to the chartroom and called the Captain and told him and he asked me if there were any colours in the rockets. I told him that they were all white. He then asked me what time it was and I went on the bridge and told the Second Officer what the Captain had said. At about 2.45 he whistled down to the Captain again but I did not hear what was said. At about 3.20 looking over the weather-cloth, I observed a rocket about two points before the beam (port), which I reported to the Second Officer. About three minutes later I saw another rocket right abeam which was followed later by another one about two points before the beam. I saw nothing else and when one bell went, I went below to get the log gear ready for the Second Officer at eight bells.

Yours respectfully,
(Signed) *James Gibson,*
Apprentice.

Appendix D

Letter to the Editor of M.M.S.A. *Reporter* by Captain Lord

The Editor,

Mercantile Marine Service Association "reporter"

Sir,—The issue of the Report of the Court, presided over by Lord Mersey, to inquire into the loss of the *Titanic,* ends a compulsory silence on my part on points raised in the course of the proceedings which affect me as the late Master of the steamer *Californian,* and it is a duty I owe to myself and my reputation as a British Shipmaster, to do what I have hitherto been prevented from doing, for obvious reasons, in giving publicity to circumstances which the Inquiry failed to elicit, and at the same time to show that the deductions which have been drawn, reflecting upon my personal character as a seaman, are entirely unfounded.

The facts briefly and consistently are as follows: On the night of the 14th April I had been on the bridge from dark until 10.30 p.m., at that time having run into loose ice, and, sighting field ice ahead, I deemed it prudent for the safety of the life and property under my charge to remain stopped until daylight. My wireless operator had been in communication with a number of steamers up to 11.30 p.m., and he then retired for the night, after a full day's duty, but not before warning all ships in the vicinity, including the *Titanic,* of the dangerous proximity of ice.

Forty minutes after midnight I left the deck in charge of the Second Officer, with instructions to call me if wanted, and retired to the chartroom, where I lay down, fully dressed, boots on and with the light burning. At 1.15 a.m. the Second Officer informed me through the speaking tube that a steamer, which had been stopped in sight of us since 11.30

p.m., bearing SSE, was altering her bearing (in other words was steaming away) and had fired a white rocket. Meanwhile, for over an hour, my morse signals to this vessel had been ignored. The officer reported her to be steaming away, and I asked him, "if he thought it was a *Company's signal*, to morse her again and report?" The evidence of my officers from this point is conclusive that I had gone to sleep. A later message, to the effect that she was last seen bearing SW½W, proving she had steamed at least 8 miles between 1 a.m. and 2 a.m. (*Titanic* did not move after midnight), I have no recollection of receiving, and subsequent events were not regarded by the officers so seriously as to induce them to take energetic means of ensuring my cognizance of happenings, which should, and would, most assuredly have had my most earnest attention. I did not hear of the disaster until daylight, and that only after it was deemed safe for my steamer to proceed.

The evidence is conclusive that none of the responsible officers of the *Californian* were aware of the serious calamity which had taken place. That any seaman would wilfully neglect signals of distress is preposterous and unthinkable—there was everything to gain and nothing to lose. The failure to adopt energetic means of making me aware of the gravity of the signals is conclusive of the fact that my officers did not attach any significance to their appearance.

The absence of any reply to the succession of morse signals made from the bridge of the *Californian* is further evidence which is entitled to some consideration.

When I asked the Second Officer the next day why he had not used more energy in calling me, and insisted on my coming on deck at once, he replied, "If the signals had been distress signals he would have done so, but as the steamer was steaming away, he concluded there was not much wrong with her." He was the man on the spot—the only officer who saw the signals, so I think I was justified in relying upon his judgement, which ought to carry some weight.

The evidence of the *Titanic* officer who was firing her distress signals, states the steamer he had under observation "approached"—obviously not the *Californian*—as she was stopped from 10.30 p.m. until 5.15 a.m.

Captain Rostron, of the *Carpathia*, states, "Whilst at the scene of the disaster at 5 a.m. it was broad daylight; he could see all round the horizon. He then saw two steamers North of where he was (the direction of the *Californian*). Neither of them was the *Californian*; he first saw that steamer at about 8 a.m., distant 5 to 6 miles, and steaming towards the *Carpathia*." Had the *Californian* been seen by the *Titanic* before sinking, she would have been plainly in view from the *Carpathia* at this time, as she was then on the same spot as when she stopped at 10.30 p.m. the previous evening.

The conversation between my Second Officer and Apprentice, when watching the steamer referred to, was that she must have been a tramp steamer using oil lamps, and that opinion was formed by them after keenly studying the situation, and before they had heard of any disaster.

My position at the Inquiry was that of a witness only, and a nautical man rarely makes a good witness. My position was marconigramed to other steamers at 6.30 p.m., five hours before the accident, and also at 5.15 a.m., before I had heard of the position of the accident, proving my distance from the disaster as given by me to be correct.

I trust this lengthy explanation, which I ought to have made earlier, but for various reasons could not, will be the means of removing the undeserved stigma which rests upon me, and, through me, upon an honourable profession.

I am, Sir, yours truly,

(Signed) STANLEY LORD,

(*Late Master steamer "Californian."*)

Liverpool,
    14th August, 1912.

Appendix E

EVIDENCE TO SHOW THAT THE FIRST ROCKET AND FIRST BOAT LOWERED WERE PRACTICALLY CONTEMPORANEOUS

Mr *Boxhall* (*at the British Inquiry*): 15593. I knew one of the boats had gone away, because I happened to be putting the firing lanyard inside the wheelhouse after sending off a rocket, and the telephone bell rang. Somebody telephoned to say that one of the starboard boats had left the ship and I was rather surprised.

Mr H. J. Pitman, Third Officer of the *Titanic*, testified (*at the U.S. Inquiry*) that No. 7 boat was the first to go (p. 304) two or three minutes previously to No. 5 (p. 289), with No. 3 next. He saw the first rocket "shortly after" No. 5 boat left the *Titanic* (p. 293), and (*at the British Inquiry*) stated that he thought "it would be about 12.30 when No. 5 boat reached the water" (15036).

Mr. *H. G. Lowe*, Fifth Officer of the *Titanic*, (*at the U.S. Inquiry*, p. 401): I pursued the same course in filling No.3 boat as in No. 5.

Senator Smith: Did Mr Ismay assist in filling that boat?

Mr. Lowe: Yes; he assisted there too.

Smith: You found him there when you turned from No. 5 to No. 3?

Lowe: He was there, and I distinctly remember seeing him alongside of me—that is, by my side—when the first detonator went off. I will tell you how I happen to remember it so distinctly. It was because the flash of the detonator lit up the whole deck. I did not know who Mr Ismay was then, but I learned afterwards who he was, and he was standing alongside of me.

Sir Cosmo Duff Gordon (at the British Inquiry): 12496. (*examined by the Attorney-General*): Were they firing rockets at that time? Yes, they had just begun while they were lowering No. 3 lifeboat.

APPENDIX F

CAPTAIN KNAPP'S EXPLANATION OF HIS CHART NUMBER 2 (SEE PAGES 164-6)

"The outer arc around each ship is drawn with a radius of 16 miles, which is approximately the farthest distance at which the curvature of the earth would have permitted the sidelights of the *Titanic* to be seen by a person at the height of the sidelights of the *Californian,* or at which the sidelights of the *Californian* could have been seen by a person at the height of the sidelights of the *Titanic*. The inner circle around each ship is drawn with a radius of 7 miles. This is approximately the distance after reaching which the curvature of the earth would have shut out the sidelights of the *Californian* from the view of one in a lifeboat in the water.

"It appears therefore that if the *Titanic*'s position at the time of the accident was as fixed by the testimony and if it was the sidelight of the *Californian* that was seen from the boat deck of the *Titanic,* the *Californian* was somewhere inside of the arc of the 16-mile circle drawn about the *Titanic*. It further appears that if the above hypothesis be correct and if the sidelights of the other steamer could not be seen, as is testified to from one of the lifeboats of the *Titanic* after being lowered, the *Californian* was somewhere outside of the circle with the 7-mile radius drawn about the *Titanic*.

"In the case of the *Californian,* if the steamer which in the testimony given by members of the crew of the *Californian* including the Captain and the donkey engine man and others is said to have been seen by them was the *Titanic,* she must have been somewhere inside of the circle with the 16-mile radius drawn around the *Californian*. If that be the case, as the *Californian*'s sidelight was shut out by the curvature of the earth from the view of anyone in a lifeboat of the *Titanic* after being lowered into the water, then the *Titanic* must have been outside of the circle drawn with the 7-mile radius around the *Californian*.

"Further reference to this chart will show plotted a hypothetical position of the *Californian*. On the hypothesis that the *Californian* was in this position, a dotted line is drawn on the chart on the bearing given by the Captain of the *Californian* as that on which the steamer was sighted. This bearing is drawn on the chart to intersect the track of the *Titanic*. Another dotted line is drawn parallel thereto from a point on the course of the *Titanic* where she apparently was at 10.06 p.m. New York time, April 14th, that being 11.56 p.m. of that date of the *Californian*'s time, at which Ernest Gill, a member of the crew of the *Californian* in his testimony before your committee stated that the large steamer was seen by him. If the *Californian* was in the hypothetical position shown on the chart, the *Titanic* could have been seen by the officers and crew of the *Californian* at the time mentioned."

SUMMARY OF CALIFORNIAN'S LOG POSITIONS

April 13th noon: latitude 43° 43'N

April 14th noon: 42° 05'N. Altered course to N 61°W magnetic (due West or S 89°W true.)

1830:   Dead reckoning 42° 03'N, 49° 09'W—broadcast to *Antillian.*

1930:   latitude 42° 05'N by pole star (Chief Officer)

2221:   Ship stopped. Dead reckoning 42° 05'N, 50° 07'W.

April 15th noon: 41° 33'N, 50° 09'W.

SOME POINTS FROM MERSEY'S JUDGEMENT ON THE LOSS OF THE *TITANIC*

Captain Smith's responsibility

"The question is what ought the Master to have done (having received the various ice reports, but not, thought Mersey, the one from the *Mesaba*). I am advised that with the knowledge of the proximity of ice which the Master had, two courses were open to him: the one was to stand on well to the southward instead of turning up to a westerly course; the other was to reduce speed materially as night approached. He did neither. . . . Why then did the Master persevere in his course and maintain his speed? The answer is to be found in the evidence. It was shown that for many years past the practice of liners using this track when in the vicinity of ice at night had been in clear weather to keep the course, to maintain the speed and to trust to a sharp lookout to enable them to avoid danger. This practice, it was said, had been justified by experience, no casualties having resulted from it. . . . But the event has proved the practice to be bad. Its root is probably to be found in the desire of the public for quick passages rather than in the judgement of navigators. But unfortunately experience appeared to justify it. In these circumstances I am not able to blame Captain Smith."

The lifeboats

"The discipline both among passengers and crew during the lowering of the boats was good, but the organisation should have been better and if it had been it is possible that more lives would have been saved."

"Timing:

about 12.05 Order given to uncover boats under davits.

12.30 Order to swing boats out.

12.30 Order to place women and children in the boats.

"Roughly speaking the boats left at the following times:

Starboard side		Port side	
7	12-45	6	12.55
5	12-55	8	1.10
3	1.00	10	1.20
1	1.10	12	1.25
9	1.20	14	1.30
11	1.25	16	1.35
13	1.35	2	1.45
15	1.35	4	1.55
C	1.40	D	2.5
A	Floated off	B	Floated off."

652 people left the *Titanic* in boats; 712 people were saved from her. An average of 36 people left the *Titanic* in each boat.

Why were there so few in the lifeboats?

"Many explanations are forthcoming, one being that the passengers were unwilling to leave the ship. When the earlier boats left and before the *Titanic* had begun materially to settle down there was a drop of some 65 feet from the boat-deck to the water and the women feared to get into the boats. This explanation is supported by the evidence of Captain Rostron of the *Carpathia*. He says that after those who were saved got on board his ship, he was told by some of them that when the boats first left the *Titanic* the people really would not be put in the boats; they did not want to go in.... At one time the Master appeared to have had the intention of putting the people into the boats from the gangway doors in the side of the ship. . . . There is no doubt that the Master did order some of the partly filled boats to row to a position under one of the doors with the object of taking passengers in at that point. It appears, however, that these doors were never opened. . . . It is said further that the officers engaged in putting the people into the boats feared that the boats might buckle if they were filled; but this proved to be an unfounded apprehension, for one or more boats were completely filled and lowered to the water.

"At 12.35 the message from the *Carpathia* was received announcing that she was making for the *Titanic*. This probably became known and may have tended to make the passengers still more unwilling to leave the ship: and the lights of a ship (the *Californian*) which were seen by many people may have encouraged the passengers to hope that assistance was at hand."

The drowning in the water

"I heard much evidence as to the conduct of the boats after the *Titanic* sank and when there must have been many struggling people in the water, and I regret to say that in my opinion, some, at all events, of the boats failed to attempt to save lives when they might have done so, and might have done so successfully. This was particularly the case with boat number 1. It may reasonably have been thought that the risk of making the attempt was too great; but it seems to me that if the attempt had been made by some of these boats it might have been the means of saving a few more lives. Subject to these few adverse comments I have nothing but praise for both passengers and crew. All the witnesses speak well of their behaviour."

The survival of Bruce Ismay

"As to the attack on Mr Bruce Ismay it resolved itself into the suggestion that, occupying the position of managing director of the steamship company, some moral duty was imposed upon him to wait on board until the vessel foundered. I do not agree. Mr Ismay, after rendering assistance to many passengers, found C collapsible, the last boat on the starboard side actually being lowered. No other people were there at the time. There was room for him and he jumped in. Had he not jumped in he would have merely added one more life, namely his own, to the number of those lost."

The Third Class passengers

"It had been suggested before the Inquiry that the Third Class passengers had been unfairly treated; that their access to the boat-deck had been impeded, and that when at last they reached the deck the First and Second Class passengers were given precedence in getting places in the boats. There appears to have been no truth in these suggestions. It is no doubt true that the proportion of Third Class passengers saved falls far short of the proportion of First and Second Class but this is accounted for by the greater reluctance of the Third Class passengers to leave the ship, by their unwillingness to part with their baggage, by the difficulty in getting them up from their quarters, which were at the extreme ends of the ship, and by other similar causes."[1]

Percentages of survival by class

Number aboard	Saved	Percentage	
First Class			
men 175	57	32·47	62·46% saved
women 144	140	97·22	
children 5	5	100·00 (highest percentage)	
Second Class			
men 168	14	8·33 (lowest percentage)	41·4% saved
women 93	80	86·02	
children 24	24	100·00 (highest percentage)	

[1] No Third Class passengers called.

Third Class			
men 462	75	16·23	25·21% saved
women 165	76	46·06	
children 79	27	45·16	
Crew			
Deck 66	43	65·15	23·95% saved
Engine 325	72	22·15	
Catering 494	97	19·63 (including 20 women out of 23)	
TOTAL			
2,201	711	32·30	

APPENDIX I

GLOSSARY OF NAUTICAL TERMS

Bearing: is the direction of an object from the viewer usually designated in the same manner as a course, or alternatively relative to the ship's head, i.e. 20° to starboard.

Compass Error: is a combination of *Variation* and *Deviation*.

Courses: In the days before the gyro-compass, courses were given in degrees from either North or South. What would now be a course of 271° would, in 1912, have been N 89°W. Similarly a course of 100° would have been S 80°E.

True Course: is the compass course which the quartermaster steers plus or minus the *compass error.*

Deviation: is the amount which the compass needle is deflected by the magnetism of the ship on which it is located.

Falls: are the ropes which are rove through blocks from the davits to each end of the lifeboat, on which the lifeboat is lowered to the water.

Heading: is the direction the ship's head is pointing.

A Knot: is one nautical mile (approximately 6,000 feet) per hour.

Latitude: The lines of latitude are parallels measured North and South from the Equator. Each degree of latitude is made up of 60 minutes (designated ') and each minute is approximately one nautical mile.

The Titanic's *Lifeboats:* rested on deck in wooden chocks beneath their davits, which were turned outboard when necessary by means of large handles inserted in the gearing.

Sailing-ship's Lights: A sailing vessel only carries the sidelights mentioned below and the stern light.

Steamship's Lights: A small steamer, when not stopped, is required to carry one white light on the mast showing from right ahead to about 20°

abaft the beam on each side, and a red sidelight on the *port* side showing from right ahead to about 20° abaft the beam on the port side, and
a green light showing similarly on the *starboard* side. She must also
carry a stern light which covers the rest of the circle—i.e. from right
astern to about 20° abaft the beam on each side. A large steamer in
1912 carried all these lights and could also carry another light abaft
the mast light and higher than it—also white and with the same arc
of visibility.

Range of Visibility of Lights: The coloured sidelights are only required to
be visible for 2 miles, but are usually visible for a greater distance
depending materially on atmospheric conditions; the mast lights
are 5 miles, but again will usually be seen further—especially in the
exceptional conditions described in this book.

Longitude: The meridians of longitude divide the earth into segments like
the segments of an orange, each meridian making a right angle with
the equator and each parallel of latitude. Longitude is measured East
or West from Greenwich.

Master's Certificate: This is a practical as well as a theoretical qualification. It means that a man has served a four-year apprenticeship or
cadetship, then passed his Second Mate's Certificate, served another
eighteen months or so, a good proportion of which has to be in
charge of a watch, and sat for his Mate's Certificate, and then served
another period of time, again in charge of a watch, before sitting for
his Master's.

Extra Master's Certificate: is mainly an academic qualification of a far
higher standard than Master's, which can be taken by anyone who has
passed for his Master's, but is unnecessary for the ordinary practice
of shipmasters. It is a testimony to the ability of the holder and to his
desire to attain the highest possible professional qualification.

Points: When a *bearing* is given in points, i.e. two points on the *starboard*
bow, each point is 11¼° (⅛ of 90°). Thus four points on the bow is 45°.

Position: is designated by the intersection of the *longitude* with the *latitude*
on the surface of the earth in the same way that a grid reference system works on a map.

Fixing Position: Each sight taken of a heavenly body will give one position line at right angles to the *bearing* (direction) of that body. Thus, during the daytime a "fix" cannot be obtained until two or more sights have been taken of the sun after it has been allowed to alter its *bearing* sufficiently to make a good angle between the position lines obtained from each. At twilight, morning and evening, it is possible to fix the ship more accurately by taking several stars almost simultaneously, the intersection of the position lines thus obtained being the position at that moment. From this it can be seen that the sun or stars *bearing* roughly North or South will give an accurate longitude.

Variation: is the amount by which the North of the magnetic needle in the compass differs from the direction true North Pole.

TITANIC FILES RELEASED
BY THE MINISTRY OF TRANSPORT,
JULY 1964

The author wrote to the Parliamentary Secretary to the Minister of Transport on January 1st, 1964, asking for permission to see the *Titanic* files, and was refused. Six months afterwards Mr Tom Driberg, M.P., acting for Mr Leslie Reade, an author, prevailed upon the Minister of Transport to make these files public and they were taken from the Ministry to the Public Records Office.

There follows a brief analysis of some points underlined by the files; unfortunately the omissions are more significant than the papers themselves:

(1) File M 16307 contains voluminous reports from St Petersburg about the movements of the Russian *Birma* (*see pages* 271-3), proving that the Board and their Law Officers had ample evidence that Captain Stulping did not agree the *Titanic's* CQD position, but placed the wreckage well to the south and east of the official position. Captain Stulping's report states that he arrived at the CQD position at about 7.30, saw the ice-field to the *east*, and that in negotiating it (*see* chart *page* 272), he met the *Carpathia* steaming west at full speed at 12.15—*nearly seven hours after he had arrived at the CQD position*, and several hours after the *Carpathia*, steaming in the opposite direction, had left the wreckage.

(2) The Liverpool management of Leylands was right behind Captain Lord: extract from their letter accompanying *Antillian's* Log when it was required by B.O.T. ". . . We think in justice to the Captain of the *Californian* we should draw your attention to the recorded Marconigram

THE *TITANIC* AND THE *CALIFORNIAN*

received by the *Antillian*, which gives the *Californian* position at 6.30 p.m. on the 14th, and this is consistent with the position at 10.30 p.m. when the engines were stopped for the night. . ."

(3) The *Californian*'s deviation book (*see page* 238) *was* in Lord Mersey's hands *before* the judgement; therefore his failure to give any reasons for his arbitrary dismissal of the *Californian*'s Log Book positions argues that the deviation book supported the Log Book evidence.

(4) The reasons for the Board's failure to prosecute Lord for the misdemeanour Lord Mersey had censured him for (*see page* 269) are many and too varied to detail in this appendix. But it is possible that they all stem from the unfortunate attempt of the Mercantile Marine Service Association—in their efforts on Lord's behalf—to implicate the *Mount Temple* as the mystery ship. See files M 22457, 23448, 25669, 26040, 29545, 31921, 25042, in Part 6 of MT 9 920 at the Public Records Office.

(5) A report from British Naval Attache, Washington, is probably indicative of how the "steamship" theory gained ascendancy over "sailing ship" theory for lights seen from *Titanic*. Having heard Boxhall's evidence at the Senate Inquiry (about the lights), he wrote, ". . . I formed a high opinion of his (Boxhall's) straightforwardness, which was also shared by American Naval officers seated near me . . ." This passage, alone in his report, is marked with a vertical red ink line down the left-hand margin.

(6) The files tell of a growing volume of reports from many countries, particularly the United States, of ships which could have been near the disaster at the material time, and which fitted the description (*see index*, "mystery ship"). There is little evidence of follow-up action.

(7) Official British view in Washington coincided with popular view of Senatorial Investigation: ". . . Although it is generally admitted that Senator Smith is one of the most unsuitable persons who could have been charged with an investigation of this nature . . ." and ". . . much of which (evidence) was, owing to the conspicuous incompetence . . . of Senator Smith . . . irrelevant. . ."

(8) The Government was under continuous pressure to set up an Inquiry independent of the B.O.T. Typical question for the Prime Minister is in File M 12097: whether, ". . . having regard to the position of the Board of Trade in the *Titanic* disaster, he will consider instituting some other

Inquiry and one in which the Board will not be in charge of the proceedings." This was referred to the lawyers by the Board, but their replies are lost—only the question remains in the file.

(9) There was also continuous pressure to call third-class passengers at the Inquiry (in view of serious discrepancy of percentage lost with First class). As we know, none were called.

(10) The davit files (marked "for public release *1960*") show that the officials of the B.O.T. were concerned only with THE RULES when considering lifeboat accommodation (*see pages* 43-7). An early file refers to 32 boats under davits; later ones to the number the sister ships eventually carried—16. This complied with THE RULES; there are scores of minutes to the effect.

(11) Lord Mersey was appointed a Wreck Commissioner a week after the loss of the *Titanic*, on April 23rd, 1912—*for the purpose of the Inquiry*—and he resigned as a Wreck Commissioner on October 23rd the same year.

(12) Perhaps the first "disaster" file sets the tone. A telegram from the Editor of the *Belfast Evening Telegraph* asks the Board to wire number and capacity of *Titanic*'s lifeboats (immediately following first news of loss). An official has neatly inserted the figures the Editor requires on the file, and directly underneath a "top" official of the Board has minuted—equally neatly—"Reply Board cannot give any information on the subject". This reply was accordingly sent.

There is a postscript: the Editor wrote an Editorial—a splendid editorial—and the author, feeling similarly afflicted with officialdom adopts it for the final words in this book: ". . . it is with regret that we state with the fullest sense of responsibility, that never in the history of hidebound officialdom has there been such an instance of crass stupidity and ineptitude as has been exhibited on this occasion . . . It is only by reason either of the gross incompetence, sheer idleness or hidebound red-tapism of the responsible officials that the public were not supplied with the fullest and most authentic particulars"—*Belfast Evening Telegraph*, 17.4.1912.

BOOKS CONSULTED

The Loss of the Titanic, by Lawrence Beesley, William Heinemann Ltd. (U.K.); Houghton Mifflin Co., (U.S.A.).

The Ismay Line, by Wilton J. Oldham, Charles Birchall and Sons.

Titanic and Other Ships, by Charles Lightoller, Nicholson and Watson.

Home from the Sea, by Sir Arthur Rostron, Cassell and Company.

Of Ships and Men, by Alan Villiers, George Newnes Ltd.

Transcript of the British Inquiry into the loss of the *Titanic*.

Transcript of the U.S. Senate Inquiry into the loss of the *Titanic*.

Journal of Commerce edited edition of the British *Titanic* Inquiry, Charles Birchall and Sons.

Tramps and Ladies, by Sir James Bisset, Angus and Robertson.

ROGERSTONE

3.3.17

Lightning Source UK Ltd.
Milton Keynes UK
UKOW05f0711310117
293268UK00017B/350/P